A JOURNEY IN LANDSCAPE RESTORATION

Published by
**Whittles Publishing Ltd.,**
Dunbeath,
Caithness, KW6 6EG
Scotland, UK
www.whittlespublishing,com


© 2020 Borders Forest Trust

ISBN 978-184995-472-3

Printed by Severn, Gloucester

# A JOURNEY IN
# LANDSCAPE
# RESTORATION

## CARRIFRAN WILDWOOD AND BEYOND

## EDITED BY PHILIP AND MYRTLE ASHMOLE
### FOR BORDERS FOREST TRUST

*We dedicate this book to all those people who care for,
or work to restore, natural environments around the world*

Borders Forest Trust is an environmental charity formed in 1996
to conserve, restore and manage native woodlands and other
natural habitats for the benefit of people and wildlife. BFT support
community woodlands, habitat restoration, and education projects.

**www.bordersforesttrust.org**

 @bordersforesttrust          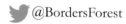 @BordersForest

**www.carrifran.org.uk**

# CONTENTS

**Boxed contributions in Parts I, II and III from the following additional people:**
    Ann Goodburn, Cat Barlow, Crinan Alexander, Duncan Halley, Kate Holl,
    Konrad Lohse, Lynn Cassells, Malcolm Lindsay, Mark Rayment, Richard
    Clarkson, Robin Sloan, Roger Key, Rosy Key, Sarah Eno, Stephen Hewitt, Steve
    Sloan, Tim Frost

**Sketches by:** *Chris Rose, John Wright*

**Poem by:** *Terry Astley*

**Contributors of photographs (apart from writers)**: *Andrew Jarrott, Anna Ashmole,
Dave Bone, Dominic Ashmole, Gillian Dawson, James Barton, James Short, Rachael Coyle,
Patricia and Angus Macdonald, Robin Sloan*

*Photographs by Philip Ashmole except where acknowledged or in blue boxes, in which photos
are normally by the authors of the boxes*

**Maps by:** *Myrtle Ashmole, Nicky Hume*

# FOREWORD

I first came across the Borders Forest Trust on an RSPB field trip, where we saw the early realisation of the Carrifran Wildwood vision. As a native woodland enthusiast with a long-held frustration at the wasteful, denuded state of many Scottish landscapes, this ambitious and inspiring project gripped me. Here was evidence that something practical could be done to bring new, diverse life to the hills. Now as a patron of the Trust, I am delighted to see this work progress and to witness nature's rapid response when debilitating influences are removed.

Over several generations, people have become used to their surroundings and don't always appreciate what has been forsaken through our history of land management. Awareness of the consequences has come late, after we've begun reaching ecological tipping points, with loss of biodiversity and climate change. Now we have a young generation concerned about the impact of these environmental crises on our futures. It is all too easy to feel hopeless and overwhelmed by such global issues, but increasingly we are seeing how individual positive steps can make a difference. Key to the way forward is the recognition that nature can provide solutions if we act to bring our natural environment back into good health.

Our forests, peatlands and waterways are prime examples of ecosystems that regulate climate and bring other benefits to society, but whose functions have been compromised by centuries of damage. The Carrifran Wildwood is a success story serving as a beacon, demonstrating that we can put valuable ecosystems on a trajectory to recovery. This initiative has far-reaching impact through inspiring others and providing an example from which we can learn good practice and repeat elsewhere. The outreach work of the Borders Forest Trust extends this influence further by providing advice and support to land managers keen to play their part in a more sustainable future.

The role of people is a central strand of the Trust's vision to create a rich tapestry of native woodlands and wild places, cared for by local communities. If our native woodlands are to be valued and appreciated by society, they must become part of life's experience. The benefits of a walk in a wood for our physical and mental well-being are officially recognised by our health care system. Encounters with woodland wildlife and connection to myths and legends provide artistic inspiration and create lifelong impressions on young and old visitors.

Establishing and managing such woodland visions also includes involving people as volunteers and employed staff with knock-on economic benefits to local communities. The perilous state of our natural habitats and the past damage we have inflicted on them means we can't simply walk away and hope nature will do the rest. Management and interventions are needed to give the best options for species and habitat restoration. Just as an injured patient's broken limb can heal unaided, surgery and nursing care ensures a more thorough recovery and avoids serious complications. The great advantage of ambitious landscape scale projects is that there is room for a variety of management types from low impact, minimal intervention areas now so rarely seen in our woodlands through to more intensive yet sustainably managed areas with economic activity including farming, forestry and wildlife tourism. The current suite of Borders Forest Trust sites show this varied approach in action.

Having come so far, so effectively, there is still much to be done and more support needed to achieve the wider vision for a diverse and vibrant landscape that functions well and supports a rich biodiversity. The establishment of Carrifran Wildwood and the Trust's further work in habitat restoration is the beginning of a change in the way we look after our environment (and revive the Wild Heart of Southern Scotland).

*Clifton Bain*
*Patron, Borders Forest Trust*

# PREFACE

Lots of people don't read prefaces at all. Some people only read a preface after finishing the book, as if it were an afterthought. Why bother to read someone else's thoughts, especially if they are longer than a soundbyte? Why not just plunge straight in and read the book? After all, that's why you picked it up, and we can all make up our own minds, thank you.

But you must read this one. It is emphatically <u>not</u> an afterthought: I want you to share the dream and be inspired by it, as I was. And the dream you will read about in the first part of this book is by no means over. It started more than a quarter of a century ago and it will continue for centuries to come, and everyone who shares in it will help to keep the dream alive.

Alive. That's what Carrifran valley now is. Alive with trees and flowers and birds and insects. This is a project about people putting nature first, giving it its true place as leader and indicator of what is important, acknowledging and re-establishing the proper place of Mankind within the natural world.

You will read the story of how the Wildwood came into being, and the dedication and tenacity behind the project. Backing the whole idea was a unique commitment to the science behind the restoration work, noting a baseline and monitoring the progress of establishment and the changes taking place. Much of these data are included in the second part of this book and make some serious reading, but they have proved an essential tool in ensuring the Wildwood serves as an inspiration and educational resource. Understanding the intricate relationships between species and habitats is important but it is a complex subject. In modern society, we have been slow to acknowledge the connection between humans and nature; to value ecosystems even if they do not appear to be immediately beneficial. We have only now started to recognise that our own long-term survival as a species depends on the support of a robust, thriving and diverse base in the natural world.

But if you take anything from this book, let it be the passion behind that science, the untiring support that has been devoted to a project which some said could never happen, the energy of those whose time and voluntary effort have gone into making the dream come true. Wildness doesn't need defence, but it does need defenders.

There is much emphasis now on the involvement of local communities and their interest in their local environment. In an area of low density population, it is not easy to raise enough interest and financial support initially, nor to keep up the momentum to see a vision realised. Yet rather than simply empowering local people, we have drawn support from a wider group, who form a community of interest, seeking to support visions like ours because they may not have any such opportunities offered locally.

This community of interest is now finding a wider voice thanks to modern communications. It showed its support for habitat restoration when The Borders Forest Trust extended their habitat restoration work beyond Carrifran by the acquisition first of Corehead Farm and the Devil's Beef Tub, and then Talla and Gameshope Estate. These three sites give the Trust ownership of approximately a third of the Wild Land Area called Talla-Hartfell, as identified by Scottish Natural Heritage (now Nature Scotland). While each site has its own characteristics, together they demonstrate the Trust's commitment to *Reviving the Wild Heart of Southern Scotland*. The greater scale of our Wild Heart sites gives scope for restoring a variety of habitats typical of this area and is now attracting a new generation to connect with the vision and contribute to the creation of a natural resource for all to enjoy.

There is no copyright or restrictive covenant on *Reviving the Wild Heart of Southern Scotland*. The Borders Forest Trust has always wanted to share its vision, to have it replicated by others on their own pieces of land, on whatever scale. So it is a great pleasure to include near the end of this book insights into other projects started by groups with similar environmental aims to our own. If the Trust's work has in any way inspired these partners in spirit, we are quietly proud. They may find it as much of an initial challenge as we did, but our story may give them the determination to continue if an injection of optimism is needed. Be bold in purpose, be consistent in execution and be passionate in vision.

The restoration of valleys and uplands in this part of Scotland to their previous splendour is not yet complete. We still have work to do to reach that point and then, even more importantly, to ensure its survival. I am proud to have shared in the dream and been part of making it come true; creating a visible inspiration to others to hold onto that vision and ensure it becomes a wider and more common reality. Even if you, the Reader, never see the transformation of our hills from green desert to wooded slopes where nature holds sway, I hope you will be inspired to endorse and protect what The Borders Forest Trust has started. And take it further. Future generations need to ensure the dream does not die: the belief, single-mindedness, stubbornness, dedication and financial support which grew into Carrifran Wildwood and which now extend over the hills into other parts of the Wild Heart of Southern Scotland deserve to prosper. I urge you to read on!

*Rosalind Grant-Robertson*
*Chairman, Borders Forest Trust*

# ACKNOWLEDGEMENTS

A large number of people have contributed to this book, many of them volunteers. A huge thank-you to all of them, both for responding to the request to write something, and for patience during the laborious process of stitching together a single tapestry from so many pieces of different shapes and sizes. We offer special thanks to John Thomas, who pulled together the basic structure of Part III and accepted much fiddling with it over the ensuing months; his input was much appreciated. We are deeply indebted to Crinan Alexander, who spent several days labouring over an early printout of the whole book, and whose input at a critical stage significantly improved it. We also wish to thank Nicky Hume for help with the maps and helping to manage a special feature of InDesign.

We are much indebted to Chris Rose and John Wright for the original sketches of birds that enliven the pages, and to the photographers whose images have enabled us to illustrate so many aspects of the work of Borders Forest Trust. We offer special thanks to Patricia and Angus Macdonald, who made two flights to capture remarkable aerial photos of the Wild Heart, to Bill Goodburn who piloted the plane from which Philip took photos in 1996, and to Pete and Viv Reynolds who captured a wonderful image of denuded Carrifran and its surroundings from their microlite.

We wish to apologise to all our relatives, friends and colleagues who have lived through the months when we have been so preoccupied with the book that many other things have fallen through the cracks.

Keith Whittles, Kerrie Moncur and Sue Steven at Whittles Publishing have shown extraordinary patience in discussions over matters of design and in dealing with the glitches in our manuscript, as well as planning initial publicity for the book. It has been a pleasure working with them on this book, as it was with our Tenerife one, and we again offer them our sincere thanks.

We also offer heartfelt thanks to the individuals who have contributed to the funding of the book. Their help epitomises the generous spirit of all the supporters of Borders Forest Trust, both in terms of gifts and of work done for free, which has been key to the ability of our small environmental charity to punch so much above its weight, leading the revival of parts of the Scottish borderlands and creating ripples that may have an influence in places far away.

# CONTRIBUTORS

**Adrian Manning**, landscape ecologist and conservation biologist, Australian National University

**Andy Wilson**, Site Officer at Borders Forest Trust and overseas expedition leader, with a passion for the outdoors and nature

**Anjo Abelaira**, Chairman, Lowther Hills Ski Club

**Ann Goodburn**, geographer and a founding member of the Wildwood Group

**Anna Craigen**, Community and Education Officer, Borders Forest Trust

**Anna Lawrence**, University of the Highlands and Islands; consultant, social forester and member of the Wildwood Steering Group

**Cat Barlow**, Project Manager, South of Scotland Golden Eagle Project

**Chris Miles**, botanist, previously Southern Scotland Unit Manager, Scottish Natural Heritage

**Chris Rose**, wildlife artist and long-term supporter of Carrifran Wildwood

**Clifton Bain**, Patron of Borders Forest Trust, nature writer and Director of IUCN UK Peatland Programme

**Crinan Alexander**, botanist, former staff member Royal Botanic Garden Edinburgh and long-term member of the Wildwood Group

**David Long**, naturalist and bryophyte specialist, Royal Botanic Garden Edinburgh

**Duncan Halley**, researcher (including comparative ecology and landscape history Scotland/Norway) for Norwegian Institute for Nature Research

**Ed Iglehart**, founder member (and self-appointed Hon. Janitor) of Southwest Scotland Community Woodlands Trust and Taliesin

**Elizabeth Kungu**, bryologist, Royal Botanic Garden Edinburgh

**Fi Martynoga**, founding member of the Wildwood Group, writer, editor and former Trustee of Borders Forest Trust and Reforesting Scotland

**Hugh Chalmers**, first Project Officer for Carrifran Wildwood, now with Tweed Forum; Trustee of Reforesting Scotland and Borders Forest Trust

**Jane Bower**, molecular genetics scientist and manager of a major ecological restoration project in the Scottish Borders

**Jane Rosegrant**, member of the Wildwood Steering Group and CEO of Borders Forest Trust from 2012 to 2018

**John Savory** (1943-2020) research scientist, ornithologist and long-term volunteer tree planter and bird recorder at Carrifran

**John Thomas**, Vice-chair of Borders Forest Trust and member of the Wildwood Steering Group, previously Trustee of John Muir Trust

**John Wright**, wildlife artist and Eagle Officer, South of Scotland Golden Eagle Project

**Kate Holl**, Woodland Adviser, Scottish Natural Heritage

**Kevin Cumming**, Langholm Initiative Project Manager, with qualifications and experience in conservation and management of protected areas

**Konrad Lohse**, population geneticist at the Institute of Evolutionary Biology; his group uses genomic approaches to study butterfly speciation

**Lynn Cassells**, previously Site Officer and later Trustee of Borders Forest Trust, now farming with partner Sandra on Lynbreck Croft, Cairngorms

**Malcolm Lindsay**, amateur naturalist with special interest in Lepidoptera

**Mark Rayment**, School of Natural Sciences, Bangor University

**Mary-Ann Smyth**, geo/environmentalist, founder of Crichton Carbon Centre in Dumfries

**Myrtle Ashmole**, biologist, artist, writer and founding member of the Wildwood Group

**Nicky Hume**, Treescapes Project Officer, Borders Forest Trust

**Nicola Hunt**, Head of Land Management, Borders Forest Trust

**Paul Short**, Partner, TreeSurv Woodland Management

**Peter Robinson**, ecologist and previously Project Manager for Cree Valley Community Woodlands Trust

**Philip Ashmole**, biologist and writer, Trustee of Borders Forest Trust and Coordinator of the Carrifran Wildwood project

**Reuben Singleton**, Director - Tweed Ecology, naturalist and stooriefit

**Richard Clarkson**, Grey Mare's Tail Reserve Manager at the National Trust for Scotland

**Rob Soutar**, ecologist and instigator of mountain woodland restoration in Galloway Forest Park

**Robin Sloan**, long-term volunteer, but a tiny cog in a ground breaking machine

**Roger and Rosy Key**, environmental consultants, both retired from Natural England (Head of Invertebrate Conservation and Monitoring Ecologist)

**Rosalind Grant-Robertson**, Chairman of Borders Forest Trust and long-term member of the Wildwood Group

**Roy Watling**, formerly Senior mycologist, Royal Botanic Garden Edinburgh, working mainly in boreal regions and SE Asia

**Sarah Eno**, Trustee of Borders Forest Trust, previously with Scottish Natural Heritage

**Scott Speed**, Stalker, with three decades of experience, for Borders Forest Trust

**Stephen Hewitt**, Entomologist and currently Research Associate with National Museums Scotland

**Steve Sloan**, previously Chairman of Borders Forest Trust

**Stuart Adair**, Habitat Ecologist, consultant and long-term member of the Wildwood Group

**Terry Astley**, naturalist and writer with a lifelong love of the natural world

**Tim Frost**, previously Woodland Site Manager for Borders Forest Trust

# INTRODUCTION

The primary aim of this book is to provide an account of a pioneering initiative in ecological restoration, written not by those who view its progress from outside but by all the people – volunteer activists, amateur experts, professional tree planters and environmental managers – who are playing their diverse roles in making restoration happen in the Moffat and Tweedsmuir Hills, an area that we call 'The Wild Heart of Southern Scotland'.

More than 40 people have written pieces for the book, in very different styles, and some readers may find it lacking in coherence. We hope, however, that this defect is outweighed by the opportunity to see the work in the round, not laid out like a management plan, which can seem fairly remote from the hands-on work in the hills in every sort of weather.

The book is in three Parts, in roughly chronological order. Part I provides a brief account of the conception and birth of Carrifran Wildwood, and of the ante-natal planning and fundraising that enabled the early years to be so effectively employed immediately after the 650 hectare valley of Carrifran became the property of Borders Forest Trust on Millennium Day. It explains how the foundations of a restored woodland and moorland ecosystem were laid within the opening decade of the 21st Century, with financial support especially from the Forestry Commission, the National Lottery and the David Stevenson Trust, as well as many hundreds of generous individuals. A more detailed account is available in our 2009 book *The Carrifran Wildwood Story*.

Part II is devoted to the remarkable changes at Carrifran that have been documented since the planting of the first trees, twenty years ago. Early changes in the vegetation were caused by the removal of the sheep, cattle and feral goats that had denuded the landscape during the previous millennium. Later we began to see changes in the ground vegetation caused by increasing shade from planted trees, and in summer 2008 and subsequent years, the annual surveys provided data on the colonisation by bird species adapted to the new three-dimensional woodland environment. The invertebrate fauna also diversified, though information is less complete.

Part III describes how – as Carrifran Wildwood was becoming established as a notable feature of the Southern Uplands – Borders Forest Trust was able to expand its vision, aspiring to restore natural ecosystems and wildlife communities on a landscape scale, under the banner 'Reviving the Wild Heart of Southern Scotland'. In 2009 the trust purchased Corehead and Devil's Beef Tub, a historic area at the source of the River Annan, where low intensity sheep farming continues alongside large-scale woodland establishment; and in 2013 BFT was able to buy Talla & Gameshope, contiguous with Carrifran and including some of the highest and most remote parts of the Scottish Borders.

The contributors to Part III illuminate the 'nuts and bolts' of rewilding; the hard slog – as much behind computers as on the hillsides – that must underpin the ambitious vision if it is to come to fruition. It shows how contractors and hundreds of volunteers, under the guidance of experts, undertake the rewarding task of restoring the full beauty and diversity of life to poor hill land, bringing benefits to livelihoods and wellbeing alongside partial repayment of an ancient debt to nature. The book finishes with a set of essays showing that Borders Forest Trust does not stand alone – diverse and inspiring projects are under way in many parts of southwest Scotland, and may serve as beacons to others who allow themselves to dream of a better future.

*Philip and Myrtle Ashmole*
*Editors*

# PART I
# MAKING A DREAM COME TRUE

# HOW IT ALL BEGAN

*Fi Martynoga*

## PEEBLESSHIRE ENVIRONMENT CONCERN AND THE 1993 CONFERENCE

In the beginning Philip Ashmole had an idea: "Wouldn't it be wonderful for a grass-roots group to get hold of a whole valley, from river to mountain top, so that we could put back the vegetation that might have existed before man made an impact on the landscape!" was what he shared with some of us. We were in a car, driving to Dryburgh Abbey Hotel where we were setting up a conference called *Restoring Borders Woodland*. Philip had recently retired from Edinburgh University and had become interested in Peeblesshire Environment Concern (PEC), the small group that his wife, Myrtle, Ann Goodburn, and I ran in Peebles. We had focused on global issues and then on more local ones, so his observation that the area of native woodland in the higher parts of the Scottish Borders was vanishingly small struck a chord with us.

It was just at the time that a number of grants for planting broadleaved trees had become available through the Local Authority and Forestry Commission Scotland. We discovered the uptake on grants was poor, so decided to aim the conference at land owners and managers. We then persuaded some of them with the best experience of planting native trees in the Borders, Michael Strang Steel and Richard Dalkeith (son of the 9th Duke of Buccleuch, now 10th Duke) for example, to speak to our audience. This was to encourage other landowners and farmers to come. We also brought in speakers – some with fairly radical ideas – from a variety of organisations such as Reforesting Scotland, the RSPB, Scottish Natural Heritage, Tweed Foundation, Forestry Commission Scotland, and the inspiring Trees for Life.

Everyone seemed to leave the conference with a sense of excitement and purpose. Many had the land on which to plant but Peeblesshire Environment Concern certainly didn't. The idea of creating a wildwood had to simmer for a while.

## NAÏVE HOPES FOR FINANCES AND THE SEARCH FOR A SITE

We had some fantasies about asking the Heritage Lottery Fund (HLF) for assistance in buying land but it was late in 1994 when we were galvanised by the first mention of a Millennium Forest for Scotland Trust (MFST), an umbrella organisation set up to enable woodland-related projects across Scotland to access funds from the Millennium Commission, one part of the National Lottery. Philip and Myrtle were abroad but Anna and Dominic Ashmole invited PEC supporters, and anyone else interested, to a series of meetings to discuss the possibility of putting forward a proposal to MFS, which was to be funded with National Lottery money. Thus the Wildwood Group was born: twenty or thirty dreamers sitting in a circle amid the infant woodland at Kidston Mill, the Ashmoles home near Peebles, all agog at the possibility of getting hold of money to make a dream reality.

In the end, the hope of acquiring funds so easily was dashed. We missed the deadline for the MFST applications because we did not have a site and, without one, our idea really was but a dream. We also discovered over the following months, that no public body such as Scottish Natural Heritage would be likely to provide funds for land purchase if the price was higher than the District Valuation.

Nonetheless, those initial enthusiasts were not deterred. There was something about the name 'Wildwood' that caught the imagination. It served to attract such a competent and enthusiastic set of people, for those dreamers had a remarkable range of skills that have proved very useful to the project over the years. Everything depended, however, on finding a place for the Wildwood. Yet it took time for us to form a plan and it was not until the late autumn of 1995 that we sent out a mailing to all the farmers, estates, and other landowners whose names we could discover. This was a year before the publication of Andy Wightman's *Who Owns Scotland,* and he kindly gave us access to some of his research, which proved very useful. We were asking about the possibility of purchasing a considerable parcel of land, preferably an entire valley for our wildwood.

## CARRIFRAN WILDWOOD MISSION STATEMENT

*The Wildwood project aims to re-create, in the Southern Uplands of Scotland, an extensive tract of mainly forested wilderness with most of the rich diversity of native species present in the area before human activities became dominant. The woodland will not be exploited commercially and the impact of humans will be carefully managed. Access will be open to all, and it is hoped that the Wildwood will be used throughout the next millennium as an inspiration and an educational resource.*

It was at this stage that we realised that we must be absolutely clear about the nature of our project. To a large extent it was driven by a desire to give something back to nature, rather than viewing the land primarily as a resource for humans. There was a ready consensus in the Wildwood Group that we wanted to undertake large-scale ecological restoration, but this was still too vague, and Myrtle insisted that we compose a concise statement to encapsulate our aims and to ensure that the original vision was not compromised by our successors. We adopted it while we were still searching for a site, but little amendment was needed when we found Carrifran. Two decades later, we would not change a word.

Over the next year there were several positive responses from landowners that got us excited. But these petered out quickly as farmers discovered inheritance tax complications in selling off land, or, in one case, had a change of mind at the last minute. Then, through a chance conversation with a visiting friend, I found out that a farm near Moffat might be the place to look. 'My cousin has recently bought it. I'm sure he would sell you part of it' I was told. When we saw the position of Capplegill farm on the map, we realised it contained the splendid Carrifran Valley, which certainly fitted our criteria. We had discounted it partly because it was in Dumfries & Galloway, not Peeblesshire, but in the face of our fruitless search, that suddenly seemed less significant.

*Philip Ashmole being interviewed on fundraising launch day,*
*with Dan Jones and Robert Hardy (right)*

Philip assembled a negotiating team of a lawyer and a land agent and went to talk to John Barker, the owner. He was clearly intrigued by the idea of a wildwood but his strong business instincts guided him and his initial price for Carrifran was £1 million. We walked away for six months and pursued other options, until renewed negotiations, this time with a skilled financial adviser as well, finally resulted in the suggestion that we might buy the land for a third of the original sum.

The offer came with strings. We would have to accept that John Barker would continue to graze much of the valley, reducing the area parcel by parcel for several years. He could then continue to claim subsidies and this would go some way towards offsetting the loss of a higher selling price. In fact, this suited our purpose well, as we recognised that we would not be able to plant the whole area in a single season, and continued grazing would stop the grass sward from getting out of hand. It meant, however, that we had to erect a lot of temporary internal fences to prevent the sheep from eating our young trees.

The other string was one we set ourselves. We asked for a two-year legal Option to Purchase and were granted it. If we could raise the money by the end of 1999, the valley would become ours.

## REFLECTIONS ON 100 STEERING GROUP MEETINGS

*After more than 100 meetings of the Wildwood Steering Group, attendance is always good, perhaps because of a good meal and serious discussion that continues in the meeting*

As a child growing up in the Scottish Borders I knew our round, bare hills and loved them just as they were. As an adult one summer about thirty years ago I was walking on a sunny Wester Ross day in one of those "wilderness" glens when we came across a small high fenced exclosure which had an unlocked gate and free entry. Inside was another world – a protected little square of beautiful young mixed trees, birdsong, insects, grasses, flowers, scents – a small paradise. It was my first close up of 're-wilding' – so talked about now, little noticed then. I was hooked. I became one of the friends who formed the Wildwood Group led so ably by Philip and Myrtle Ashmole in the '90s. I remember Philip's description of climbing up to the small Loch Skene above the Grey Mare's Tail just east of where Carrifan Wildwood is now and how the only trees to be seen in the vicinity were on a small islet in the middle of the loch where the sheep or any grazers could not reach! Another seminal moment!

We meet regularly in a member's house and all contribute to a meal before the meetings and intentionally we have no permanent chairman but give everyone a chance. I think this informality has really helped to keep us together for 20 years! Usually my contribution is to try to extract the Minutes from all the enthusiasm! We have several scientists but we are not just a scientific group. We discuss and make all the decisions for Carrifran Wildwood – a paradise in the Borders.

**Ann Goodburn**

### THE CREATION OF BORDERS FOREST TRUST

Initial elation was followed by panic. Could we, a small group of friends and associates, actually become landowners? A parallel development helped us out of this dilemma. Others in the Borders, notably Tim Stead, the sculptor and one of the initiators of the very first Community Woodlands in Scotland, had many visions for wood-related projects. He wanted to see much more educational work in schools, a Woodschool to train furniture makers, and better use made of local hardwoods. After discussions with MFST, we joined forces with him and others to make a bid for basic lottery support. It was successful and Borders Forest Trust was born. The Wildwood project was to be a fairly autonomous entity within the trust and the problem of ownership of our site, should we secure it, was solved.

### SERIOUS FUNDRAISING

The original set of dreamers, now styled the Wildwood Group, turned out to include more people interested in planting trees than enthusiasts for fundraising. Some arm-twisting created an effective fundraising group of about six, though none had relevant experience. Once the knowledge that public money was out of the question had sunk in, our initial thought was to try for business support. On good advice we soon gave this up: businesses prefer projects with a bigger human element and ours was strictly for nature. Instead, we focused on getting the money from individuals and small trusts.

Using talent from within the group, we designed and produced tens of thousands of copies of a brochure that stressed the potential to turn the spectacular Carrifran Valley from bare sheep-walk into lush woodland. We wrote articles for magazines and journals using brochures as inserts. We sent them to our entire social circles asking for help, then to any rich acquaintances, and finally to any celebrities we thought might take an interest.

One incidental feature of Carrifran proved extremely helpful in fundraising. A few years before we had it in our sights, a hill walker had spotted an unusual bit of wood sticking out of a peat-hag on Rotten Bottom, just above the valley. It proved to be around 6000 years old: the oldest Prehistoric yew bow ever found in Britain. Wanting to understand the context of the find, the National Trust for Scotland, which owned nearby land, raised money from Strongbow Cider to pay for core samples to be taken by archaeologists through more than three metres of peat at the site. These gave us 10,000 years worth of pollen data: one of the longest pollen profiles in Scotland, which later helped us decide on the species to plant.

Initially, though, it was the story of the find itself that gave real interest to our brochure. We sent a copy to one celebrity, the actor Robert Hardy, whom we knew had written a book on archery. Moreover, he had a house in Peeblesshire, so the project was potentially of local interest to him. It was! He really served us very well by coming out to do photo-shoots at Carrifran, and again at the Royal Botanic Garden Edinburgh, to launch our fundraising campaign. The press coverage on the following day was impressive.

The Fundraising Group had, early on, made a decision to appeal for large sums of money. Anyone prepared to donate £250 or £500 became a Founder and received a thank you letter from Philip, as well as a certificate to show their special connection with the project. We offered the two rates because we felt strongly that the less well off who gave generously (£250 was a considerable sum in 1998/9) should not be seen as second-class donors compared with

## WORKING FOR FREE

Early in the Wildwood project we established a feature that still sets it apart from most comparable initiatives: we decided that to maintain the grass-roots character of the Wildwood project, volunteers would play a central role and not be optional extras, and that any task that could be done by volunteers would be done by them rather than being handed over to Borders Forest Trust staff or to consultants. We realised that we would sometimes need professional help, but there was lots of expertise within the group and we always tried to maximise its use, establishing the norm of working for free. Fundraising has been almost entirely by volunteers (though donations are handled by BFT staff), the main ecological planning was done by volunteers (though many of these were relevant professionals) and we often receive free advice on legal and land agency matters. Seed collecting has always been the responsibility of volunteers, and visiting groups are normally shown around by volunteers, allowing our few overstretched staff to get on with the tasks that only they can do.

**Myrtle Ashmole**

those who could afford more. The gamble paid off. Over the months we built up to 500 Founders and as Millennium Day (the date set for the purchase) approached, we were two-thirds of the way to our £350,000 target.

A little last-minute panic and flurry around securing a bridging-loan was soon allayed. A final appeal to friends and supporters, one or two of whom gave sums up to £25,000, found us with nearly £400,000 in the bank at the end of 1999. Two other factors had assisted us. One was a careful appeal to small trusts. They were often quite slow in responding and a lot of work was involved, but in the end came up with various sums that added up to about one fifth of our total.

The other was a most useful bond we forged with the John Muir Trust (JMT). We felt we needed the backing of a more established group than BFT, which was still in its infancy. JMT has a big following in Scotland and overseas. Its avowed interest in wild land accorded with our desire to create a wild place (remember this is before 'rewilding' was a recognised word or concept). The trust did not give us money but generously allowed us to write an article about the Wildwood project for their journal at the start of our fundraising campaign, and to insert copies of our brochure in the same issue; the result was extraordinary, with funds immediately starting to pour in. We owe them a debt of gratitude for their support at a crucial moment, and much value our continuing association with them.

## HOW TO CREATE A WILDWOOD

We were lucky enough to have a forest ecologist in the group, Adrian Newton, working at Edinburgh University but living in Peebles. This enabled us to organise a high profile Edinburgh University/Borders Forest Trust conference. In autumn 1997 we assembled more than 150 ecologists and foresters in the Royal Botanic Garden Edinburgh to establish the principles for restoring deciduous forest in the south of Scotland, a task distinct from the efforts that were already under way to bring back extensive Caledonian pine forests in the Highlands. The well-known speakers and the range of expertise among the delegates raised credibility, and undoubtedly helped us when we put forward proposals to plant hundreds of acres of new deciduous woodland and to change the whole ecology of Carrifran.

At the conference we heard about the pollen record and about the sad history of the woodlands of the Borders, and we soon decided that we should attempt to recreate the type of vegetation that was present at about the time the Rotten Bottom Bow was lost. Its owner would probably have been one of a mobile band of Mesolithic hunters six thousand years ago. A little later in time, people would start to settle, to have domestic herds, and to cultivate crops. But that hunter lived just before any major human impact was made on the landscape, when the woodland that had developed after the last retreat of the glaciers had reached its greatest diversity and really could be described as wild.

An early practical decision was to make use of the Woodland Grant Scheme of the Forestry Commission to establish broadleaved woodland in most of the lower part of Carrifran valley. A big scheme like this required an elaborate Environmental Statement to support the grant application and we thought we might need to employ a consultant. But Adrian convinced us that we could prepare the document in-house, and he agreed to lead the communal process. The Statement had to take into consideration that Carrifran Valley is part of the Moffat Hills Site of Special Scientific Interest (SSSI), principally because of the presence of certain rare

*Carrifran as a brown desert, winter 1998*

plant species found only at high altitudes. It also had to consider the archaeological features within the valley, so money to pay for a proper archaeological survey was duly sought.

Through most of 1998 we met monthly in a Peebles pub to develop our plans, sometimes joined by senior foresters or other experts who offered sage advice. Adrian circulated a draft of a chapter of the Environmental Statement before each meeting and it was then scrutinized, paragraph by paragraph, by the Ecological Planning Group, a sub-group of the main Wildwood Group with a range of skills in forestry, landscape, botany and ecology. Those without relevant specific skills weighed in with aesthetic judgments and distinct points of view. The discussions were lively, but slowly a fully democratic plan was evolved. Although this was principally aimed at convincing the Forestry Commission Scotland (FCS) that we had an appropriate planting plan, it also served to show our competence to Scottish Natural Heritage and Dumfries & Galloway Council, as well as to other potential funders. When it was finally submitted, FCS approved it without modification and remarked that it was one of the best management plans they had seen, which we took as an accolade to our grass-roots, diverse and talented group.

## TOWARDS MILLENNIUM DAY

As Millennium Day approached, we realised that Borders Forest Trust were on the brink of ownership of one of the finest valleys in the south of Scotland. It was magnificent in scenic terms, but we knew that it was ecologically degraded, and we were on a mission to

*Carrifran in summer 1996, producing some lamb and beef, but an ecosystem at the nadir*

demonstrate how it could once again come to function as a natural upland ecosystem, more beautiful and with far greater diversity of plants and animals than the surrounding denuded sheep-walk and spruce plantations.

Acceptance of our Environmental Statement by the FCS paved the way for success in obtaining our first government funding, to support planting of nearly half a million trees in the lower parts of Carrifran, creating 300 hectares of native woodland. This funding came with a few awkward strings, of which the most serious was the stipulation that the grant-aided planting could only include 10% of 'shrubs'. This rule was clearly a legacy of a time when the only role of the Forestry Commission was to grow harvestable timber: it was inappropriate for 'conservation woodlands' and has since been relaxed. But at the turn of the century, although we had considerable freedom in proportions of major tree species, all the species classed as 'shrubs' (including Hazel, Hawthorn, Blackthorn, Juniper, as well as all the roses and smaller willows) had to be crammed into the 10% that was allowed.

This was ridiculous in an ecological restoration project, but in the end it did not cramp our style too much, because we had a fairy godfather. David Stevenson, former owner of the Edinburgh Woollen Mill, agreed to help us to the tune of over a hundred and fifty thousand pounds for propagating trees, and this – along with the availability of many dedicated volunteer tree-planters – has enabled us to add in tens of thousands of extra shrubs (and some trees) after completion of the main planting. We are still going on with this 'enrichment planting', making the composition of the new woodland a better approximation of what was probably there in the distant past.

In January 2000, however, we tried to hit the ground running, making the best possible use of the grant aid. Because of our two-year option on the site, we had had time to do all our planning in advance, as well as raising the money. We knew how we wanted to programme the planting, and volunteers had been making trips to surviving ancient woodland fragments in our area to collect the seeds needed to ensure that when we became owners of Carrifran there would be saplings ready for us to plant. Some were in back gardens, but most were in two local commercial nurseries, since we had quickly realised that as we would be planting tens of thousands of trees each year, a group of amateurs could not expect to grow them all.

Furthermore, a far-sighted person in the newly established Borders Forest Trust had realised that once we were involved in large scale planting and fencing contracts, we would need a professional project officer. Scottish Natural Heritage agreed to fund a position for a year full-time, and for several subsequent years part-time. Hugh Chalmers was in post by the time we actually bought Carrifran, and he takes up the story now.

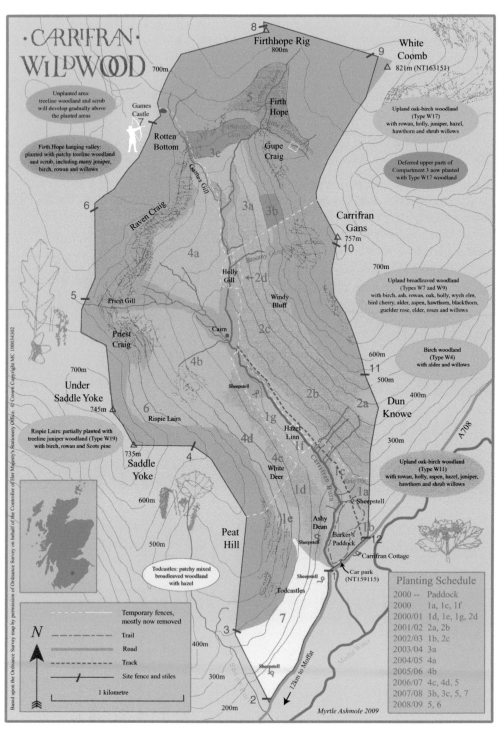

Map of Carrifran, showing outline of planting plan for the first decade

# BRINGING BACK THE TREES

*Hugh Chalmers*

*Hugh Chalmers*

STARTING FROM SCRATCH

The offer of Project Officer funding from Scottish Natural Heritage (SNH) came late in the day. They had been persuaded that this was a valid use of public funds as without a dedicated person to move work along, there would be complete reliance on volunteers, and there was a lot to do on site. A job description was assembled and an advert distributed. SNH funding would be sufficient for a full time post for one year and several further years at part-time. At the time I had been a Farm Wildlife Adviser with the Farming & Wildlife Advisory Group (FWAG) for around five years, based in the Borders. It was a great job, and I had learned a lot during that time, especially working with farmers and the agriculture department to implement the first agri-environment scheme in the area, the Central Southern Uplands Environmentally Sensitive Area Scheme, which focused mainly on the loss of heather on the hills, the lack of native trees and the degraded state of watercourses. However, it was obvious that whilst the scheme was full of good intentions, it was not going to be particularly effective, despite significant money being paid to farmers to reduce sheep numbers and to erect fences.

The opportunity to be a key player in a project which could make a real difference to a dramatic valley in the Southern Uplands was very attractive, but had to be balanced with job security (with a mortgage and two young children!) At the interview I was offered the job and I accepted. A life changing decision!

On 1st December 1999 I made a small office space on my cottage landing and arranged for a computer to be delivered – there was no room at the BFT Green Shed, so I would work from home. It seems like another age, as mobile phones were just becoming commonplace, and the internet was equally new. I spent time with Philip and Willie (McGhee, the Director of BFT) and other Wildwood Group members, getting to know the actors in the drama about to unfold – Forestry Commission staff were important, as were SNH, but also the looming threat from a local group – the Friends of Moffat Water – who were opposed to our plans to relocate around 40 feral goats from Carrifran.

The priority was to carry out the work detailed in the Woodland Grant Scheme five-year contract, where we were obliged to plant around 40ha (60,000 trees) per year for the first five years. Fencing, tree seed gathering and growing, herbivore management, taking on contractors started in earnest. Carrifran in 2000 was not fenced, except for a small length beside the Polmoody plantation and a poor fence across Rotten Bottom.

*Oak woodland established on Rum by Peter
Wormell in the 1960s, which we visited in 2001*

## A RUM EXPERIENCE

In September 2001, ten members of the Wildwood Group visited a number of native woodland planting sites on Morvern, Mull and the Isle of Rum. On the SNH owned island of Rum National Nature Reserve, large and small areas of trees had been planted by Peter Wormell the first warden, and we walked among closed canopies of oak and birch. We were particularly impressed by the small patches of plantation at Harris, on the exposed west side of Rum, where a wind sculpted edge formed a bulwark to storms straight off the Atlantic – if trees could survive here, they could survive at Carrifran! I re-visited Rum in 2018 and was dumbstruck by the state of the woods around Harris – they were completely trashed by horses, highland ponies and red deer, the fences being in an advanced state of disrepair. What had been an inspiration to the Wildwood group had now become a warning! Herbivore management is everything when establishing new native woodland.

**Hugh Chalmers**

*Planted oak woodland on Rum in 2018, devastated by red deer after the fences broke down*

We needed a 11 kilometre fence (mostly above 600m asl.) to keep out domestic sheep and feral goats. We decided that a deer fence would be pointless, as deer would get in, and a tall wire net would be torn down each winter, especially when ice formed on the wire, combined with high winds. We agonised over the design, and came up with a fence of seven mild steel line wires, posts at 2m spacing made of slow grown Russian pine, which had been well preserved. Even the fence staples, which hold the wire to the fence, were specially barbed, so as not to pull out easily. We were fortunate to take on Charlie McCrerie, a fence contractor from Denholm. He and his team (with the aid of a helicopter lift) put in very long days over the first summer, and by the end of August we had a secure site to establish the Wildwood.

There was always some tension about whether or not we would be able to establish trees and so fulfil the WGS contract. We had taken the 'King's Shilling', so if we failed, all the grant money (eventually over £400,000 from Forestry Commission) would need to be paid back with interest. Experience with our first efforts at planting in April 2000, behind a temporary electric fence to exclude sheep and goats, caused some concern. The Rowan saplings had flushed (the buds had grown into fleshy, soft, leaves) and they looked good, until a fierce wind (probably a mini-tornado) visited the valley and blew all the leaves off! Earlier on, planted saplings were blanketed in snow, which held them in an icy grip, with the top few inches exposed. The ensuing wind and icy hail then proceeded to scour the bark and buds off the trees. I also witnessed a young holly sapling being torn out of the ground by a whirlwind and flying up the valley! Together with sheep and goat incursions, worries about tree diseases, and nibbling from deer, it was a challenging start.

However, there were encouraging times too, such as the great invasion of enthusiastic volunteers on the first Sunday of the month during the first few years, planting hundreds of trees, constructing a basic shelter in an old sheep gathering stell (to shelter volunteers from the cruel combination of horizontal rain just above freezing point!). We also had some large trees to plant, especially holly which were now five years old and had been grown on in volunteers' gardens – I planted these with Michael Matthews, who had coordinated their production in the firm hope that they would find a suitable home. I would often meet people walking in the valley (on days of good weather) who would reveal themselves as Founders of the Wildwood. Their enthusiasm for the project was encouraging but also a bit daunting, as the pressure was on to succeed. Knowledge and advice from successful new native tree planting projects was important too, especially 'Trees for Life', who were doing great things in the Scottish Highlands.

Over the first seven years at Carrifran, we planted about 40ha, around 60,000 trees, per year. This was too big a job for volunteers, so the planting was done by three main contractors – Treesurv, David Cairns and James McCallum – with areas marked out for each them. They placed 30cm canes in summer, followed by a spot herbicide treatment. Trees were delivered in October and then planting began, with a 20cm vole guard used to protect delicate and juicy stems. The contracting teams worked steadily through to April. Despite a lot of discussion on how to make the job easier, perhaps using machines or horses on steep ground, it was obvious that grit, determination and a good level of fitness was the key, and planters would load up their planting bags with 20kg of trees and vole guards and slog up the steep slopes, time after time. They only stopped if the tree bundles were frozen together. It was a pleasure working with them.

## INSPIRATION FROM NORWAY

The montane zone is the land above the tree-line, but below the dwarf shrub/heather line, and in the Southern Uplands of Scotland is probably between 500m snd 700m. Juniper, Dwarf Birch and a number of upland willow species would grow there, but they are almost entirely absent in the Southern Uplands due to a long history of grazing and burning. Only tiny remnants survive, mostly on cliffs inaccessible to grazers. The South West of Norway provides a vision of the diversity which could flourish again in Scotland. The climate, geology and soils of the two regions have been shown to be remarkably similar, and a summer walk in the hills of SW Norway always inspires budding and more experienced restoration ecologists. To walk among twisted Birch, Dwarf Birch, Juniper, Heather, Blueberry, willows and stunted Pine is surely one of nature's greatest pleasures, though tinged with sadness when one recalls the comprehensive loss of habitat back in Scotland.

**Hugh Chalmers**

*Trollheimen, Norway c.900m with Downy Birch, riparian Downy Willow and Juniper, and with Dwarf Birch nearby, above Scots pine*

## MOUNTAIN BIRCH

Until recently the highest woodland in Scotland was Creag Fhiaclach, at 640m asl above Loch an Eilein in the Cairngorms. It was even stated that it represented the natural tree line, and to this day you can find an interpretive sign in Glenmore stating that this shows the climate there is even harsher than in Scandinavia! It's not true, though. Weather records then and now clearly indicate that the climates of SW Norway and of the Highlands are closely similar. And now that grazing pressures have been reduced in parts of the central Cairngorms, pines are pioneering up to 900m and beyond on Meall a' Bhuacaille and in the northern corries, which is just where you would expect the transition to the alpine zone to be, by comparison with places of the same climate and geology in SW Norway.

This is great news of course, but – something is missing. In northern mountain regions around the world, the natural pattern is for pines or spruces to dominate to a certain height, about 700-750m in climates like the Cairngorms. They are succeeded above it by the 'birch belt', usually open in character and always dominated by a special form of Downy Birch *Betula pubescens*, though pines and other species like Juniper, Aspen and Rowan are often scattered within them; and then – before fading gradually into the alpine zone – the ' willow region', a mosaic of low bushes, grasses, herbs, and Heather in which montane willow species are common, though not usually dominant. The missing element in Scotland is the 'tortuosa' form of Downy Birch. It is not a subspecies, at least in the usual colloquial usage, but a stable high altitude form. It is freely interfertile with lower ground forms, and a spectrum of intermediate forms are common in the transitional zone, but it nevertheless maintains its characteristics despite a line of contact with lower ground forms up and down every glen in the mountain regions of northern Eurasia. This indicates that there is something in the genetic material of the form that allows it to live at these higher altitudes.

The form appears to be extinct in Scotland, as is so much else of the higher altitude woodland flora and fauna. Possibly a few cling to cliffs here and there, as with the montane willows. The highest birch woodland in Scotland seems to be at about 560m near Newtonmore, well below the limit for the tortuosa form in similar climates elsewhere. Attempts to plant low ground origin seedlings at higher altitudes have failed. Tortuosa is usually low in height, rarely more than 3m and towards its limits, often not above 1m. It usually branches strongly from low down, so that it has only a short, or even no, 'trunk'. The branches are often tortuous in form (hence the name). In part this can be due to the weight of snow in winter, but in part it is genetic. This woodland type supports a diverse flora and fauna, much of it requiring the habitat and much of it extinct or very rare in Scotland. It is much more productive biologically, and potentially economically (through hunting and grazing at moderate densities), than the current artificial habitats at those altitudes, and it has other beneficial social and economic effects such as stabilising slopes and reducing peaks and troughs in runoff. Restoration of treeline woodland at these altitudes is desirable, and on the evidence available it needs birch of this form to achieve it. Where to get it? The choices are to try to breed back from any remnants clinging to cliffs in Britain, or to bring in seed from similar climates, for instance in SW Norway, where it can easily be collected in large quantities. Genetic research shows there is little variation in Downy Birch DNA on a continental scale, as would be expected in a wind pollinated and dispersed species only 10,000 years after the last Ice Age. In any case, non-native Downy Birch have been very widely planted in Scotland as amenity trees, and in some places as experimental plantations, for decades; these have bred, and will breed with trees of local provenance. Even if arguments about racial purity in Downy Dirch held any water, and the scientific data says they do not, that ship has sailed.

**Duncan Halley**

*Planted Honeysuckle on young birches.*

*Planted Ivy colonising a large Downy Birch survivor in Hazel Linn
which has put up large suckers since removal of feral goats*

## BRINGING BACK THE LIANAS

Native woodlands are not complete without the scrambling plants such as Honeysuckle and Ivy, our analogues of lianas in the forests of the tropics. Absence of Honeysuckle is typical of unhealthy woodland grazed by sheep, while Ivy is unpopular with foresters and those who view an untidy wood as one needing more 'management'. In restoring a Wildwood we are trying gradually to hand over control to nature. Unmanaged natural woods - almost unknown in Britain - have ancient and partially dead trees as well as young ones, and everywhere there are fallen trunks, branches and twigs, all contributing to the complex layer of rotting leaves and wood on the forest floor, home to an extraordinary community of small animals, fungi and microbes. When the main planting at Carrifran was under control, some of us searched out survivng stands of the pale-flowered wild Honeysuckle - not the brightly coloured ones grown in gardens - growing in local ancient woodland remnants, and cut long strands to take home. We then cut them into sections with two nodes and bundled them in water in batches for distribution to gardening friends who were prepared to grow them on, using a variety of approaches. Rooting in damp sand - with one node above ground and one below - is followed by planting out in compost or soil, producing plants ready for taking to Carrifran in the following year. After almost a decade of this work a couple of thousand Honeysuckles are flourishing in the Wildwood, though more are needed in the areas planted most recently. Bringing back Ivy is at an earlier stage, but some Ivies have been planted and hundreds more are in the the pipeline.

**Myrtle and Philip Ashmole**

RESTORING MONTANE SCRUB AT CARRIFRAN

Although the montane scrub so far established at Carrifran is limited in extent, it has required a significant and sustained effort by volunteers. We don't have the luxury of a track from the valley bottom up to the 700m hanging valley which is Little Firthhope, an ascent of 550m, the last part of which is quite steep and exposed. However, it is possible for tracked vehicles to take a long way round to carry the thousands of saplings needed close to the site. To date there have been around 15 'high camps', where hardy souls carry up tents to the site and spend the weekend restoring the montane forest. There is a great deal of camaraderie during these events – conditions can be challenging. We ensure that there is at least one qualified Mountain Leader during these weekends. Despite that, incidents do happen.

One memorable weekend we felt the urge to walk to the top of Firthhope Rig in the fading light after a hard but rewarding day planting juniper and downy willow. There were long runnels of snow stretching down 100m from the top of the steep slope, and these looked like a handy and rapid way back down to camp. I went first, launching head first on slippery waterproofs, quickly reaching top speed and coming to a halt by spinning round and using my feet to brake. Chris, from Devon, came next. I don't think he had experienced much snow in Devon, and seemed not to consider the need to brake. As he sped down towards me, I realised drastic measures were required, so I jumped on top of him as he whizzed past me, and made sure we stopped before the rocky scree! Chris was surprised, grateful and sore! Reflecting on his experience later in the tent with whisky and chocolate, he concluded that it was a one-off, but unforgettable experience!

Dave Bone, an astronomer from Manchester is another character who has been at the heart of the montane scrub restoration. He is the definition of indefatigable, and is just as at home among Himalayan peaks as the round shouldered hills of the Southern Uplands. He will regularly bivvy out up high and have hundreds of trees planted before other volunteers have stirred from their sleeping bags.

We recently altered the high-camp weekend arrangements and now lie low beneath the crags on a Friday or Saturday night, based around an ex-army arctic bell tent at the foot of Firthhope Linn. This avoids the need for volunteers to lug camping gear beyond the 400m contour, although they do have to do the rest of the climb on Saturday and again on Sunday. It also places us in a sort of flexible siege position, ready to strike up high in the morning either to Firth Hope, the hanging valley on Carrifran between 600 and 750m above Firthhope Linn, or to the planting sites close to Games Castle, Rough Craig and Stirk Craig – the latter two at the head of the Gameshope valley – and thus part of the River Tweed catchment. This is where we will join up two major BFT sites – Carrifran and Talla & Gameshope – with a common new habitat. This work will be on-going for the next decade or so, so we will need new hardy recruits for this rewarding task.

With over 35,000 willows and Juniper already planted at high levels on Carrifran (though of course not all of them still alive) the high-camp volunteers share the vision of a restored montane scrub zone, where, like in Norway, there is the full range of natural vegetation. There is also the hope of the whole suite of creatures one day living in the montane zone, including birds such as black grouse, who are struggling to survive in south Scotland. The Montane Scrub Action Group, of which BFT is an active member, has been instrumental in bringing this 'Cinderella' habitat to the attention of ecologists and the wider public. It suffers badly from the 'shifting baseline' syndrome; it's so long ago since this amazing habitat was removed by fire and grazing, that we have almost forgotten that it ever existed.

### Foot & Mouth and its aftermath

During the Foot & Mouth outbreak in 2001 (when millions of sheep and cattle were destroyed to control a widespread viral infection) we were not allowed to go on the land at Carrifran. The sheep had been culled (though not the 40 or so feral goats), but we were not allowed to cull deer. One big problem was that we had just taken delivery of around 25,000 delicate native tree saplings, cell-grown and wrapped in plastic bundles of 15. We decided to water them until the next planting season in October. This proved to be a bad idea. The water supply from the Spring at Keld Pot, quickly dried up, so we divided the trees among volunteers to water them at home in their bundles of 15. We should have paid to have them returned to the nursery to be re-potted and grown on properly, but the cost would have been considerable. The 70% of trees which did survive were badly weakened, so when we planted them out, they either died or took many years to recover. As a result, the cost of replacing dead trees, extra weed control and worry, taught us that we should always plant well-grown and vigorous saplings.

### The problem of Bracken

As there was only around 8ha of Bracken at Carrifran we decided that we would simply hand cut around small planted trees for a few years until the trees got their heads above the luxuriant fern. Volunteers in June and July could be used to whip or cut the stems around the trees, whilst enjoying the natural charms of early summer in the valley. After the end of the first season, we knew we were in trouble; the Bracken grew really strong (being released from sheep and cows trampling and browsing) and some groups of volunteers refused to go anywhere near bracken as its sap is carcinogenic. On hot days swarms

*Incompetently sprayed bracken*

of head-flies would gather around us, tree saplings would suffer 'Sheffield Blight' – being cut by sickles accidentally, and on wet days (there were many) we would be soaked in minutes. Through persistence, we did manage to get most trees to survive, but some were completely swamped by the Bracken and lost.  Bracken needs to be taken seriously.  On the southern tip of Carrifran, where planting was started later than in the main part of the valley, we used a helicopter to spray around 20ha of Bracken with the approved chemical Asulox. This area was part of the SSSI site and the consent  from Scottish Natural Heritage required us to cover up other fern species, especially the uncommon Parsley Fern. The timing of such spraying is critical and weather caused delays, with the result that it was not fully effective. The trees there are growing well, but at what harm to the wider environment? Another attempt at control, with contractors using knapsack spraying, was done in windy weather and led to embarrassing patterns on the hillside. Lots of lessons learned.

## Deer Control

From the very start of the Wildwood project, we knew that deer, and roe deer in particular, were a serious challenge to establishing a new native woodland. Roe deer have no natural predators in Britain, and we thought that they would be more attracted to the valley as we removed the sheep and goats over the first five years, so our tender broad-leaved saplings would be at risk. Deer clearly had to be excluded or culled. A deer fence round the whole site did not seem a realistic option, so we resorted to control using firearms, as described later.

One incident in 2004 had brought my thoughts to a conclusion. In June, I spotted two roe bucks part way up the Peat Hill side of the valley among newly planted trees. It was the start of the rut, and they were sparring together, using their sharp antlers to clash and push each other – it looked like a fair match. I walked towards them to chase them away from the young trees with their delicate and tasty leaves. They were too engrossed in combat to take any notice of me – such is the influence of testosterone. They eventually moved on, but I realised that I was on their territory. Things would need to change.

The ethics of deer control was something we had discussed in the Wildwood Ecological Planning Group, and we were aware that our supporters would need to work through the sometimes painful realisation that to create a new native woodland at Carrifran using ecological restoration principles, we would need to mimic natural predation as much as is possible, although the law in Scotland required shooting with a high-powered rifle. Unlike our ancestor who left his weapon at Rotten Bottom 6,000 years ago, we would not be using bow and arrow.

Unfortunately, deer hunting in Scotland (particularly of red deer stags) is often associated with an elite class of individuals who pay significant sums to take a trophy. We were convinced that this 'sport shooting', where the hunters pay for the experience of deer stalking, especially when they take 'trophy' of an impressive head of antlers, was not the way to organise our cull. There is always the worry that management of trophy hunting will be more motivated by ensuring that a trophy is present on the site, than that damage to trees is kept low by reducing densities of deer of both sexes. To us, the more acceptable model is that of non-elite hunting in Scandinavia, where there is a widespread hunting culture and trees can regenerate freely.

Even after taking the decision to cull, uncertainty remained over whether we could keep deer densities down to a level that would allow our newly planted trees to grow for long enough for them to get out of danger from deer. As far as we knew, this had not been done at this scale before, as any similar broad-leaved plantings had been smaller and at a lower level where deer fencing could be used.

In our ambitious scheme, a well-run and extensive deer control effort would be needed, or all our planting efforts would be in vain. We therefore measured the effect of browsing on the trees in our grant-aided planting while they were becoming established, using a standardised method, and this gave us good information on the extent and severity of damage. If it was excessive, extra trees were planted to maintain the required densities, and the shooting effort was increased.

The practicalities of budgeting for the deer control were obvious. Some figures we found suggested that it might take between 30-80 hours of effort to cull a roe deer – we really had no idea. In practice, over the last 18 years at Carrifran, a steady average of 25 deer per year have been culled, at a cost of around £5,000 per year. Our most recent figures show that it takes around 12 hours of effort by our professional deer stalker to cull one roe deer at Carrifran – a remarkably low figure which reflects the skill of the individual. Nonetheless, deer culling remains a major item in the budget, and we look forward to the growth of our planted trees putting them out of danger, and in the long run to the time when culling by lynx enables enough trees to regenerate naturally to maintain the Wildwood.

Photo: Robin Sloan

*Volunteers planting at Carrifran, 2015*

# PART II

# SEEING WHAT NATURE CAN DO

*.... and the birds come back*

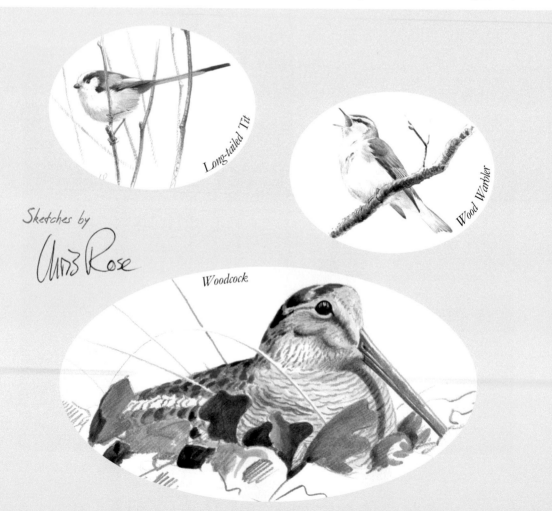

*Long-tailed Tit*

*Wood Warbler*

*Sketches by*

*Woodcock*

*Remnant woodland with notable plant life, Holly Gill*

*Relict Downy Birches below newly established Oak-Birch woodland with Blaeberry in Broomy Gutter*

# VEGETATION RELEASED FROM DOMESTIC GRAZING

*Stuart Adair*

### SUMMARY OF PLANT LIFE IN 2000

The plant life at Carrifran in the year 2000 consisted of the short-cropped, largely tree-less vegetation associated with – and so typical of – long-term pasturing and extensive grazing of domestic farm animals and muirburn (burning of vegetation to encourage grasses and heather and prevent woodland restoration). The virgin forest had long since gone and been largely replaced by the wiry leaved swards of Mat-grass and Bent and Fescue grasses and various forms of heath. A few tiny fragments of the old forest clung on in inaccessible places such as cliffs, ledges, steep ravines and wherever domestic animals (and feral goats) could not gain access.

Although these fragments were very small (and could barely be described as woodland proper) they did provide vital refugia for both trees and shrubs, along with a suite of herbs, ferns and mosses, so typical of our ancient indigenous woodlands. About nineteen native species of trees and shrubs had survived in such places. The bulk of the growth consisted of Downy Birch and Rowan with Ash dominant in one spot and Hazel and Hawthorn scattered throughout. Willows, too were fairly common if never extensive. Smaller woody plants and climbers such as roses, Honeysuckle and Ivy had also managed to cling on. Among the associated flora were typical woodland and/or shade loving plants such as Wood Sorrel, Wood Anemone, Dog Violet, Sanicle, Red Campion, Wild Strawberry, Barren Strawberry, Slender St. John's-wort, Wood Crane's-bill, ferns such as Male Fern, Hard Fern, Lemon-scented Fern and Common Polypody and a suite of mosses including Common Tamarisk-moss, Broom Fork-moss, Swan's-neck Thyme-moss and Common Haircap. As ever, in sheep country, there was the odd bit of spring and flush with interesting vegetation and degraded

*Lower part of the Holly Gill cliff in 1996: a refuge for plants excluded from elsewhere*

*Maturing stand of planted Hazel and Downy Birch woodland*

blanket bog. Various forms of dry, montane and alpine heath struggled on despite the ovine predation, as did rich tall-herb vegetation on high cliffs and ledges. But, on the whole, the area was very typical open and botanically impoverished 'sheep walk'.

## SUMMARY OF CURRENT VEGETATION

So, what happens when farming and direct management is removed from such a situation? The answer to this has long been debated by natural historians, ecologists and botanists and Carrifran offers a rare opportunity to study this 'for real'. The story so far (after twenty years) is one of positives upon positives. Rarely (or rather, not at all) in the Southern Uplands, has such a thing ever been tried let alone witnessed. For 'students of plant communities' like myself, the results could hardly be more pleasing or satisfying. Free from the hungry mouths of sheep and goats, the plants have come 'alive'. The vigour (and entirely unscientific) notion of happy plants is now there for all to see. All too often, the science behind natural history can be very dry and boring but looking upon Carrifran now it fills one with emotion and, frankly, simple joy. Where once, beleaguered plants looked almost plaintive, as if crying out for release from their ovine prison, they now look at you with a charmed smile, even a wink. The dry science of all this has been well captured and published and need not detain us here. What should interest us is not the detail (which species has done what etc) but the overall progress – the beginnings of actual functioning ecosystems – the ultimate goal of ecological restoration. The prevailing nature conservation thinking of 'managed diversity' seems to pale in comparison to nature 'let free' to do her own thing. Picking out particular species and communities (as professionals call the associations of plants) is very difficult and, could, frankly, detain us with another book entirely.

Photo: Stuart Adair

*Forest floor with leaf-litter, seedlings, woody debris, fungi and mosses*

As it happens, the author comes from generations of Border shepherds and my father, a retired shepherd himself, once asked me: '*So, whit happens whin thon yows cam aff the knowes thin?*' The following paragraphs aim to, at least in part, answer that question.

## PLANTED WOODLAND

More than 650,000 native trees and shrubs have been planted at Carrifran since 2000. When trying to establish native woodland, one does not just use the 'scattergun' approach, whereby native trees species are just scattered randomly across a space and left to sort themselves out over time. Rather, one looks to match the prevailing natural conditions as far as is possible. At Carrifran, we have used local geology, soils, climate and existing plant life (in conjunction with what we know of the vegetation history through ancient plant pollen captured and stored in deep peat such as at Rotten Bottom) to determine the most appropriate type of natural woodland to be established in each situation. On the middle and lower slopes three main woodland types have been established: upland Oak-Birch woodland; upland mixed broadleaved (or Ash-Elm) woodland; and slope/flush Alder-Ash woodland. Reflecting the prevailing nature of the climate, geology and soils, Oak-Birch woodland is the most widespread type with Ash-Elm and Ash-Alder stands confined to areas with suitable moist, flushed, wet and richer soils. Some wet Birch-Willow woodland has been established on shallow (< 0.5m) peats with, among others, Downy Birch and Eared and Grey Willow. In addition, a scattering of Scots Pine has been planted on and around northeast facing crags. Upslope, the latter communities give way to various forms of montane scrub planting with, among others, Juniper, Downy Willow, Tea-leaved Willow, Dark-leaved Willow and Montane Goat Willow.

*Bluebells rapidly spreading in Ashy Dean, in summer 2018*

*Downy Willow - Great Wood-rush scrub (W20) developing in Firth Hope Corrie above 600m*

The maturing stands in the lower part of the glen are in good condition. The earliest plantings are nearly twenty years old and are now recognisable woodland ecosystems with closed canopy, vertical and horizontal layering, increasing and dappled shade, leaf litter and some woody debris building on the forest floor. The canopy has a mean height of about 3-5m with occasional specimens reaching 6m.

Downy Birch, Rowan and Hazel make up the bulk of the planted woodland with lesser amounts of Sessile Oak, Ash, Alder, Wych/Scots Elm, Aspen, Holly, Hawthorn, Juniper, Bird Cherry and various willows and roses. Honeysuckle, and to a lesser extent, Ivy, are also quite frequent. The older plantings show good vigour, girth, early crown development and healthy lateral branching. The most mature and healthy stands are those that were established on the deep brown earths formerly occupied by Bracken. The latter are especially suited to Sessile Oak and Hazel and with recovering plant life such as Bluebells and Lemon-Scented fern, these stands are now taking on the familiar character of Bluebell Oakwood. The montane scrub planting, as one would expect, is much slower to mature and make a real impact. Nevertheless, Downy Willow scrub is now taking on the familiar look of natural formations with Great Wood-rush, Water Avens and Lady's Mantle among others. Juniper scrub, albeit slower than the Willow scrub, is also starting to take on a more natural look as species like Blaeberry, Cowberry, Wood Sorrel, Hard Fern and Lemon-scented Fern join the Juniper.

*High altitude prostrate Juniper*

*Natural regeneration, Hazel seedling*

*Original surviving Honeysuckle, now rampant*

*Surviving ancient Rowan that has produced a forest of suckers since feral goats were removed*

*Planted Sessile Oaks (and visiting Jays) are now setting the scene for regeneration*

If the woodland is to prove viable in the longer term, successful natural regeneration (from both existing and planted populations) is essential. At the moment, and naturally enough bearing in mind the short time period, this is currently in relatively short supply but is, nonetheless, increasing. The first and most obvious form of regeneration to take place has been within the existing fragments of woodland. Free from browsing, trees, especially Ash, Rowan and Hazel, once characterised by contorted, irregular and angular branching have put up multiple vertical shoots and developed better formed crowns. In other situations, Downy Birch and several species of willows are putting out new, coppice-like growth from low, formerly heavily browsed and suppressed stumps along watercourses, and on ledges and small cliffs. Both extant and planted Honeysuckle have flourished greatly in the new conditions, climbing up trees and sprawling over the ground in quite luxuriant growth. The few surviving Ivy are spreading, but planting of this species is only now getting under way.

Regeneration of new plants from seed is still fairly scarce but becoming more common. Ash, Rowan, Hazel, Alder, Bird Cherry and Downy Birch are all producing seedlings. Rowan, Hazel and Bird Cherry seedlings are the most abundant with Rowan especially on heathery banks and more open situations. Hazel is more common

*This area with sloping wet rock provides an opportunity for Downy
Birch and Dark-leaved Willow seedlings to become established*

under the shade of maturing woodland and Bird Cherry is very common around mature
stems of the same species. Alder seedlings are less common on flushed ground but healthy
and vigorous looking wherever they do occur. Planted Aspen quickly began to produce
suckering shoots which in certain places are becoming very abundant. Downy Birch seed
from planted stock is being produced in large quantities but the seed 'rain' is currently mostly
falling onto unsuitable dense, rank vegetation and unable to make contact with bare ground
and other suitable substrates and consequently birch seedlings are still very scarce. Sessile Oak
is now producing acorns in substantial numbers in a few
areas and jays have been recorded in the woodland; given
the abundance of suitable ground conditions, one would
imagine that Oak will follow Hazel and readily regenerate
given time. Naturally regenerated willows are becoming
more and more common, especially along watercourses
and in wet, sheltered hollows.

The trends within the planted woodland can
be summarised thus: upland Oak-Birch woodland
with Bluebell is now firmly established on former
Bracken stands and Bent-Fescue swards on the lower
ground over better brown earths. Upland Oak-Birch
woodland with Blaeberry is currently establishing on
former Mat-grass swards over poorer soils on the

*Dark-leaved Willow seedling*

Notable changes in species cover since the removal of grazing stock

| Increased | Decreased |
|---|---|
| Great Wood-rush | Mat-grass |
| Northern/Bog Bilberry | Sheep's Fescue |
| Wavy Hair-grass | Bracken |
| Tufted Hair-grass | |
| Ling-heather | |
| Cowberry | |
| Common Knapweed | |
| Meadowsweet | |
| Wild Angelica | |
| Lady's Mantle | |

Notable changes in plant communities
since the removal of grazing stock

| Increased | Decreased |
|---|---|
| Blaeberry heath | Mat-grass grassland |
| Great Wood-rush tall-herb community | Bent-Fescue grassland |
| Tufted Hair-grass grassland | Heath-rush grassland |
| Heather-Blaeberry heath | Bracken |
| Planted native woodland | |

middle slopes and accounts for the bulk of the planted woodland in the glen. On lightly flushed and better soils mixed broad-leaved or Ash-Elm woodland is well established if of limited extent. In similar but wetter situations, Alder-Ash slope/flush woodland is establishing, especially on flushed slopes over nutrient-rich gleyed/wet soils. On the higher ground, the montane scrub planting is maturing, albeit slowly, and gradually beginning to resemble natural formations.

Within the developing field layers, the low, multi-stemmed growth and deep shade cast by Hazel, in particular, has altered the original field layer quite markedly. Where Bracken was once dominant, it has now thinned considerably under the increasing shade of the closing canopy. Conversely, typical woodland herbs and associates of the former bracken stands such as Bluebell/Wild Hyacinth, Pignut, Tormentil, Common bent-grass, Common Dog Violet, Wood Sorrel, Creeping Soft-grass and, most especially, mosses such as Common Tamarisk-moss, Neat Feather-moss, Glittering Wood-moss, Red-stemmed Feather-moss,

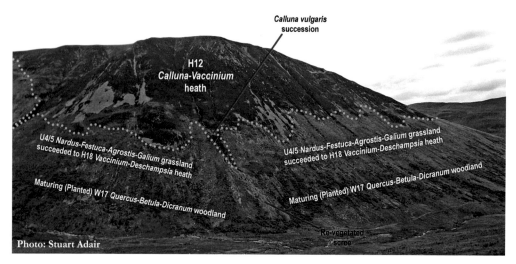

*Broad zonal patterns are emerging and taking on the character of more natural situations*

Springy Turf-moss and Broom Fork-moss, free from the vigorous competition and deep shade of the Bracken, are increasing their extent and range. Of the latter, Bluebell especially, in recent years, has increased its range greatly (and can now also be seen on fairly open ground at over 400m a.s.l).

As yet, the planted trees are having little direct impact on heathland. Nevertheless, there are occasional areas where one can see maturing Sessile Oak, Downy Birch, Rowan, Hazel, Holly and Juniper come together with Blaeberry, Ling-heather, Bell-heather, Wavy Hair-grass, Great Wood-rush, Hard-fern and Lemon Scented-fern in associations so typical of upland Oak-Birch woodlands in the Highlands and the Lake District. In other places, the field layer is becoming more reminiscent of Ash-Elm or Ash-Alder woodland, often characterised by the large tussocks of Tufted Hair-grass with occasional specimens of Barren Strawberry and other small herbs like Germander Speedwell, Herb Robert and Pignut and ever-increasing ferns such as Male-fern and Lady-fern. On shady banks by extant woodland Beech-fern is becoming very abundant. Other ferns, such as Male-fern, Broad Buckler-fern and Scaly Male-fern were slow to extend their range initially but are now becoming more prominent in the flora. In similar but wetter places dominated by planted Alder, poor-fen tall-herbs such as Wild Angelica, Meadowsweet, Marsh Thistle and Marsh Marigold and smaller characteristic herbs like Yellow Pimpernel are beginning to break the stranglehold of Rushes and Sedges that dominated the scene under the sheep.

OPEN GROUND

Ecological restoration (ecosystem recovery/rewilding) involves much more than native woodland restoration, of course. At Carrifran, long established, poor, sheep-related vegetation such as acid grasslands have been all but completely replaced by heathland and tall-herb vegetation. Blaeberry and Great Wood-rush especially have increased their

*Resurgent mountain flowers above 450m, in gully below Priest Craig that was probably formed by a flood in 2003; Mountain Sorrel, Sea Campion, Mossy Saxifrage, Lady's Mantle and Wild Thyme*

*Bog Bilberry, Cloudberry and Crowberry at 700m on Carrifran*

Photo: Stuart Adair

*Mountain Sorrel is one of the species that have escaped from their refuges on the crags and now occur along the length of Carrifran burn; this one is at 189m a.s.l.*

*A single clump of Alpine Saw-wort was discovered in a small, rather inaccessible gully below the top of the waterfall; the species was later found spreading on an open slope a few hundred metres upstream in Firth Hope*

Photo: Chris Miles

*A single individual of Wood Bitter Vetch has survived at Carrifran on an inaccessible ledge on Raven Craig*

**Notable plant species status and confirmed additions since 2000**

| | Present in 2000 | Present in 2020 | Additions since 2000 |
|---|---|---|---|
| Alpine Foxtail | Y | Y | |
| Pale Forget-me-not | Y | Y | |
| Mountain Sorrel* | Y | Y | |
| Roseroot* | Y | Y | |
| Sea Campion* | Y | Y | |
| Mossy Saxifrage* | Y | Y | |
| Wood Bitter-vetch | Y | Y | |
| Wilson's Filmy-fern | Y | Y | |
| Alpine Meadow-rue* | Y | Y | |
| Serrated Wintergreen | Y | Y | |
| Mountain Male-fern* | Y | Y | |
| Alpine Willowherb | Y | Y | |
| Dwarf Willow* | Y | Y | |
| Oblong Woodsia** | Y | Y | |
| Alpine Cinquefoil | N | Y | Y |
| Lesser Twayblade | N | Y | Y |
| Bog Bilberry*** | N | Y | Y |
| Alpine Saw-wort | N | Y | Y |

\*      Indicates species has colonised new ground
\*\*    The Oblong Woodsia was bolstered by translocation in c. 2000
\*\*\*  Northern/Bog Bilberry was originally recorded here by Derek Ratcliffe in the 1950s but was not relocated until 2010

extent enormously – recovering from either suppressed populations within former grassland in the case of the former or expanding out from small scattered stands in the case of the latter. Ling-heather regeneration is less extensive but nevertheless widespread, especially coming down gullies from existing moorland above and along steep banks by watercourses. On sunny, drier south and southwest facing slopes, the latter is often joined by Bell Heather, which has also increased greatly since the time of purchase. Crowberry and Cowberry have also increased both their range and extent. Some of the heath is incredibly species-rich in comparison to the usual managed, species-poor, burned and grazed heaths so typical of our uplands, with the Ling-heather sharing the ground with

### EU Habitats Directive Annex 1 Habitats occurring at Carrifran

| Annex 1 Habitat | Condition at Carrifran in 2020 |
| --- | --- |
| Alpine and subalpine heaths | Favourable, improving. Some increase in extent of alpine heath. Translocation of bearberry into the latter. Vast increase in extent of boreal heath |
| European dry heaths | Favourable, improving. Vast increase in extent |
| Blanket bogs (Priority habitat) | Favourable, improving. Bog restoration works undertaken. Huge increase in extent of the notable plant species Bog Bilberry |
| Montane acid grasslands | Favourable, improving. Some increase in extent. Some increase in coverage of Dwarf Willow and Woolly Fringe-moss |
| Tall-herb communities | Favourable, improving. Vast increase in this community. Originally confined to inaccessible cliffs and ledges in Firthhope Linn and Holly Gill especially. Now widespread right along the course of Carrifran Burn and coming down to 180m a.s.l. Including notable plant species such as Mountain Sorrel, Roseroot and Sea Campion |
| Acid Scree | Favourable, improving. Increase in coverage of Parsley Fern |
| Plants in crevices on acid rocks | Favourable. Location of rare/notable plant species Brittle Bladder-fern and Wilson's Filmy-fern |
| Plants in crevices on base-rich rocks | Favourable. Location of rare plant species Holly-fern. |

*The Moffat Hills were designated as a Special Area of Conservation (SAC) under the EU Habitats Directive in 2005. The qualifying interest for this international designation includes eight Annex 1 Habitats. These habitats and their current conditions at Carrifran are listed above.*

*Landscape restoration in action: planted native woodland and recovering plant communities after 20 years. The grazing-sensitive Mountain Male-fern (seen here in foreground among recovering heath) has increased in abundance dramatically since the removal of sheep and goats and is indicative of the positive changes in the flora over the past two decades*

other dwarf-shrubs like Blaeberry, Crowberry and Cowberry, tall-herbs such as Great Wood-rush, ferns, including the relatively rare Mountain Male-fern, small herbs such as Tormentil, Common Dog Violet and Wood Anemone, grasses including Wavy Hair-grass, a suite of typical upland mosses and Reindeer Lichens such as *Cladonia portentosa* and *C. arbuscula*.

Degraded blanket mires are recovering (aided by some remedial works) with peat builders such as Sphagna (bog mosses) and Cotton-grasses colonising formerly bare peats. The once very rare and notable Northern/Bog Bilberry has increased its extent at least a hundredfold and almost certainly more, especially in the recovering mire around the head of the Little Firthhope Burn. Planted Bog-myrtle is marking out the water tracks over the surface of mires and now looks very natural.

One of the most important of the upland vegetation types occurring at Carrifran – wind-clipped summit moss-heath – is beginning to show its true status and extent, with the patterns of wind buffeting becoming more obvious as the low growing carpet gives way to taller vegetation wherever the influence of the wind recedes. Characteristic species of this community such as Woolly Fringe-moss and Dwarf Willow are expanding their range and being joined occasionally by new additions to the summit flora such as Goldenrod.

Springs and associated flush vegetation have changed little in their floristic composition since the removal of stock. The vegetation has become more rank but as yet, all the key species are flourishing and have been joined occasionally by notable species such as Mountain Sorrel. The rare Alpine Foxtail has increased its stature in response to the more vigorous growth after the withdrawal of stock. In the absence of poaching by stock, cushion mosses such as the distinctive bright yellow-green Fountain Apple-moss have thickened up noticeably.

But perhaps the most eye-catching changes in the flora have come through the spread of previously scarce tall-herbs. The latter were confined to inaccessible ledges and cliffs high up in the narrow ravines and small gorges of Firthhope Linn, Holly Gill and other similar places at the time of purchase, when sheep and goats were still present. Since then, the tall herbs have escaped from their previously confined stations and come both downhill and downstream and spread all along both the margins of the Carrifran Burn and, especially, within formerly bare in-channel gravel bars and shelves. Among the more noteworthy of these plants are Mountain Sorrel, Roseroot and Sea Campion – species so typical of mountain cliffs and ledges, now coming down as low as less than 200m a.s.l.

The list of plants that have colonised these areas includes Great Wood-rush, Water Avens, Lady's Mantle, Early Purple Orchid, Wood Crane's-bill, Common Bird's – foot – trefoil, Common Knapweed, Wild Angelica, Common Valerian, Meadowsweet, Primrose, Colt's-foot, Marsh Ragwort, Common Milkwort, Ribwort Plantain, Ling-heather and many, many more – all of which can be seen in some places within an area of perhaps no more than c. 10 x 10m – very species-rich vegetation indeed by upland standards. In the medium to long-term though, such plant communities may prove to be somewhat ephemeral and come and go naturally as heavy catastrophic flooding periodically re-sculptures the scene and the process of gain-loss-gain is repeated in exactly the type of dynamic ecosystem, governed by natural processes, that is so desperately lacking in most of our semi-natural habitats.

## Notable plant species

Notable plant species form one of the core qualifying interests of the Moffat Hills SSSI/SAC and the Carrifran portion has its fair share.

At this early stage, it is, of course, still too early to draw any definitive conclusions, but after nearly two decades without grazing by domestic stock or feral goats, not only have the original notable plant species recorded in the glen survived and flourished, expanding their range from cliffs, ledges and other inaccessible places onto open ground, the list has in fact grown with several new additions recorded since the stock were removed. Mountain Sorrel, Roseroot, Sea Campion, Alpine Meadow-rue, Pale Forget-me-not, Mossy Saxifrage and Dwarf Willow have all expanded their range, in the case of Mountain Sorrel, Roseroot and Sea Campion quite considerably including down onto the lower ground. Alpine Fox-tail has not yet been

*Planted Bog-myrtle flourishing on the mire south of Holly Gill*

recorded at new stations but the original population is stable. The Red Listed, Vulnerable species Holly Fern has one of its only stations in southern Scotland at Carrifran. Other notable plant species occurring at Carrifran include Hoary Whitlow-grass, Alpine Willowherb and Serrated Wintergreen.

New additions to the flora since the change of management include Northern Bilberry which has expanded its coverage enormously from a scattering of plants first re-recorded (it was first recorded here by Derek Ratcliffe in the 1950s) on the edges of peat hags in 2010 to cover extensive areas of the mires around the head of the Little Firthhope Burn. Alpine Saw-wort has been recorded for the first time as have Alpine Cinquefoil and Lesser Twayblade. The population of the rare fern Oblong Woodsia in the Moffat Hills was bolstered by translocations into Carrifran in 2000, having previously only been recorded in neighbouring Black Hope.

## Summary of Changes since 2000

The first striking thing (other than the planted trees themselves) that greets you now at Carrifran is the near complete transition from grassland to heath as the sheep and goats no longer nip the young Blaeberry, Ling-heather, Cowberry and Bell Heather daring to peek their heads above the grassy sward. This alone would have been enough for many but there is more… tall-herbs have come out of their refuges and are asking to play with the other plants. Such previously shy, and somewhat elusive, montane beasts as Mountain Sorrel have come down among the commoners and are happy to play on the low ground with the mere Knapweeds of the world. The Wood Anemones have conquered vast new areas previously only available to their sheep-friendly cousins. The sub-arctic and boreal heaths of the Moffat Hills have long been noted for their conservation value. Now, with the pincer-like mouths of sheep and goats removed, the heaths have expanded their extent greatly and are

*Vaglaskogur, a birch woodland in Iceland with Small Cow-wheat, Wood Cranesbill, Common Wintergreen, Yarrow, Stone Bramble, Lady's Bedstraw and Autumn Hawkbit, and Northern Butterfly Orchid were also flowering in the wood*

*Vaglaskogur birch woodland in Iceland with Meadow Buttercup, Wood Horsetail, Wood Cranesbill, Hawkweed, Tufted Hair Grass, Meadowsweet, Lady's Mantle, Dandelion and Water Avens*

## WHERE HAVE ALL THE FLOWERS GONE? (AND HOW TO GET THEM BACK)

Since the 1960s, deer numbers in Scotland are known to have steadily increased, and grazing by deer and other herbivores is now considered to be a major cause of the poor biodiversity in wildlife protected areas. In the woods, deer browse on Bramble, Honeysuckle and other flowering plants so that these are unable to flower, fruit and set seed. As a consequence, there is very little nectar and no fruit or seeds to feed all the insects, small mammals and birds that might otherwise be there. Several hundred years of deer and sheep browsing in Scottish woods has left them without their 'filling': everything in between the canopy and the ground – especially the flowers – has been eaten out. Woodland managers and advisers are used to this, but have for so long been focused on getting trees to regenerate, that they have almost failed to notice that woods are actually much more than just the trees…

In 2017, with the help of a Churchill Fellowship, I created a project to visit woods in other parts of Europe where herbivore impacts have historically been high, but where they are now much lower, and where climate and geology are comparable to Scotland, to find out what woods can look like when they don't support such high numbers of herbivores. I found that woods where herbivores had been excluded for longest now had the richest understorey. Icelandic woods that had been free from the impacts of large herbivores (deer and sheep) for more than 100 years were carpeted with flowers! Iceland has not always been as treeless as it is today. When it was first settled in 900AD, the island was described in the Icelandic Sagas as "wooded from firth to fell". Although the island has no native herbivores, Norse settlers brought their livestock, and by the early 1900s overgrazing had virtually eliminated Iceland's forests.

To try and halt the woodland loss, about 100 years ago some of the remnants were fenced to protect them from grazing. Herbivores have yet to be re-introduced to these woods, but despite more challenging enviromental conditions than here in Scotland, these woodlands are thriving, and full of flowers. Plants such as Wood Cranesbill, Hawkweed, Stone Bramble, Northern Bilberry and Lady's Mantle provide important nectar, pollen and fruit for a wide range of associated species. Such an abundance of flowers is rarely seen in comparable Scottish woods due to the universally high levels of grazing, but where herbivores have been excluded for long enough, we find that the vegetation has recovered some of the more sensitive flowering plants, such as in the un-grazed woodland

*Abundant flowers under a Hazel canopy on a tiny un-grazed Argyll island. Species include Ivy, Honeysuckle, Bluebell, Wood Cranesbill, Sanicle, Pignut, Wild Garlic, Primrose and Lesser Celandine*

in Argyll (above), hinting at what could be achieved with very low levels of grazing across the wider Scottish landscape. But how is it that woods that have had no herbivores for so long could still be the most biodiverse, as herbivores are a natural part of every ecosystem?

A wood in good condition has 'filling' (or understorey), which is the source of biomass that supports many woodland species – either as food or habitat. Currently many plants that would naturally inhabit our native woods are not only absent, but even when present, they are rarely able to flower and complete their life cycles. Honeysuckle, Bramble and Ivy occur in many woods but rarely flower and fruit. Mostly they just exist as stunted, over-grazed plants in the sward. If they cannot fully develop as plants, then the insects, animals and birds that might live on or in them are probably also not there. The woodland ecosystem is not working properly.

With so little growth in the woodland understorey a single regenerating young tree or shrub is unlikely to escape browsing, so for ecosystem recovery to happen, herbivore numbers must be dramatically reduced. Once the 'filling' is restored, herbivore browsing can be supported, without noticeable impact on the ecosystem, but every wood has an ecological carrying capacity, and if herbivore numbers exceed this then woodland condition will decline until ultimately a return to ecological exhaustion occurs once again. So whether or not fences are used to achieve the initial reduction in impact, once ecological health is restored, herbivore impact must be contained within the carrying capacity of the woodland in order to maintain ecological health.

The difficult truth is that most of our woods are currently in a state of ecological exhaustion as a result of centuries of overgrazing, and now need a period of respite so they can recover. So although herbivores are a natural part of every ecosystem, if the ecosystem is exhausted, it requires time without herbivores in order to recover. All that is needed in most places to ensure this recovery is a dramatic reduction in herbivore numbers, and patience. Landscape-scale forest ecosystem restoration through herbivore reductions has happened in Norway and Iceland, so it can happen in Scotland too!

**Kate Holl**

*Sea Campion and other plants flourishing in the open at the top of Firthhope Linn*

*Wood Anemones flourishing at about 450m above developing planted woodland*

becoming more species-rich – aided by the recent translocation (transplanting) of the rare dwarf-shrub, Bearberry – which adds to the original mixture of Ling-heather, Crowberry, Cowberry, Blaeberry, Bell Heather and Reindeer mosses and lichens. The Sphagnum Bog Mosses grow luxuriantly, now free from the all prevailing trampling feet of the Asiatic herbivores. The deep peats of Rotten Bottom are now growing again for, perhaps, the first time in centuries – building future pollen records with the massive upturn in tree pollen recorded at this very moment but stored for a many a century to come. Pollen itself, is now a plenty as the plant life, now free from sheep, flowers much more profusely and regularly than when under constant ovine assault. The planted woodland is now starting to resemble natural upland forest and montane scrub and, in many places, could easily be mistaken for natural regeneration.

So, then, has it all been worth it? In terms of natural history, ecology and the advance of nature conservation in these islands, I think the answer is an unqualified yes. All of the Annex 1 Habitats for which the site is designated as a Special Area of Conservation (and thus of international importance) have either increased their extent or species-richness, or both. On a personal level, it has been quite the best and most positive thing the author has ever been part of.

*Starry Saxifrage, Opposite-leaved Golden Saxifrage and Fountain Apple-moss: the moss clumps in front and behind are male plants with the disc-like male 'flowers' at the stem tips; in front left are also some globose capsules of the same moss, on long stalks, arising from a group of female plants*

John Wright

♂ Lesser Redpoll – 26·4·19

# RETURN OF THE FLOWERS: A RESTORATION GALLERY

## Philip Ashmole, Myrtle Ashmole and Stuart Adair

In this section we aim to provide a glimpse of the main habitats that visitors to Carrifran Wildwood can expect to encounter, along with thumbnail illustrations of some of the plants that now make a walk through Carrifran such a satisfying experience. A whole suite of wildflowers had almost disappeared from the landscapes of the Southern Uplands, but many of them were waiting in the wings and are now filling the stage at Carrifran.

Carrifran has long been known for the presence – in the few places inaccessible to the sheep and even to the agile feral goats – of a number of scarce montane plants. The refuges were either on cliffs in ravines, most spectacularly on the cliff at Holly Gill, and on the steepest parts of the larger crags, especially Raven Craig. Over the last 20 years it has become obvious that some of these surviving species had been producing seeds in their refuges for many centuries, which had been dispersed by wind and water and then germinated, only for the seedlings to be shaved off by the domestic herbivores and not even noticed by botanists. Removal of the sheep and goats was quickly followed by discovery of groups of these special plants, along with other more widespread ones, growing along the burnsides, and also in the hanging valley that we call Firth Hope and on the plateau around the rim of the valley.

On the slopes of the valley and in the bogs and flushes at lower levels the recovery of the wildflowers is also under way. Bluebells have appeared under bracken low down the valley and were clearly long-term suppressed survivors, but have also appeared at over 400m in two quite separate parts of the upper valley, evoking a distant past in which oakwoods carpeted with bluebells may have covered large areas at Carrifran. The recovery is already startling, but there are doubtless more surprises in store.

In the following pages we have collected together images of some of the plants that we have found extending their range at Carrifran in the last decade. We have grouped them roughly into species characteristic of different habitats, found in different parts of the valley and up above it, but of course the boundaries between these are indistinct and many species could have been included in more than one group.

The gallery was created by Myrtle Ashmole and the photos were taken opportunistically by the authors. There are obvious gaps, but we hope that they will convey a flavour of the complex and diverse ecosystem that is natural to the hills of Southern Scotland but is unfamiliar to most local people as well as to visitors from elsewhere.

Carrifran is now the most botanically rich part of the Moffat and Tweedsmuir Hills and the regenerating flora is indicative of the recovering ecosystem. Two decades is a short period, and we hope that two centuries hence, Carrifran will be well on its way to full maturity.

*Marsh Marigold*

*Alpine Foxtail*

*Wood Anemone*

ALPINE MEADOWS, WITH GLOBEFLOWER,
AND THE RIM OF THE PLATEAU

Starry Saxifrage

Water Avens

Cloudberry

Heath Spotted Orchid

Dwarf Willow

Bog Bilberry & Crowberry

CRAG AND RAVINE SURVIVORS

*Wood Bitter-vetch*

*Sea Campion*

*Soft Downy-rose*

*Goldenrod*

*Roseroot*

*Mountain Sorrel*

*Mountain Pansy*

*Burnet Rose*

*Dark-leaved Willow*

SCREES

*Wood Sage*                    *Lady's Mantle*

*Wood Sorrel*

*Mossy Saxifrage & Parsley Fern*

*Woolly Fringe-moss*

*Wild Thyme*

*Cowberry*

*Meadow Buttercup*

SLOPES OF THE VALLEY

*Common Bird's-foot-trefoil*

*Wood Anemone*

Bugle

Blaeberry

Goldenrod & Tormentil

Mossy Saxifrage

Mountain Sorrel

Harebell

TALL HERBS AND BURNSIDES

*Mountain Sorrel & Sea Campion*

*Greater Bird's-foot-trefoil*

*Common Knapweed*

*Wild Angelica*

*Water Avens*

*Meadowsweet*

*Valerian*

*Cuckooflower*

*Wood Crane's-bill*

SURVIVORS UNDER THE BRACKEN AND IN OTHER SHADY PLACES

*Pignut*

*Primrose*

*Wood Sorrel*

*Barren Strawberry*

*Common Dog-violet*

*Slender St John's-wort*

*Germander Speedwell*

*Greater Stitchwort*

Bogs, MIRES AND FLUSHES

*Early-purple Orchid*

*Bog Asphodel*

Marsh Thistle

Hare's-tail Cottongrass

Butterwort

Grass-of-Parnassus

Round-leaved Sundew

Devil's-bit Scabious

Ragged Robin

Hooked Scorpion-moss

*Hard Shield-fern*

*Scaly Male-fern*

FERNS AND THEIR ALLIES

*Stag's-horn Clubmoss*

*Oak Fern*

*Maidenhair Spleenwort*

*Beech Fern*

*Broad Buckler-fern*

*Lemon Scented-fern*

*Fir Clubmoss*

*Carrifran valley in summer 2004*

*The valley five years later in summer 2009*

*Ten years later in summer 2014*

*And the valley fifteen years later in summer 2019*

Photos: John Savory

# BIRDS AS INDICATORS OF ENVIRONMENTAL CHANGE AT CARRIFRAN

*John Savory*
*1943-2020*

We live in an era that has been called the 'Anthropocene defaunation' in which global biodiversity and biomass of wild animals (especially invertebrates) are declining at an alarming rate. So there is some consolation in knowing that what we have achieved at Carrifran Wildwood is now widely recognised as an exemplar of how ecological restoration can help to reduce this trend. The Rewilding Britain charity, for example, has highlighted Carrifran as 'inspirational' on its website since its launch in 2015. The most convincing evidence of the success of our woodland habitat restoration comes from regular systematic surveys of birds, which, as in other contexts, are sensitive indicators of environmental

*Carrifran valley with adjacent Black Hope at upper left and*
*Polmoodie plantation lower right, October 2015*

Photo: P. and A. Macdonald/Aerographica

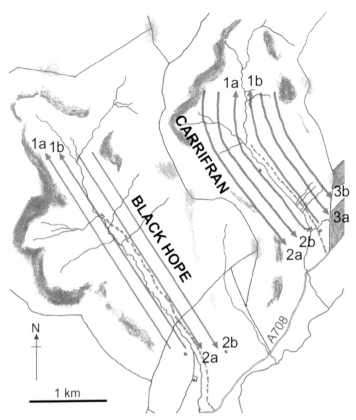

*Figure 1. Plan of Black Hope and Carrifran valleys, showing (numbered) transects walked in systematic bird surveys*

*Nests at Carrifran of meadow pipit (left) and lesser redpoll (right)*

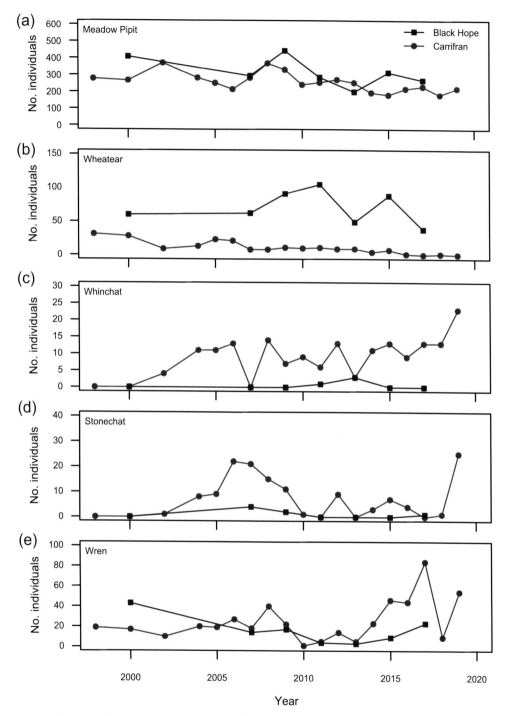

*Figure 2. Comparisons between Black Hope and Carrifran in numbers of meadow pipit, wheatear, whinchat, stonechat and wren recorded in surveys in different years*

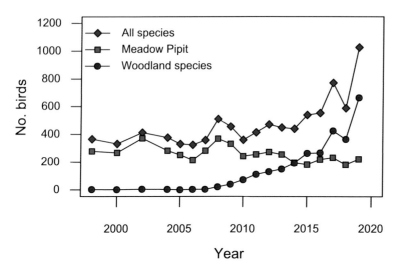

*Figure 3. Total numbers of birds recorded in surveys at Carrifran, of all species, meadow pipit and all woodland species*

change that can be monitored fairly easily. In the adjacent valley Black Hope, where the environment has remained unchanged and where there have also been bird surveys, we have a good comparator for the observed responses at Carrifran.

As well as the surveys of birds, there have been other surveys at Carrifran, of small mammals, bats, fish, invertebrates, plants and fungi, that are dealt with elsewhere in this book. Records have also been kept of all birds (and other wildlife) that have been seen and reported on visits to Carrifran by participants in the project (I volunteered there in most weeks from 2003 until 2018) and other naturalists. These incidental bird records come from all parts of Carrifran at all times of year and provide information that supplements that coming from the regular surveys which are done along fixed transects in May and June. A blackcock lek (display area) next to the boundary fence has been monitored annually for bird attendance since we discovered it in 2006. More information came from our use of a Bushnell trail camera for a few months in 2014-15. This chapter concentrates on the birds at Carrifran.

As part of the Wildwood Group's development of a coherent monitoring plan for Carrifran, Peter Gordon, a member of the Group who was then RSPB Borders Conservation Officer, recognised the opportunity the project gave for studying colonisation by birds in newly developing broad-leaved woodland. He also recognised the value of the topographically very similar adjacent valley Black Hope, with its continued use as sheepwalk and absence of planted trees, as a comparator for monitoring change at Carrifran, where grazing animals (sheep, cattle and feral goats) were removed at the outset and trees planted. In 1998 and 2000, therefore, he initiated systematic bird surveys at Carrifran and Black Hope respectively.

These surveys were conducted at Carrifran in 1998, 2000, 2002, 2004 and every year thereafter, and at Black Hope in 2000, 2007 and every alternate year thereafter. Each valley was surveyed on one day in May and one day in June (never both on the same day), using a method similar to the BTO's annual Breeding Bird Survey (www.bto.org/volunteer-surveys/bbs/taking-part/survey-methods). On each survey day, two observers each walked either three (at Carrifran) or two (at Black Hope) widely spaced (c.200m apart) parallel linear transects totalling 6km, covering most of the valleys below 450m (so most of the planted area at Carrifran), as chosen by Peter Gordon for his first surveys (Figure 1). For each valley, the total distance surveyed by both recorders on both days was thus 24km. All birds that were seen or heard while walking these transects, including any flying nearby, were identified, counted and recorded, and care was taken to try not to record the same bird more than once in each transect. Although the behaviour of many recorded birds indicated they were holding breeding territories, and some nests were found incidentally, no attempt was made to verify this, or to relate their presence to detailed description of habitat. The results of the surveys were stored on two spreadsheets (Excel), one for Carrifran and the other for Black Hope. Occasional sightings of birds that were obviously flying over the valleys and heading elsewhere (geese, gulls, osprey) were excluded from these data.

Up to and including 2019, a total of 52 bird species have been recorded in the May and June surveys. Of these, 26 were at both valleys, 23 were at Carrifran only (hence probably responding to the removal of grazers and planting of trees there) and three were at Black Hope only. Some of the species recorded at both valleys (in low numbers) have shown changes over time. Thus, woodpigeon was absent until 2007 and since then has been seen more at Carrifran, whereas skylark, ring ouzel and pied wagtail have been largely absent at Carrifran since 2004 but continue to be recorded occasionally at Black Hope. No list of the 52 species recorded in the surveys (or of the incidental bird records) is given in this chapter because its main aim is to focus on birds' responses to the environmental change at Carrifran.

Until 2013, by far the most numerous bird recorded at both valleys was meadow pipit, a species of open country (Figure 2). This remains the case at Black Hope, but since 2015 meadow pipits at Carrifran have been overtaken by the total number of colonising woodland birds (Figure 3). A decline in meadow pipits at Carrifran, which is already apparent, is inevitable as their ground nesting habitat is gradually depleted by the developing woodland there. Wheatear was initially abundant in both valleys, particularly Black Hope where it has remained the second most numerous species (Figure 2). At Carrifran, however, it declined after the first few years, probably because the growth of grass and other ground vegetation following the removal of grazers made it less suitable as breeding habitat. The closely related whinchat and stonechat, which inhabit scrubland and heath, were more common at Carrifran than at Black Hope from 2004 onwards (Figure 2). Neither species has shown consistent change thereafter and both are occasionally scarce or absent, presumably reflecting mortality associated with their respective overwintering strategies (whinchats migrate to Africa whereas most stonechats remain in Britain).

From the first surveys in 1998 and 2000, wren numbers have been variable in both valleys (Figure 2) and the lowest counts probably reflect high mortality in hard winters like 2009/10, 2010/11 and 2017/18. Although it occurs in a wide range of habitats, and high counts were recorded in rocky areas and cleuchs at both Carrifran and the almost treeless Black Hope, it is nevertheless most common in deciduous woodland. Increasing counts at Carrifran in 2014-2019 (apart from the low count in 2018 which followed a hard winter) may thus reflect colonisation of new woodland habitat.

The only birds recorded in the earliest surveys that are associated with woodland more closely than wren were two chaffinch and one willow warbler at Carrifran and one chaffinch at Black Hope. In both valleys they were observed where there were sparse relict trees and shrubs. After the first planted trees at Carrifran became established, chaffinch was

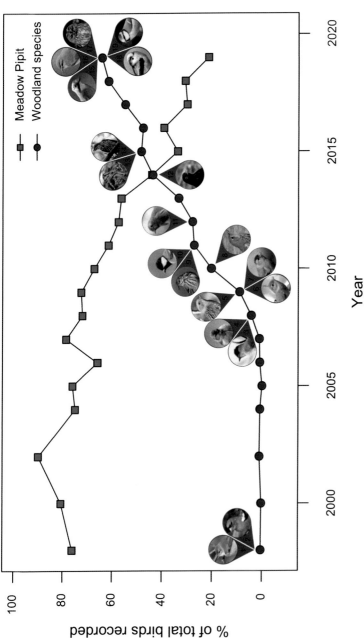

*Figure 4. Proportion of Meadow Pipits and all woodland birds (as percentage of total for members out numbers all birds recorded in surveys at Carrifran) and the years of first appearance of different woodland species*

## Year of species colonisation at Carrifran

1. Willow Warbler (1998)
2. Chaffinch (1998)
3. Blackcap (2008)
4. Lesser Redpoll (2008)
5. Dunnock (2009)

6. Garden Warbler (2009)
7. Siskin (2009)
8. Mistle Thrush (2010)
9. Tree Pipit (2011)
10. Great Tit (2011)

11. Robin (2012)
12. Blackbird (2014)
13. Woodcock (2015)
14. Song Thrush (2015)
15. Jay (2019)

16. Wood Warbler (2019)
17. Tawny Owl (2019)
18. Long-Tailed Tit (2019)
19. Blue Tit (2019)

recorded from 2002 and willow warbler reappeared in 2005 (but not in the surveys until 2006). From 2008 onwards, which happened to be when the intensive planting programme at Carrifran ended (but when most of the valley was still only sparsely wooded) numbers of both species increased greatly and other woodland species also started featuring in the surveys (Figure 4).

To the best of our knowledge, our monitoring at Carrifran over 20 years provides the first continuous record anywhere of colonisation by birds in newly planted broad-leaved woodland, with an appropriate unplanted comparator (Black Hope). Our dataset is probably also the first to describe the sequence of colonisation by woodland birds in such changing habitat. Thus, following the willow warbler and chaffinch at Carrifran at the outset, another 17 species have since been recorded there. Sequentially, these were blackcap and lesser redpoll in 2008, dunnock, garden warbler and siskin in 2009, mistle thrush in 2010, tree pipit and great tit in 2011, robin in 2012, blackbird in 2014, woodcock and song thrush in 2015, and tawny owl, wood warbler, jay, long-tailed tit and blue tit in 2019 (Figure 4).

In terms of avian biodiversity, the total number of species recorded in the surveys at Carrifran (species richness) diverged from that at Black Hope after about 2011 (Figure 5a). However, a simple count of recorded species disregards information on how many individuals were recorded for each species, and hence is disproportionately influenced by the number of rare species. A more reliable way to summarise biodiversity, especially when making comparisons between sites or over time, is by using diversity indices. The Shannon-Wiener index (Shannon H') is one such commonly used index that is calculated using the proportion (or relative abundance) of individuals of each recorded species relative to all individuals recorded at a surveyed site. As with species richness, the Shannon H' indices for avian diversity at Carrifran and Black Hope diverge over time, with Carrifran showing higher diversity after 2013 (Figure 5b). On a global scale, avian biodiversity is greatest in woodland habitats worldwide, so such increases at Carrifran are to be expected. Moreover, previous studies have shown that bird species diversity is closely correlated positively not only with overall breeding density (hence the use of diversity indices) but also with foliage height diversity (hence increasing numbers of species in new developing woodland). An increase in the Shannon H' index at Carrifran after 2013 seems explicable considering that 2013 was five years after the intensive planting programme ended in 2008, when much of the valley was wooded with established and growing trees and shrubs of different species and varying height.

In terms of actual numbers of birds recorded (on two days in May and June) the two woodland species that have increased most at Carrifran, willow warbler and chaffinch, are ubiquitous throughout Scotland and were present in the area at the

*Willow warbler, the most numerous woodland bird at Carrifran*

outset. Willow warbler is the most numerous species and in 2019 it reached a total of 275 individuals recorded (Figure 6) thus outnumbering meadow pipit (Figure 3) for the first time. Next comes chaffinch, then lesser redpoll, then robin, blackcap and tree pipit. While the latter two species are still increasing, robin did not recover in 2019 from its crash in numbers in 2018 following a hard winter. Also increasing in lower numbers are dunnock, garden warbler, great tit and siskin. Then there are some 'minor players' which have yet to show consistent increases, namely tawny owl, woodcock, song thrush, blackbird, mistle thrush, jay, wood warbler, long-tailed tit and blue tit.

The relative increases over time in numbers of individual birds of different woodland species at Carrifran (Figure 6) presumably reflect variation in their respective optimal habitats and food supply during the breeding season. Some species, like warblers and robins, are mainly insectivorous, whereas others, like finches, are mainly granivorous (seed eaters). So the fact that the willow warbler population is increasing faster than those of other woodland species must be at least partly due to increasing availability of invertebrate food in the developing woodland. It is known that oaks, willows and birches are the most important native trees in Britain for sustaining insects, and these species account for roughly 80% of all (c.700,000) planted trees in the valley. Chaffinches and lesser redpolls are no doubt profiting from the annual supply of seeds from downy birch which accounts for more than half the planted trees. Also, like wren, the habitat requirements of willow warbler and chaffinch may be less specialised (i.e. they are 'habitat generalists') than those of other woodland species ('habitat specialists'). With regard to robin numbers, it is not clear why they failed to recover at Carrifran in 2019 after their crash in 2018, considering that they did recover at another woodland (Glenlude) being monitored not far away.

Growth rates of populations of woodland birds are at least partly dependent on production of young each year, their survival and longevity, and their propensity to return

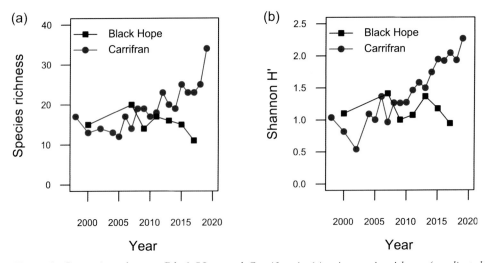

*Figure 5. Comparisons between Black Hope and Carrifran in (a) avian species richness (unadjusted numbers of species) and (b) the Shannon-Wiener index (Shannon H'), a more reliable measure of diversity which takes account of variation in numbers of individuals of each species recorded*

to their natal habitat. The migratory willow warbler, for example, usually rears six young per year whereas the non-migratory chaffinch usually rears four. The average lifespan of the willow warbler is two years while that of the chaffinch is three years. Some of the changes in numbers of individual species at Carrifran may also reflect broader population trends across Scotland. These are shown for the 10 years from 2007 to 2017 in the BTO's 2018 Breeding Bird Survey Report (www.bto.org/our-science/projects/bbs/latest-results/population-trends). Thus, there have been substantial (>20%) increases in lesser redpoll, blackcap and tree pipit (all of which increased at Carrifran), smaller (10-20%) increases in meadow pipit and song thrush, little change (<10%) in willow warbler, wren, robin, great tit, blackbird and siskin, substantial decreases in wheatear and stonechat, and smaller decreases in chaffinch, garden warbler and dunnock. It should also be pointed out that nearly all recorded species, which presumably come to Carrifran to breed, are present in the valley only from about April to September. Outside that period, most birds move elsewhere in Britain (some not far) or migrate to Africa (most warblers) and only a few robins, wrens, dunnocks, finches and tits may remain. Our incidental records at Carrifran also show that fieldfares, redwings and blackbirds come regularly in autumn and winter to feed on the various crops of berries that are available.

At the start of the breeding season, in April or May depending on species, birds arrive and immediately take up the territories which are essential for breeding and which they defend against competitors. The case of the willow warbler at Carrifran is of particular interest because not only is it now our most numerous bird but it also has one of the longest migrations (from sub-Saharan Africa) for a bird of its size. Synchronisation and dates of arrival in breeding habitat have been well studied in migratory birds. Synchronisation of willow warbler arrival at Carrifran is evident every year. In 2019, for example, a large number were calling throughout the valley on 21st April, declaring their territorial ownership (and birds that have bred the previous year show territorial fidelity) but none were there a week earlier. We can also get an idea of the timing of their arrival each year from the dates of our first incidental records. These show that, from 2005 to 2008, when their numbers were very low, they arrived in early May, but from 2009 onwards, which is when their numbers started increasing (Figure 6) they have been consistently arriving at least one week earlier, in late April. This difference may be explained by the fact that young willow warblers are known to arrive later than older birds, so those few records in early years may have been of young birds. Competition for breeding territories is also known to cause earlier arrival of migratory birds. However, at present, this is unlikely to be the case with the willow warblers at Carrifran because their preferred scrubby habitat is still increasing in much of the valley, so we can predict further population growth. There can also be competition for territories between species. Blackcaps and garden warblers, for example, which share the same habitat, are known to defend their territories against each other as well as against members of the same species. It has even been proposed that blackcaps mimic garden warbler song in a deliberate attempt to discourage incoming birds from setting up nearby territories.

Upper limits to population sizes of different species at Carrifran are inevitable eventually, as their preferred habitats become fully occupied. There will also be other gradual changes in the avifauna as the ecological succession of woodland progresses slowly from pioneer

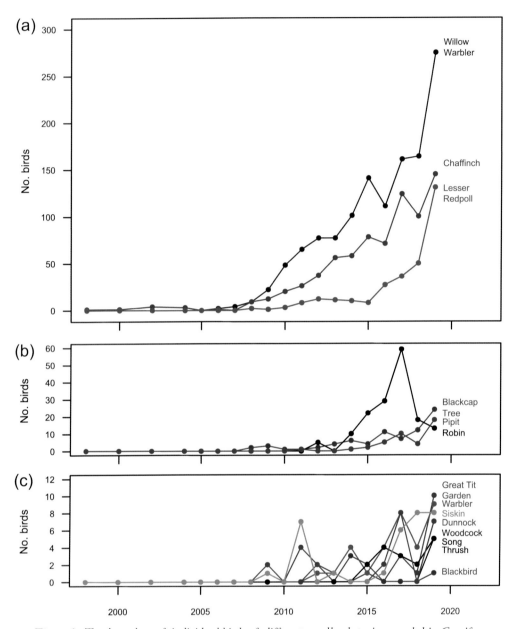

*Figure 6. Total numbers of individual birds of different woodland species recorded in Carrifran.*

and building stages towards a mature climax community. In a recently published paper (Colonisation by woodland birds at Carrifran Wildwood: the story so far. *Scottish Birds* 36:2, 135-149, 2016) I made predictions of which bird species would decline or colonise in the short-term and long-term. The species I predicted would decline in the near future (before 2025) was meadow pipit, and decliners in the distant future (after 2025) were whinchat, stonechat and goldfinch. Predicted colonisers in the near future were sparrowhawk, long-eared owl, jay, goldcrest, long-tailed tit, blue tit, coal tit, chiffchaff, whitethroat, treecreeper, spotted flycatcher, bullfinch, greenfinch and goldfinch. Of these, jay, long-tailed tit and blue tit were recorded for the first time in the 2019 surveys and most of the others have been recorded incidentally at other times. Predicted colonisers in the distant future were goshawk, stock dove, tawny owl, green woodpecker, great spotted woodpecker, wood warbler, nuthatch, pied flycatcher and redstart. These are all species associated with mature woodland, so it was surprising that two of them, tawny owl and wood warbler, were recorded for the first time in the 2019 surveys, when there is no new woodland at Carrifran that can yet be called mature.

The raptor that is seen most regularly at Carrifran and Black Hope is the buzzard, usually in ones or twos and often in the air being mobbed by crows or ravens (also recorded regularly). It is an opportunistic feeder that can take a wide variety of prey and carrion, but it feeds mostly on small mammals, especially voles which are ubiquitous in both valleys. Kestrels also feed mainly on voles, but they have been recorded less frequently than buzzards and are currently in decline across Scotland. There have been occasional sightings of short-eared owl and long-eared owl and they too feed mainly on small mammals. The former was recorded for the first time in a June survey in 2017, when it was probably breeding. Peregrines breed regularly at Carrifran and Black Hope and are usually recorded in the May and June surveys. They feed almost exclusively on medium-sized

## A CHANCE ENCOUNTER

'Trips' of passage Dotterel are infrequently recorded in the Moffat Hills, so it was a nice surprise on 29th August 2015 to find five individuals on Carrifran's Racomitrium heath near the summit of White Coomb. The most recent previous record was a sighting on Lochcraig Head from 26th May 2006, when a visitor to Grey Mare's Tail reported seeing seven. There are several older records, the most noteworthy being a record of ten from White Coomb summit on the 8th May 1995. Breeding of Dotterel in the Southern Uplands has occasionally been recorded in recent decades, but generally sightings in the Moffat and Tweedsmuir Hills are of birds passing through during late April or more often in May. An autumn passage is less commonly recorded. So our decision to take a break from fencing work and make the short walk to White Coomb summit was rewarded with a rare sighting, and luckily Gillian Dawson – one of several volunteers helping me on the day – had a phone to record our chance encounter.

**Richard Clarkson**

and smaller birds, and the meadow pipit common in both valleys is known to be among their prey. Sparrowhawks also feed on small birds and have been seen at Carrifran in recent years (but not yet in the surveys). Merlin, another predator of small birds, was seen a few times in the early years. A golden eagle called Roxy that was radio-tagged in Galloway in 2010 flew over a few times and is now known to be breeding elsewhere in the

Borders. Introduction of young eagles by the South of Scotland Golden Eagle Project (*www.goldeneaglessouth of scotland.co.uk*) could mean there will be more frequent sightings of these impressive birds in future.

Attendance by blackcocks and greyhens (male and female black grouse) at the dawn lek next to the boundary fence (at 495m altitude) has been monitored annually in late April in a single visit involving an overnight camp. When the lek was first discovered in 2006 there were five displaying cocks and this number increased consistently to a maximum of 11 in 2012. There then followed a crash to six cocks in 2013 and three in 2014, the number has remained at two to four since then; three were present in 2019. One or two greyhens also attended in most years, and they sometimes perch on the fence apparently to better observe the displaying and competing cocks without getting chased by them. Perhaps this is why leks elsewhere are quite often sited next to fences. The declines in numbers of blackcocks in 2013 and 2014 were also recorded at other leks being monitored across southern Scotland and their cause is unknown. The May and June surveys at Carrifran show that, although greyhens sometimes nest in heather there, there is no evidence of any increase in black grouse in response to the tree planting. Regular attendance by cocks at some leks can commence as early as September and end in June. Greyhen attendance, on the other hand, is for a much shorter period, in late April and early May, and only one successful mating is required for fertilisation of

Photo: John Savory

*Blackcocks displaying at the dawn lek at Carrifran with a greyhen perched on a fence post.*
*Inset: her choice here is between just two*

a clutch of eggs. The fairly even spacing of a few miles between adjacent known leks suggests that some cocks may fly considerable distances every dawn in order to display on their particular defended spot of ground. They are powerful fliers and when he was Project Officer Hugh Chalmers once saw a blackcock outflying a chasing peregrine in level flight along Carrifran Gans!

So to conclude, this chapter shows how our ecological restoration work at Carrifran Wildwood has fundamentally changed the bird community there from one that was essentially dominated by just one open ground species, meadow pipit, to a much more varied and dynamic one now dominated by larger numbers of several woodland species. In other words both the biodiversity and the biomass of the avifauna have been enhanced. The details of this change, as described here, were entirely dependent on the information obtained in our annual bird surveys, and credit must go to Peter Gordon for his foresight in initiating surveys at Carrifran and Black Hope at the outset. Two senior researchers on the staff at Edinburgh University have participated in the surveys in the past two years, and have agreed to continue the monitoring at both valleys in the long-term. They appreciate the importance of this growing dataset which may well be unique in global terms. And it will be of great interest to see how many of our predictions of colonisation by different woodland birds at different stages of ecological succession are borne out in years to come.

## REPTILES, AMPHIBIANS AND FISH

Common (viviparous) lizards have been recorded at Carrifran in most years, from March to August and in all parts of the valley, including one that came into a tent during a volunteers' high planting weekend at Firth Hope in April 2007! Adders are also present but have been recorded in only two years and their cast skins were found in two other years.

Common toads are scarce, having been seen in only two years. Common frogs, on the other hand, have produced frogspawn every year in March in a few semi-permanent puddles on the main track, fed by water draining from above. The resulting tadpoles grow into froglets from May to late June. In most years several palmate newts can also be found in one or two of these puddles, and have been observed eating tadpoles, even depleting them entirely on a few occasions. In years when weather is warm and dry in spring and early summer, most of the puddles dry up leaving dead and dessicated tadpoles and newts on the track. There is a permanent lochan high up next to the boundary fence above Firth Hope, at 715 m altitude, where large numbers of frogs gather for mating. This was discovered during a fence check in April 2013, when males at the edge of the lochan were seen and heard croaking and at least 50 pairs were mating.

The only fish in the Carrifran Burn that have been seen in the valley itself are stone loach and brown trout parr. However, a series of electrofishing surveys by the Annan Fishery Board from 1997 to 2017, lower down the burn near the A708 road bridge, showed the presence of European eels and Atlantic salmon fry and parr, as well as brown trout (and possibly sea trout) fry and parr and stone loach.

**John Savory**

## MAMMALS

The 11 km boundary fence at Carrifran is stock-proof but not deer-proof. Sheep get in occasionally from adjacent ground, when the fence is partially buried in snow for example, but the feral goats on adjacent ground have never done so. Roe deer, which encroach regularly by jumping over the fence, are controlled by shooting. Numbers shot have remained consistent over the years, averaging about 20 per year (and one in every four visits by stalkers) since 2005, and bucks shot have accounted for 61% of the total. One Sika stag was shot in 2013 and they are known to occur elsewhere in the vicinity. As many of the roe deer originate from the adjacent Polmoodie conifer plantation, which is currently being felled, their numbers encroaching may decline but they will presumably become harder to see as the Carrifran woodland gets denser. Like other browsing mammals, roe deer have preferences for certain tree species. Oak, ash, aspen and rowan are preferred to downy birch, which accounts for more than half the trees in the valley, and alder is least preferred. Young oaks have been heavily browsed in places but those with well established root systems remain healthy and develop a bushier growth form. In addition to the deer, at least 20 other species of smaller mammals have been recorded at Carrifran. The trail camera used in 2014-15 produced photos of fox, badger and brown hare in several locations. Evidence also comes from direct observation, footprints in mud or snow, scats (faeces, which often show what has been eaten) holes in the ground where badgers have been rooting for food (which promote germination of tree seeds), and the unmistakable trails these low-slung and powerful animals create when moving directly up and down the valley sides. There are at least three badger setts; they and foxes use the whole area, including the highest ground along the boundary fence, and brown hares are replaced by occasional mountain hares above about 400m. Rabbits in the vicinity have only rarely entered the valley and otters along the Moffat Water sometimes leave spraint where the Carrifran Burn passes under the A708 road bridge. Stoats and weasels are present and a probable pine marten (rare in the area) scat was found on the track from the car park in January 2018. Red squirrels probably originating from the Polmoodie plantation have been seen occasionally since 2012 in the lower part of the valley where there are hazelnuts for them to eat in early autumn. Short-tailed (or field) voles are common wherever grasses dominate the ground vegetation and they provide an important food source for many of the predators that are present (foxes, mustelids, buzzards, kestrels, owls). Their numbers fluctuate according to a roughly 4-year cycle and this variation influences the numbers of predators. Bank voles were also recorded in a survey in 2010-11 based on analyses of DNA in faeces deposited by small mammals in tubes baited with food placed regularly along eight transects. This survey was organised by Andy Riches, Mammal Society Recorder for the Dumfries and Galloway Region.

Vole guards were used to protect the stems of the young trees that were planted, and voles, like deer, have preferences for certain species. Vole damage to bark at the bases of hollies and willows, for example, was often seen where the guards gave imperfect protection. Wood mouse and house mouse are also present. The distinctive black faeces of hedgehogs have been found a few times but moles are more common, judging from fresh mole hills seen every year in many places, including up high and especially around the dry stone shelter at the end of the main track where there are presumably plenty of earthworms and other invertebrates for them to eat. Common shrews have been found dead on the track in most years and a dead water shrew was also found in 2014. Their presence and also that of pygmy shrews was confirmed in the 2010-11 small mammal survey. A Southern Scotland Bat Survey in 2016 by the Scottish Wildlife Trust, based on identification of different species' calls in several locations, indicated that soprano pipistrelles are more numerous than common pipistrelles, and that there are at least three other species of bat present.

**John Savory**

*John Savory explaining the bird survey work at Carrifran to staff of Scottish Natural Heritage in 2015*

Greyhen flushed off the east side of valley
Carrifran - 27·10·19

John Wright

# INVERTEBRATE RECOVERY
# AT CARRIFRAN

*Reuben Singleton*

A walk through the Border Hills in high summer can be both an exhilarating and a sobering experience. Wide open vistas with few people are a rare thing to experience today but any joy at being out in the sun and the wind, always the wind, is tempered by the knowledge that the lack of wildflowers and associated large insects is not evidence of a healthy ecosystem.

A typical walk over the hills in June will see you walking across close-grazed turf studded with the whites, yellows and purples of Heath Bedstraw, Tormentil and Thyme. Butterflies can be abundant but restricted to Small Heath and the occasional Common Blue. Wetter areas knee-deep in rushes provide some welcome variation in habitat and here Green-veined Whites flutter in their hundreds over the lime-green sward. Occasionally the observer is lucky enough to be rewarded by the sight of a richly coloured Small Pearl-bordered Fritillary butterfly flopping over the rushes, stopping only to take nectar from Ragged-robin and Bugle, or concentrating on finding a mate. Day-flying moths with the exception of the ubiquitous grass-moths (Crambid species) are rare. Only the fleeting glimpse of a large brown moth zipping by on the wind serves to provide any variety, most likely a Fox Moth or a Northern Eggar.

The contrast with a walk through Carrifran in 2019 could not be more stark. All the plants found on the open hill are still there but with a very different growth form. The Tormentil and Heath Bedstraw are now trailing though a luxurious sward of grasses and have been joined by a diverse suite of herbs, while the thyme forms deep fragrant purple cushions. The omnipresent breeze of the open hill (how often do you ever see motionless wind turbines) has gone, disrupted and moderated by the mosaic of young trees which now characterise the valley. The importance of cover or shelter for wildlife is often under-estimated by ecologists but it shouldn't be; after all what are the three things we require to survive? – food, water and shelter.

Now that the influence of the wind has reduced, it is possible to sit for a few minutes in the sunshine in the lee of Birch and Aspen grove and contemplate the changes that have taken place in less than twenty short years. The most striking thing is how many more days per year it is now possible to sit in the same spot wearing only a t-shirt. Years before, the fleece jacket would have been a constant companion and rarely relegated to the backpack. Now basking in the unfortunately still too rare Scottish summer sunshine it is possible to contemplate the hum of insects going about their business, no longer drowned out by the sound of the wind. Looking around there are Blaeberry Bumblebees attending to the cushions of Thyme and Narrow-bordered Five-spot Burnet moths nectaring on Common Knapweed no longer shorn to the ground by grazing livestock. The butterflies of 20 years ago are still here though the proportions of the species have changed; Small Heath and Green-veined White butterflies are less common now but the numbers of Common Blue and Small Pearl-bordered Fritillary have exploded. These species have been joined by a recent arrival from the south, the Large Skipper, and it is surely only a matter of time until it is joined by its diminutive relative, the Small Skipper. In late summer, August onwards, the valley is alive with Scotch Argus butterflies.

It is the night-time denizens of the valley where the most significant recorded changes have occurred. In the early years of the project two entomologists, Keith Bland and Jeff Waddell undertook a series of moth trapping sessions in the Carrifran valley, providing an excellent baseline of the moth fauna prior to the widespread planting of trees. Jeff recorded 68 species over the summer of 2003, most of these being characteristic species of open ground. Of these, 52 species were recorded as generalist species with only five species regarded as being typical of woodland habitats. In recent years, moth recording has been undertaken on an opportunistic basis by a number of observers which has enabled a contemporary picture of the moth populations to be drawn.

Today the number of moth species recorded at Carrifran has more than doubled to 159 species, with surely many more to be found with continued recording effort. Almost all of the characteristic species of open ground found on the site in 2003 are still being recorded, with local species characteristic of open moorland such as Northern Deep-brown Dart being recorded for the first time in 2018. The number of species seen as woodland specialists have increased markedly since 2003 from five to around 20 species. These include Clouded Silver, Common Lutestring, Least Black Arches, Nut-tree Tussock and Peach Blossom. Some of the recent arrivals have been of considerable interest with the micro-moth *Nemophora degeerella* recorded in 2015 being the most northerly record of this moth at that time. It has subsequently been recorded further north in Peeblesshire indicating that this is a species which is expanding its range as a result of climate change. In similar vein, the Large Skipper butterfly was recorded at Carrifran in 2019 for the first time, another species that is expected to move north as the climate becomes warmer.

One of the by-catches of moth traps are night-flying caddis-flies and craneflies which has resulted in a handful of common species being recorded at Carrifran including the attractive Hairy-eyed Cranefly, *Pedicia rivosa*.

Some of the species being recorded at Carrifran today have always been there, but the establishment of trees and shrubs in the valley has created new niches for them. The July Highflyer is a moth with larvae that feed on a range of low shrubs and trees. Recently its caterpillars were observed defoliating Downy Willow at 500 m in Broomy Gutter. Downy willow is a rare shrub in Scotland and has been planted at high altitudes at Carrifran with a view to creating a natural treeline of montane scrub. This is certainly one moth which lives up to its name.

Good mothing nights are few in the uplands with a full moon and clear skies. Low temperatures, heavy rain and strong winds all sound the death knell for a successful mothing expedition. Consequently, the few days before a prospective trip are marked by the time spent on various weather forecast websites and apps. Experience shows that the Norwegian Weather Institute through its weather forecast website (www.yr.no) provides the most reliable indicator of weather conditions at Carrifran rather than the crop of home-grown alternatives.

## CARRIFRAN'S BUTTERFLIES MARK THE BEGINNING OF THE DARWIN TREE OF LIFE PROJECT

The Darwin Tree of Life project launched in November 2018 by the Sanger Wellcome Trust has set itself a truly ambitious mission: to generate genome reference sequences for the entire flora and fauna of the British Isles. Much like the human genome project, this permanent scientific resource promises to transform biology. Butterflies were an obvious group of choice for the pilot phase of the project: there are few wild creatures that delight and fascinate us in the way butterflies do.

Thanks to the efforts of generations of naturalists, we have a near complete knowledge of the ecology of our native butterfly fauna. Citizen science recording schemes run by Butterfly Conservation continue to be powered by the enthusiasm for butterflies and allow us to track changes in range in real time. With 59 regularly recorded species, UK butterfly diversity is manageable and identification easy. More importantly, a broad and enthusiastic group of biologists has already coalesced around the prospect of this wonderful resource. These range from evolutionary biologists interested in the fundamental forces behind genome evolution and speciation to conservation geneticists who are using genetic data from museum collections to identify the drivers of past extinction events and current range shifts.

Unlike the initial human reference genome, which is an amalgam of many individuals, each genomic reference generated by the Darwin Tree of Life initiative will be based on individual specimens. Given that these genomic voucher individuals will be studied by the scientific community for decades to come, it made sense to choose populations which have both an interesting past, and a long-term future (ideally including continued monitoring). With the enthusiastic support of Philip and Myrtle Ashmole and the Wildwood Steering Group, my lab set out to record the butterfly fauna of Carrifran (see list below). For each of the 14 species we encountered we collected a small number of individuals to be used for whole genome sequencing by the Darwin Tree of Life project. Our butterfly survey was light touch (recording presence/absence during four monthly visits, May - August) and most of the species we encountered had been recorded at Carrifran before. However, we were excited to find strong populations of Large Skipper, a species currently expanding northwards which had not previously been found at Carrifran, and Scotch Argus, an emblematic upland species of southern Scotland with a shrinking range.

*Much travelled Painted Lady*

*Small Pearl-bordered Fritillary
on Wood Cranesbill.*

## BUTTERFLIES RECORDED FROM CARRIFRAN IN 2019

| | | |
|---|---|---|
| *Pieris napi* | Geen-veined White | abundant May-Aug |
| *Anthocharis cardamines* | Orange-tip | very abundant May |
| *Aglais io* | Peacock | very abundant |
| *Aglais urticae* | Small Tortoiseshell | abundant |
| *Vanessa atalanta* | Red Admiral | regular |
| *Vanessa cardui* | Painted Lady | large influx in July |
| *Boloria selene* | Small Pearl-bordered Fritillary | very abundant |
| *Argynnis aglaja* | Dark Green Fritillary | recorded previously, not in 2019 |
| *Aphantopus hyperantus* | Ringlet | common July |
| *Maniola jurtina* | Meadow Brown | common |
| *Erebia aethiops* | Scotch Argus | July-Aug |
| *Coenonympha pamphilus* | Small Heath | abundant June-Aug |
| *Lycaena phlaeas* | Small Copper | recorded previously, not in 2019 |
| *Polyommatus icarus* | Common Blue | single sighting near sheepstell |
| *Ochlodes sylvanus* | Large Skipper | strong population |

*Scotch Argus.*

Given that butterflies are the best studied invertebrate group, it is surprising how little is known about their deeper history. When, where and how did the species we find in the UK now split off from their closest evolutionary relatives? From which glacial refuge and how quickly were the British Isles colonised after the last ice age? How evolutionarily distinct are UK populations? Which genetic changes matter for adaptation to man-made changes in land use and climate? The genomic reference sequences generated from the Carrifran samples contain within them information about the history of many thousands of genetic ancestors which will be studied by the scientific community to answer these and many other questions. Of course the sequencing of Carrifran's butterflies marks only the very beginning of much larger endeavour. The success of the Darwin Tree of Life project will ultimately depend on the coordinated efforts and perseverance of many enthusiasts who know and care about our flora and fauna. Not least in this respect, Carrifran will serve as an inspiration!

**Konrad Lohse**

A SELECTION OF MOTHS FOUND AT CARRIFRAN

*Opposite page*
*Clockwise from top left: Puss Moth; Nut-tree Tussock Moth; Northern Eggar;*
*Lesser Swallow Prominent; Longhorn Moth*

*This page*
*Clockwise from top left: Garden Tiger; Peppered Moth; Scalloped Hazel Moth;*
*Poplar Hawk Moth just emerged*

## A NEW BUG FOR SCOTLAND

A visit by Carlisle Natural History Society (CNHS) to Carrifran in July 2016 resulted in the collection of a rather special bug, the Hemipteran, *Orthotylus virens*. Stephen Hewitt swept several specimens from Bay Willow in the lower valley which turned out to be the first Scottish records.

*Orthotylus virens* was first reported as British in 1917 by CNHS members F. H. Day and J. Murray from separate sites in Cumberland. The following year, Day made a more detailed study of the population he had discovered on Cumwhitton Moss east of Carlisle and established that it was restricted to Bay Willow. Following this lead, the bug was then discovered on the same foodplant at Hayton Moss nearby and at further sites thereafter.

A review of the status of Hemipteran bugs in the UK in 1992 found it to be restricted to the northern English counties of Cumberland, Westmorland and Yorkshire, though it could be found readily in these areas. It was predicted in that review that "more populations will ultimately be found in the north of England, and perhaps also in Scotland".

The bug appears to enjoy Bay Willow bearing catkins in sunny situations and this was the case at Carrifran. Given the native woodland at Carrifran has all been planted in the last 20 years, with the exception of a few trees along the main watercourses which did not include Bay Willow, it must have become established at the site within this period. The Bay Willow planted at Carrifran was sourced from a local population at Riskinhope, Selkirkshire, approximately 10 km to the north-east. The willow seedlings were germinated from catkins collected there in August 1997 by Philip Ashmole, and were planted at Carrifran in 2000. Because the eggs of the bug are laid on young wood, there is no question of direct introduction of the bug at the time of planting, even assuming it could survive on such young plants. It seemed likely that the Bay Willow at Carrifran had been colonised from an overlooked population of the bug nearby.

Later that month, Stephen Hewitt visited Riskinhope, finding *Orthotylus virens* to be present there as well, sweeping specimens off Bay Willow both with and without catkins. In August 2016 Stephen went on to find the bug on catkins in the Ettrick Valley.

**Stephen Hewitt**

## THE NORTHERN DART IN THE SOUTHERN UPLANDS

The Northern Dart *Xestia alpicola* is a very special arctic-alpine moth which is usually found at high altitudes in the UK. It is a priority species in the UK Biodiversity Plan and is listed on the Scottish Biodiversity List as a species of conservation importance. Its UK stronghold is in the Scottish Highlands but there has long been a suspicion that it would occur on the highest hills of the Southern Uplands, with old records for the Cheviot, North Pennines and Lake District.

Two intrepid moth recorders, Malcolm Lindsay and Teyl de Bordes, launched a mission in 2013 to find this moth in the Tweedsmuir Hills. The moth has an odd life cycle with adults emerging only every other year, being scarce or absent in the intervening year. The caterpillars overwinter twice, taking two years to mature before pupation. Light trapping efforts in 2013 drew a blank, but perfect conditions on the night of 11th July 2014 resulted in the capture of 65 specimens between 711m and 790m altitude. This was the largest trapping count of the species recorded in the UK.

The moth was recorded at another site in the Tweedsmuir Hills in 2018, where an even more remarkable 112 moths were trapped by the same recorders. Malcolm continued his rich vein of form in 2019 when he and Chris Whitmore recorded the moth on the Cheviot on the Scotland-England border where a single specimen had been found 44 years before. It appears that the Cheviot and Tweedsmuir populations, though appearing to be identical in morphology, emerge in different years.

It is considered likely that the Northern Dart will be present at both Carrifran and Talla & Gameshope and it is proposed that it would be a good mascot for the 'Wild Heart of Southern Scotland'.

**Malcolm Lindsay**

Even the Norwegians cannot be relied upon completely; too many times Moffat can be enjoying 20°C sunshine, while up at Carrifran hill fog can mean 12°C and a strong breeze. A challenging location indeed!

A typical moth-trapping session at Carrifran involves arriving an hour before sunset at the road-side carpark before 'sherpaing' the paraphernalia (generator, moth traps, camp chairs, butterfly nets, collecting pots, field guides, midge repellent, pork pies, beer and whisky) up the hillside to the chosen trapping location. As dusk falls, anticipation builds as moths start to emerge and can be netted as they traverse the hillside. In the past couple of years roding Woodcock and the creaking-gate sound of young Long-eared Owls begging for food has added atmosphere to the proceedings. Midges are unfortunately an occupational hazard for fieldwork in this part of the world, but along with other small insects they provide food for the Pipistrelle bats that are now commonly seen hawking the prolific insect populations in the valley. It will be some time though, before there are nooks and crannies in any trees to provide roosting sites for bats.

# A VERY WET INSECT SURVEY

A cancelled entomological research trip to northern Norway with Dr Steve Compton, Reader in Entomology at the University of Leeds and expert on the small parasitic wasps of the Chalcidoidea gave us the opportunity for all of us to make a four day invertebrate recording visit to Carrifran at the end of the first week in August 2019.

A very bad weather forecast for most of our available time led to a very early start from Yorkshire on Thursday 8th and a desperate race against the weather to get traps in for the first day for a least a brief recording session on the Thursday afternoon. We met Philip Ashmole and Borders Forest Trust's Site Officer Andy Wilson in the Carrifran car park at 10:30 and Andy saved us a huge expense of time and energy by transporting all our trapping equipment up to the confluence of Games Gill and Firthhope Linn on the quad-bike. Meanwhile Steve started up from the car park, sweeping for small flying insects from the vegetation while it was still dry.

Lack of time prevented our climbing much further up the valley than our drop-off point. We quickly set up a line of six water traps (bright yellow bowls filled with water plus preservative) which catch insects by stimulating their settling response on flowers. We also set up a Malaise interception trap. How this tent-like apparatus works will be familiar to anyone who has camped in a classical ridge tent, where insects climb to the highest point of the interior in order to escape. By situating a collecting bottle at that highest point the insects can be collected and, if well situated along a flight line, can rapidly sample insects flying through 2m x 1m area of airspace. Finally, a 10-minute vacuum sample, made by inserting an insect collecting net in the air-intake of a petrol-engined leaf blower, was taken of moss, plant litter, the base of various vegetation types, bare ground and riverside shingle.

Racing down the valley with the remainder of our equipment we set up three more sets of water and Malaise traps in areas of different vegetation and repeated the vacuum samples, with the lowest back down in the woodland just above the car-park. Ominous dark clouds building from the south circumvented any delay and we immediately set off back up the valley to begin retrieving the furthest traps before the deluge, eventually meeting Steve still working his way along with his sweep-net and pooter. We managed to collect all our traps before the

*Organising entomological equipment*

True darkness comes late at this latitude at mid-summer and if there is a full moon then it never becomes properly dark and it is possible to walk around in the middle of the night without the need for a torch. On such clear nights the stars can be breathtaking with the Milky Way stretching brilliantly across the sky from horizon to horizon. Not for nothing is the nearest town of Moffat designated as Europe's first "Dark Sky Town".

Moths start to arrive at the traps in numbers about an hour after sunset. This is accompanied by the frenetic swishing of butterfly nets and the potting of specimens for identification. Most of this occurs next morning as the colour of moths is badly washed out by artificial light, particularly that provided by modern LEDs. The arrival of moths is not constant with pulses of moths arriving throughout the night. Like us, different species arrive and leave the party at different times with some early birds and some seemingly determined not to make their entrance until the bitter end.

rain began and were pleased to see that they had made a fair-sized catch in such a short time. As we returned along the track we were treated to the sight of dozens of Scotch Argus butterflies, a fine Golden-ringed dragonfly (*Cordulegaster boltonii*) and numerous northern dumbledor beetles (*Anoplotrupes stercorosus*).

Overnight a major storm with torrential rain and gale force winds swept across Britain causing widespread damage and flooding, and we awoke on Friday to find our car at Tushielaw parked in five inches of standing water. Had our equipment remained out the Malaise would have been flattened and the water traps flooded and the catches lost. The continuing heavy rain made further recording work impossible and we took the litter samples back to Philip and Myrtle's house at Kidston Mill and transferred them into Berlese extraction funnels in Myrtle's greenhouse. These funnels work by producing a gradient of a naphthalene insect-repellent vapour which forces the insects to flee towards a collecting pot. More heavy rain overnight gave way to weak sunshine on the Saturday morning and we dashed back to Carrifran and quickly set up three further rows of water traps in vegetation types in the lower valley we had not visited on the Thursday. Back to Kidston Mill where we picked up the Berlese funnels and found they had worked admirably with clean, easy to sort samples of litter-dwelling insects and then dashed back to Carrifran to collect the water traps as once again more ominous cloud arrived from the south west. The traps had again worked well and we managed to pick up the last of them as the first raindrops began to fall. The rain continued for the rest of the day and overnight and, with no prospect at all of clearer weather on the Sunday, we retreated south to begin the sorting and identification of the invertebrates we had found.

So far we have identified 40 species of beetles, 12 species of true bugs 14 species of flies and 29 species of other invertebrates. The hoppers, parasitic wasps, spiders and most families of flies have been dispersed to experts around the country for identification. The most notable records so far are a boreal ensign-scale insect (*Arctorthezia cataphracta*) that feeds on the roots of a wide variety of plants in moss at high latitudes, and a thick-legged flower beetle (*Oedemera virescens*) which is a Nationally Rare species, albeit with a distribution centred in south-west Scotland. According to the National Biodiversity Network database the scale insect record is the first for Southern Scotland.

**Roger & Rosy Key**

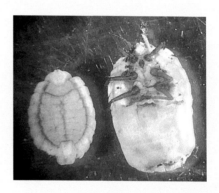

*Arctorthezia cataphracta, a boreal ensign-scale insect found during the 2019 survey at Carrifran*

The wider Wild Heart of Scotland area hosts a number of nationally scarce moth species including the Broad-bordered White Underwing, Northern Dart, Northern Arches, Small Chocolate-tip and Thyme Pug. In 2019, a micro-moth, the Bearberry Bell (*Epinotia nemorivaga*) was found in a valley near Drumelzier at its only known site south of the Cairngorms. Some concerns have been voiced that the removal or reduction of livestock grazing will result in the decline of some of these species but there is little evidence of this to date. The expansion of dwarf shrubs such as Cowberry and Bearberry is likely to result in more habitat for species like the Broad-bordered White Underwing, Northern Dart and the Bearberry Bell, while species such as Thyme Pug which prefer open scree habitat are likely to persist as their habitat will remain largely unchanged. The status of the Small Chocolate-tip provides the most cause for concern as the larvae appear to prefer scattered Eared Willow bushes in open locations. They do however use Aspen trees, particularly young suckering growth of which there should be no shortage in the relaxation of livestock grazing. Monitoring of this moth's fortunes should be a priority in the coming years.

Invertebrate recording at Carrifran has not been restricted to Lepidoptera (butterflies and moths), with considerable work also undertaken on species groups such as beetles (Coleoptera) and spiders (Arachnida). Because spider communities are more critically linked to structural habitat diversity than plant species availability, due to them being carnivores, it would be expected that the thicker sward resulting from the removal of grazing would result in a positive effect on species numbers. Pitfall trapping surveys by Philip Ashmole in 2000-01 and 2017, with species determination by Bob Merritt and Edward Milner, have resulted in an impressive 122 spider species being recorded at Carrifran to date; this number is set to increase considerably as the woodland becomes well-established. In 2017, Philip was able to station a group of four traps in different habitats at 700-800 m altitude on White Coomb resulting in 12 species new to Dumfriesshire. This has helped the 10 km square in which Carrifran sits to become the most diverse square for spiders in Dumfriesshire.

In July 2019 a comprehensive collecting expedition approach over three days led by Roger Key resulted in several hundred invertebrates collected. A series of survey techniques were used including pitfall trapping, sieving of leaf litter and suction trapping which deploys a giant vacuum cleaner to suck small invertebrates off vegetation.

A comprehensive picture of the invertebrate populations at Carrifran is unlikely to be attained until such time that it is possible to harness the technological advances of DNA metabarcoding at an affordable cost. Until such time, diligent surveyors will continue to record notable species, particularly in the more inaccessible areas of the site.

The future is exciting: as the woodland matures extremes of microclimate will continue to be ameliorated and increasing deadwood habitat, both standing and lying on the ground, will provide niches which don't currently exist for a range of invertebrate species. These deadwood-dependent invertebrates will speed up the availability of nesting and roosting sites for birds and bats as well as offering additional food sources for other species. To pump-prime this process, consideration should be given to the import of deadwood from long-established woodland sites elsewhere in southern Scotland.

*Green-veined White*

# CARRIFRAN FUNGI: THINGS ARE CHANGING!

*Roy Watling*

While it is always interesting to visit a new locality to study the fungus flora (mycota), it is of greater interest to visit a site repeatedly and study the development of the mycota over time; Carrifran is such a site! It is also comparatively rare to be able to compare the resulting records with well-established data sets from areas geographically close-by. Thus, in the 20-year study completed at Dawyck in Peeblesshire (over the watershed from Carrifran), the different fungal species number a little over 1,550, although this is a long-established woodland with many exotic introductions. However, it gives some idea as to the potential of an area in this part of Scotland. With intense scrutiny a diverse range of fungi can be found, whether in rough pasture or areas with an arborescent element. Early observations at Carrifran were made in the grazed areas of denuded sheep walks; these formed a base-line study allowing us to see what fungi have been found in the intervening years. It is imperative though, to understand that this account is just a small window into the local fungus flora as fungi are not necessarily visible every year, even though they may be present. Observations made in Malaysia by E J H Corner in the 1930s showed that there may be intervals of up to 40 years between re-appearance of fruiting bodies and in the UK similar gaps of various lengths are known.

The Carrifran project is now twenty years old, though observations on the fungi began long before planting commenced. These gave an idea of the fungi of naturally grazed pasture-woodland which presumably persisted until the high-stocked introduction of sheep and cattle. It has been suggested that many of the fungi recorded in sheep-grazed areas in Scotland spread over the adjacent countryside from gaps and glades in earlier primaeval woodland (Watling, 1984). An alpine-montane element, which persists today, of Alpine Brittlegill (*Russula nana*), a putative ectomycorrhizal associate with Dwarf Willow (*Salix herbacea*) and *Lichenomphalia alpina* & *L. hudsoniana*, both basidio-lichens, has probably been around on the higher ground from early times. This is probably true also of the Saxifrage Rust (*Puccinia saxifragae*), which attacks Starry Saxifrage (*Saxifraga stellaris*); it is found today at 610m. To these must be added two much larger fungi, which may have a boreal distribution in Scotland and are now found fruiting along the track at Carrifran: Pedicellate Puffball (*Lycoperdon caudatum*), with long sterigmatic tails to the basidiospores and *L. norvegicum*. The recent Carrifran record of the latter is the first for the British Isles, although it has long been expected. *L. norvegicum* has a very strong resemblance to the common Jewelled Puffball (*L. perlatum*), already recorded from the area. It has been suggested (Pegler et al. 1995) that *L. caudatum* and *L. norvegicum* grow in similar habitats to each other. Also collected in recent

*Three species of puffball are found at Carrifran, including* Lycoperdon norvegicum *illustrated here. The Carrifran record is the first for the British Isles but it may be more widely distributed because few people examine the basidiospores under the microscope, where they are seen to be almost smooth in contrast to those of the common L. perlatum also found near trees at Carrifran, which it resembles macroscopically but differs in its warty spores. L. foetidum is the third species of puffball but is darker in colour and favours more open grassland areas, including those quite high up*

surveys, the Ergot fungus (*Claviceps purpurea*) and Choke Grass (*Epichloe typhina*), both parasites of grasses, undoubtedly formed part of the old community.

A key problem with any fungal survey is that identification of the larger types, at present anyway, is mostly based on the appearance of their fruiting structures, sometimes then confirmed by microscopy. Identification of the smaller types, which grow on stems and bark etc., relies almost entirely on microscopic examination. The latter include parasitic species, such as the rust-fungi and the hypertrophy-inducing fungi, as well as saprobic taxa. The second group has four species recorded for Carrifran: *Taphrina torquenetii* on leaves of Alder (*Alnus glutinosa*), *T. amentorum* on Alder catkins, *T. aurea* on leaves of Aspen (*Populus tremula*), and Pocket Plum (*T. pruni*) on Blackthorn (*Prunus spinosa*). These species are all associated with the newly planted areas. The larger fungi also have a full range of life styles from the ectomycorrhizal genera *Lactarius* and *Russula,* and the ubiquitous Deceiver (*Laccaria laccata*) to litter-rotters such as the Butter Cap (*Rhodocollybia butyracea*) and the saprobic Wax-caps (*Hygrocybe* spp.) and Pink Gills (*Entoloma* spp.). The last two make up part of the CHEG (*Clavaria, Entoloma, Hygroybe & Geoglossum*) conservation formula used to assess the quality of grassland. For Carrifran the figure of 37 makes the area of International importance. Lignicolous fungi are rare due to the current deficiency of woody substrates in the area but these are expected to increase as this resource becomes more available. However, *Oxyporus populinus*, not confined to poplar wood as suggested by its name, was found on an old stump by the stream in the earliest excursions and more recently the less-common *Chromocyphella muscicola* was found on old wet alder wood – quite a find as it is so small. As far as the micro-mycota are concerned, species can be found nearly all year round, many depending on a single substrate or group of suitable substrates, e.g. *Venturia rumicis* on the leaves of Broad-leaved Dock (*Rumex obtusifolius*), or various species confined to the previous year's Umbelliferae stems. Several species which might be expected at Carrifran have either got there by invasion from neighbouring woodland or have persisted in an asexual stage e.g. Grass Twist (*Lidophia graminis*) whose imperfect stage is sometimes called *Dilophospora alopecuri*. It deforms the developing shoots of a range of grasses, not just *Alopecurus*. Also included would be the Birch Rust fungus (*Melampsoridium betulinum*). This has a form on alder, found on later excursions to Carrifran, which is considered by some authors to be the separate species *M. hiratsukanum*. Such reticulate patterns make the true pattern of a species in a single locality difficult to ascertain. Undoubtedly planting trees, the fundamental concept of the project, is paramount in the establishment of a rich fungus flora. Glimpses of the benefits of planting, especially in Barker's Paddock (the area nearest to the Car Park), where willows and Alder grow, show how habitats for flourishing fungi can be created. The larger club fungi 'Bracken Club' (*Typhula quisquillaris*) and Pipe Club (*Macrotyphula fistulosa*) have both been recorded and follow the establishment of wet thickets. In the dense undergrowth of these woodland strips several small terricolous species are present, including Bonnet Fungi such as the bright orange *Mycena acicula* and *M. pterigena,* which is confined to fern petioles, and *M. bulbosa*, restricted to the basal parts of *Juncus* culms. Other similar small agarics are the Parachute fungus *Marasmius setulosus, Rorimyces rotula* with its sticky stem and *Hemimycena tortuosa* with twisted hairs entirely covering the small white mushroom, clearly observable with a lens. Micro-species e.g. species of *Pyrenopeziza* and *Pseudopeziza* and their relatives were very probably present before re-afforestation and *Hymenoscyphus scutula*, related to the dreaded Ash dieback (*H. fraxineus*) probably already existed in the area; although an ascomycete it accompanies small mushrooms in damp areas.

*Xerocomus ferrugineus, a bolete typical of Scottish hills, at nearly 650m on Gupe Craig with Dwarf Willow (Salix herbacea) nearby. It is associated with Dwarf Willow and possibly also with Birch (Betula spp.)*

*Gymnosporangium cornutum. The horn-shaped fruiting structures are the asexual stage of this rust-fungus on Rowan (Sorbus aucuparia). It is common in Scotland, less so in England and was probably an original inhabitant of the Scottish wildwood. The 'horns' collapse releasing air-borne spores which infect the stems and leaves of Juniper (Juniperus communis). The resulting lesions, the alternate sexual stage, are insignificant unless wet, when they swell producing orange blobs. The disease is perennial and may be revealed at other times of the year as characteristic swellings on the stems.*

That fungi can be introduced from elsewhere is shown by the occurrence of the jelly fungus Pale Staghorn (*Calocera pallidospathulata*), only recently described but advancing north ever since; it was found on discarded conifer wood. *Gloeophyllum sepiarium*, another conifer inhabitant is common throughout the area; it too must have been introduced. On Bamboo canes used as stakes along the trackside at Carrifran is the dark-coloured powdery asexual (conidial, anamorphic) stage of *Apiospora montagnei*, often separately called *Papularia arundinis*. It is common on bamboos and other exotic grasses in gardens although less commonly recorded on some native Gramineae.

But where do all these fungi come from? The spores of most fungi are generally air-borne and may also be spread accidentally on the roots of any planted tree or on the boots of visitors to the area. Naturalists go from site to site on their travels, oblivious as to what they might be doing! Fungi require a favorable environment in which to germinate and suitable conditions for the germlings to continue flourishing. Not all is then straightforward as the fungus may fall prey to invertebrates or be out-competed by mycelium (the usually unseen vegetative growth) of more vigorous fungi already in-place. Experiments in Svalbard have shown suppression of fruiting in certain taxa after irrigation of plots with acid-rain (Alexander, pers. comm.). This suggests that changing the type of nutrient alters the fruiting pattern of larger fungi.

There are also apparently successional patterns in the fruiting of larger fungi, and this is reflected in the position of fruiting-bodies under the tree-canopy. Some species may occur in very small but persistent 'nuclei', which only spring into growth when there is a favorable change in the environment. Thus wax-caps in an area of Fair Isle under observation showed re-establishment of a whole range of species on cessation of manuring (Riddiford & Watling; in press). The mycota of any site are a distillate of all these elements and vary from site to site, with ultimately a few common denominators.

It's been suggested that 'strimming' might reflect the situation before herbivores were removed when at least some of the fauna had not adapted to the new environment, thus relieving, for instance, the pressure on breeding Orange Tips, and probably other invertebrates unknown to us. By 2018 there had been a noticeable decrease in the numbers and species of the larger fungi. The grass and other tall herbs had produced a rank under-storey causing some of the larger fungi to fruit only at the trackside, e.g. Brown Rim (*Paxillus involutus*). Other similar species were not observed either because they had not fruited or were so scarce they had been missed. A small field-test undertaken earlier at Dawyck involved mowing a strip in the grassland on the southern border, after which fruiting bodies were soon seen.  These fungi were probably there all the time, but their 'fruiting' was suppressed by the long grass. In the very short time between mowing and fruiting, mature fruiting mycelium could not have developed from dormant spores or from spores colonizing from elsewhere. The year 2018 was notable for the appearance in several places along the track of *Amanita betulae*, recently recognized as distinct. It seems to me that where this fungus has been seen elsewhere in Scotland it favours partially disturbed habitats in which to grow or produce fruiting bodies. Perhaps as the canopy forms at Carrifran we will experience changes like this and with time colonization by fungi may be as envisaged by those who initiated the project.

Perhaps the current long grass at Carrifran results from residual nutrients held in the soil-profile from dung deposited before the removal of the sheep. The presence of Mottle-gills (*Panaeolus*), Brownies (*Psilocybe*), Round-heads (*Stropharia*) and various Inky Caps (Coprinoids) suggest that a lot of dung was deposited in the past. A much lower deposition-rate may now be maintained by Roe Deer.

*The author at Carrifran explaining micro-fungi to a group of mycologists from the South of Scotland Fungus Group during a 2019 foray, arranged in celebration of his 80th birthday*

On acidic substrates in the areas surrounding the re-forested areas at Carrifran, it's been noted that the peaty soils are home to species of *Hypholoma e.g.* Sphagnum Brownie (*H. elongatum*) and Olive Brownie (*H. myosotis*) and various species of *Galerina*. Indeed, Bog Bell (*G. paludosa*) grows amongst the *Sphagnum*, accompanied by 'The Sphagnum Greyling' (*Tephrocybe palustris*) which is probably parasitic on the moss.

It is almost impossible to return an area such as Carrifran to the state before sheep were introduced, as some of the flora and fauna will have adapted to the intervening regime and will have to do so again now that re-forestation is taking place. Heavy grazing over a long period has led to a downward spiral which the new management system should stop and hopefully even reverse. Until recently, we could only tell of changes in the fungus flora by the appearance of fruiting bodies, but things are changing as a range of fungi can now be identified using molecular techniques. It is now possible by sampling the soil or other substrates colonized to ascertain whether a fungus is present in the absence of a visible fructification. In this way it should be possible to see if certain fungi have persisted through these changing times or have re-colonised the area without showing themselves by producing fruiting bodies. Perhaps when the next anniversary comes around more will have shown their heads!

This account is just a brief overview of Carrifran fungi, based on a few visits over several years, but should give an idea as to the complexities of the mycota, complexities which are not restricted to Carrifran - and they will all change with time.

### References

Corner, E.J.H. (1935) *The seasonal fruiting of agarics in Malaya. Gardens Bull. Straits Settl. 9: 79-88.*

Pegler, D.N. & Lassoe, T. & Spooner, B. M. (1995). *British Puffballs, Earthstars & Stinkhorns. Royal Bot. Gardens Kew, Richmond, Surrey, England.*

Riddiford, N. & Watling R. (in press). *Restoring grassland fungi. British Wildlife.*

Watling, R. (1984). *Macrofungi of birchwoods. Proc. Roy. Soc. Edinb. 85: 129-140.*

*The hanging valley of Firth Hope at over 600m still has lots of space for montane scrub, especially Downy Willow and Juniper. Neither of these establish easily from seed in a heavy sward, so continued planting is needed*

*Philip carrying Honeysuckle cuttings for planting and volunteers with Andy Wilson compacting removed tree tubes and vole guards for land fill*

# NATURE STILL NEEDS
# A HAND AT CARRIFRAN

*Philip Ashmole and Stuart Adair*

The ultimate aim of ecological restoration is to re-create healthy and fully functioning ecosystems that require no human intervention. In truth, we are still a very long way from this point, especially at relatively small and isolated sites like Carrifran. Realistically, control of deer is likely to be needed at Carrifran for some time to come. Otherwise, in the absence of natural predators, we would risk major loss of what has already been achieved. The same is true of maintaining stock-proof fencing, especially with feral goats still roaming the wider Moffat Hills.

*Myrtle has always hoped that the growth of trees along the track would make it less conspicuous*

Another practical matter is that there are still some tree tubes and thousands of plastic voleguards around planted trees at Carrifran. Recently volunteers have been working hard to remove them, but there is still a long way to go. Some of the tubes can be re-used in current planting elsewhere, but the voleguards are brittle and cannot be recycled, so compacting them before they go to landfill is the best we can do.

The old farm track up the valley from the road gate is not a feature that we would have wanted to create, since it reduces the feeling of wildness. However, it has been useful during the main planting phase and is a natural route to take with parties of visitors. In the long run we hope that it can be made less obtrusive, and growth of trees is already making a difference.

During recent discussions in the Wildwood Steering Group, a consensus emerged that we should continue planting various tree, shrub and plant species for some time to come. Although we want to hand over management to nature, we also want to maintain the rate at which the site approaches a more natural condition. This is primarily because of the increasing value of Carrifran Wildwood as one of very few sites where people can see and come to understand, by visiting or looking at images, what a natural environment – one not drastically affected by human activities – in the Southern Uplands might be like. Considering the time involved since the ecosystem at Carrifran was in its prime some 6,000 years ago, are a few more decades of light-touch management really something to worry about?

## BRINGING BACK THE BEARBERRY AND OTHER PLANTS

Bearberry *Arctostaphylos uva-ursi* is an attractive procumbent trailing evergreen dwarf-shrub of upland and montane heaths. It thrives on thin, dry, stony and well drained acid soils in sunny situations around 350-750m a.s.l. It grows with Heather, Cowberry and various other dwarf-shrubs, Reindeer lichens and Wavy Hair-grass among others. The flowers are delicate pink cups appearing in May to June and are important nectar sources for bees and moths. The red fruits turn black when ripe and contain four or five hard little seeds. The fruits are edible and in some quarters are considered to have health-giving properties. Bearberry is widespread across Northern Europe, North America and the Scottish Highlands but very scarce in the Southern Uplands now and is found only in a handful places such as at Drumelzier in the Tweedsmuir Hills in Peeblesshire. Given the right environmental conditions it can be fairly confidently assumed that Bearberry was far more widespread in the Southern Uplands before human activity altered the scene. This is especially true of the higher ground in the Moffat and Tweedsmuir Hills – the Wild Heart of Southern Scotland. As part of the on-going ecological restoration project in these hills, it was decided to try and expand the extent of Bearberry heath through the establishment of new populations in suitable areas. In 2017 we were advised by Scottish Natural Heritage to undertake an assessment according to the Scottish Code for Conservation Translocations to ascertain the potential for translocation (or transplanting) of this key upland heath species. This involved the identification of an appropriate source of the plant material to be collected; the resilience of this population to removing shoots or cuttings; the assessment of any potential biosecurity and disease issues; the intended propagation method; the identification of suitable recipient (establishment) sites and the aftercare of the latter and the funding of the project.

In 2018, the first cuttings were collected from one of the best and largest of the remaining populations of Bearberry heath in southern Scotland, located in the Tweedsmuir Hills approximately ten miles as the crow flies from the intended establishment site at Carrifran. The collection site was examined by a plant pathologist from Forest Research to check for any possible diseases. Having confirmed that the population was healthy, cuttings were collected and sent to local nurseries (Alba Trees and Quercus Garden Plants) and grown-on ready for planting out. In 2019 a further two collecting trips were undertaken to provide planting material for future planting.

The first planting took place in October 2019. The Bearberry was translocated or transplanted onto the south facing slopes of Gamesgill Crags at Carrifran at around 600m a.s.l. Suitable sites for the species were identified by using indicator species and ground conditions typical of existing Bearberry heath found elsewhere in the country. Thus, the plugs were planted on thin stony soils, scree and crags with Heather, Cowberry, Blaeberry, Crowberry, Wavy Hair-grass and Reindeer lichens. The translocation of this important dwarf-shrub is somewhat experimental and the success or failure of the project will take time to assess, but every effort has been made to establish the plant in similar conditions to naturally occurring examples. Further transplants will continue as plant material becomes available. Petty Whin is another common plant in naturally occurring Bearberry heath that does not occur at Carrifran and it is planned to translocate this species (and possibly others) into these areas as well at some future date.

**Sarah Eno and Stuart Adair**

The difficulties, of course, are uncertainty about what the 'pristine' ecosystem was really like, and uncertainty about the past and future changes in the physical environment that will constrain attempts to re-create that ecosystem. We have a relaxed attitude to these problems, believing that nature will lead us towards the best solution, if we use our knowledge to clear away obstacles and make suitable native species available.

*Left column: Bearberry at the donor site with Heather; with browsed Blackthorn; with fruit*

*Right column: Planting Bearberry cuttings on Carrifran at 600m; the chosen site; a cutting planted behind a rock; planters relaxing after a good day*

In this time of climate crisis, it is natural to consider whether we should adapt our plan for Carrifran Wildwood by planting some different species that might flourish there under changed conditions in the future. We might also consider sourcing stock of species that we already plant from locations where conditions resemble those predicted for southern Scotland in the future, hoping that the resulting population at Carrifran

## CONNECTING WATERSHEDS

*Searching for rare mosses on Stirk Craig*

By 2013 the establishment of montane scrub at Carrifran was well under way, so when Borders Forest Trust bought Talla & Gameshope, which meets Carrifran at Rotten Bottom, an exciting opportunity presented itself. Rotten Bottom is on the watershed – at 620m – between the Gameshope Burn flowing north and east as part of the Tweed catchment and the Carrifran Burn flowing to the south as part of the River Annan catchment. The ancient bowman could look both ways, towards the North Sea and the Solway Firth. If we established more natural vegetation across the divide, it would provide an ecological link across the spine of Britain.

In 2013, however, that link was in a parlous state. The bog at the watershed was degraded, with steep-walled peat hags between gullies carrying water which was loaded with eroding peat fragments after every rainstorm, and where the bog surface had survived at all it was a pale shadow of the live and active peat bog that had grown in thickness over ten millennia at a rate averaging about a centimetre per 30 years. Furthermore, the drier ground around the watershed was mainly degraded grassland that offered little ecological continuity between the two catchments. Removal of the sheep and goats from both sides of the watershed would provide some relief to the vegetation, but that was only the start.

In the Wildwood Group, we soon began to consider how we could strengthen this ecological link. At the altitude of Rotten Bottom it would not be appropriate to try to establish high forest, but the pollen record derived from the peat core taken there in 1994 suggested that woody vegetation

*Stirk Craig at the top of the Gameshope valley with soil suitable for montane willows*

had existed nearby in the past, and we realised that we should be able to establish montane scrub across the watershed.

However, this would be easier said than done. Volunteers or professionals planting the willows and other montane shrubs would need to climb from 170 m to over 600m, a walk taking about two hours. Access by quad is not feasible up the Carrifran valley, but plants and materials can be delivered by coming over the plateau from the upper Talla valley to the north. In 2018 we decided to establish a base camp on the Carrifran side of the watershed at about 400m, in a site giving relatively quick but steep access both to Rotten Bottom and the top of the Gameshope Burn, and to Firth Hope on Carrifran where most of our previous montane scrub planting had been focused and where we wanted to go on planting.

Funding for the work was also a potential constraint, since there would be costs in obtaining planting stock and in paying staff for weekend work, and perhaps for professional planters to finish the job. However, Borders Forest Trust had been developing close links with the Woodland Trust Scotland, and they generously funded our first large-scale planting at the watershed in spring 2019.

*Volunteers leaving the newly established Base Camp for the first day of planting around the watershed*

*Members of the Green Team planting willows, in the rain, around the foot of Stirk Craig*

Then in summer 2019 SNH suddenly announced a Biodiversity Challenge Fund, and through heroic efforts by Nicola Hunt, BFT was able to access funds to support the planting of 20,000 montane shrubs, spread among the three large sites, of which 8,500 were earmarked for developing the connection between Gameshope valley and Carrifran on suitable ground near Rotten Bottom. This opporunity also presented a challenge, since montane shrubs appropriate for conditions on our sites are not normally stocked in quantity by tree nurseries in Scotland, but we had recently been lucky with seed collections from our planted Downy Willows, and had also arranged to have cuttings from Galloway grown for us by volunteers in the Cree Valley Community Woodlands Trust. Some other montane willows were also available in smaller numbers and there was a chance of some prostrate juniper plants, suitable for the high altitude, from the Forestry Commission in Galloway. A good many years of slow growth will be needed to establish a genuine scrubby connection across the watershed, but we have made a very good start.

**Philip Ashmole**

would be genetically pre-adapted for future change. The Wildwood Group – after careful discussion – decided instead to maintain our original regime, feeling that Carrifran in the future would provide an opportunity to see whether populations with a reasonably diverse genetic base would be able to adapt to changing conditions by evolutionary change, or would gradually alter their distribution at Carrifran, making use of the great topographic variety within the site.

We shall therefore continue planting selected tree and shrub species, sourcing them from the best available localities nearby. For instance, in winter 2019-2020 we have planted hundreds more Hazel in parts of Carrifran where we would expect Hazel woodland to flourish. In the last few years we have been short of Hazel of suitable provenance, but a batch recently obtained from Galloway should add useful genetic diversity to the currently established stands. We are also planting more Sessile Oak in remote patches of bracken that indicate suitable soil, as well as more Honeysuckle and Ivy, both still largely missing from the more distant parts of Carrifran.

At higher elevations there is a need for continued planting of montane scrub species, specially Downy Willow (and other suitable willows) and Juniper. In the latter case we have come to understand that conditions in the more exposed parts of Carrifran are suitable for more genetically prostrate forms than can now be found locally, so we have recently collected seed from the Cairngorms and obtained some high-altitude stock from Galloway.

Some herb-layer plants that would be expected in natural woodland in the Southern Uplands are still missing or very scarce at Carrifran, and we hope to be able to undertake 'translocation' projects to bring in some of these 'ancient woodland specialists' that tend to have low natural dispersal powers. There are bureaucratic constraints on translocation because of Carrifran's designated status, but our ongoing Bearberry translocation project (see Box) has paved the way, as well as the translocation of the Oblong Woodsia fern (lost from Carrifran partly through the activities of Victorian fern collectors) organised by the Royal Botanic Garden Edinburgh several years ago, using stock derived from the only surviving stand in the Southern Uplands. Other species that we feel may merit translocation efforts include Wood Bitter-vetch (currently with only one known station at Carrifran), Petty Whin and Dwarf Cornel (both species not currently occurring at Carrifran), Serrated Wintergreen and Alpine Bistort (both present at Carrifran but very, very scarce). More ambitious translocations, perhaps, would include some of the rare and notable plant species recorded in the Moffat Hills but not at Carrifran. These include Black Alpine Sedge, Alpine Mouse-ear, Alpine Saxifrage, Purple Saxifrage, Hairy Stonecrop and Pyramidal Bugle. Black Alpine Sedge in particular would represent something of a challenge as it only occurs at a handful of stations on soft, crumbly cliffs in Midlaw Linn at the Grey Mare's Tail but is exactly the type of rare species that ecological restoration seeks to restore. The other big issue, of course, is the absence of large mammals at Carrifran: our rewilding is still on too small a scale to accommodate large wild carnivores and herbivores. At present our largest mammalian carnivores are fox and badger, both well established. Lynx are a realistic future possibility since they could range over Carrifran and the wider countryside, but we do not expect wolves or bears in the Southern Uplands in the foreseeable future. Among herbivores, deer are present and will require continued management, as discussed elsewhere in this book. A future beaver population is realistic for Moffatdale but probably

## PIGS ON HOLIDAY

*Tamworth pigs stirring up the ground at Knepp, Sussex*

With the first planted trees at Carrifran reaching their 20th anniversary, and with many species, such as Willow, Birch, Oak, Hazel and Blackthorn now shedding seed, our thoughts turn to the ecological processes needed to make these seeds germinate. Heavier seeds can be transported by birds or small mammals and placed in the ground where they might germinate, and hazelnuts transported by mice are a good example of this. However, the lighter, wind-borne seed can travel a fair distance (especially across frozen snow). These tiny seeds need to make contact with the soil. After 20 years of tree planting with no grazing, we now have a 'binary' vegetation cover on the lower parts of the valley – trees or thick grasses. This means that we need disturbance of the turf to allow birch and willows (and perhaps aspen) to germinate. These are pioneer trees and relatively short lived and in the course of time and with natural seed dispersal processes happening over the decades, these regenerated areas will gradually develop a more diverse range of species.

To kick-start this process, we need the agent of disturbance – the wild swine, or its equivalent, a creature at home in the Wildwood. The plan in 2020/21 is for a dozen or so domestic pigs to visit the valley. A flying herd of pigs. Flying Pigs! Beforehand we will set out a baseline survey to count any regenerating trees on the wide areas of riparian open ground (which was part of the Forestry Commission and SNH approved design), then we will bring in pigs from a farm near Galashiels, where Ben Douglas rears pigs for his roast hog business. It's a great coincidence that Ben is the grandson of Haig Douglas, who owned Carrifran in the 1970's. The pigs will stay for a month or so, being herded by a group of volunteer swine herds and led to the places (using some tasty pig nuts) where we most want woodland regeneration. If it proves that the pigs are doing too much damage to existing trees, we will end the trial. After a few years we can repeat the survey work – by then we should be able to see if the flying pigs have made a difference.

**Hugh Chalmers**

marginal for Carrifran itself with its relatively high gradient. Swine and cattle, however, merit further discussion.

The changes in ground vegetation following removal of domestic stock are documented by Stuart Adair earlier, and it seems clear that the dense sward resulting from the absence of cattle makes it hard for small-seeded shrubs and trees such as birch to regenerate except in the few places where bare ground becomes exposed by the action of water or foraging badgers.

Routing by pigs or wild boar would produce more opportunities for natural regeneration, and wild boar are present nearby, although our perimeter fence might constrain their natural colonisation of the valley. As a short-term measure, the Wildwood Group are considering bringing pigs to Carrifran for short periods to expose some bare soil and so promote regeneration.

There is little doubt that cattle in the form of Aurochs, which are known to have occurred in the Scottish Borders in post-glacial times, would have been present at Carrifran, at least on the lower ground. It is not feasible to have wild cattle at Carrifran, and bringing in domestic cattle on a permanent basis would involve bureaucratic controls and management difficulties that would be a burden to Borders Forest Trust. It would inevitably also reduce the feeling of wildness in the valley, which the Wildwood Group are determined to maintain as far as possible. A possible compromise, as in the case of swine, is to arrange short periods of grazing by cattle in summer, as BFT envisions as a future possibility at Corehead & Devil's Beef Tub.

*Carrifran valley from Bodesbeck Law - May 2017*

# PART III

# REVIVING THE WILD HEART OF SOUTHERN SCOTLAND

₱ 121 — 4·10·18

*John Wright*

# THE MOFFAT AND TWEEDSMUIR HILLS

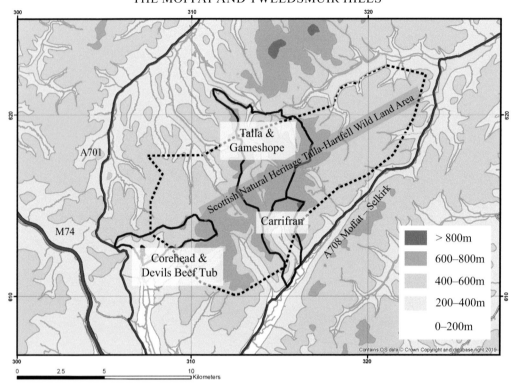

# SOUTHERN SCOTLAND

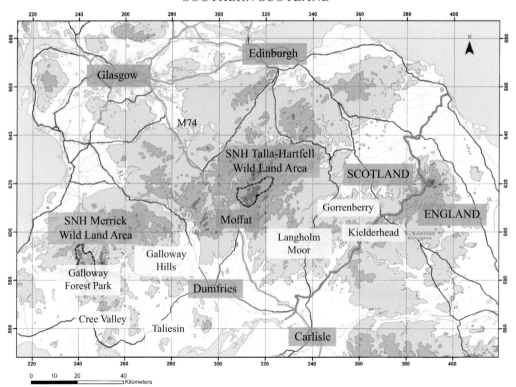

# BORDERS FOREST TRUST
# AND THE WILD HEART

*Jane Rosegrant*

In the first two parts of this book the various authors have described the genesis of Carrifran Wildwood and have documented a few of the exciting – and in some cases unpredicted – ecological changes that have already resulted from this project. In this third part we describe BFT's vision of the ecological changes that we hope to bring about on the land we now own; we also include contributions relating to other restoration projects elsewhere in southern Scotland.

While Carrifran has been an important source of inspiration to many, BFT's work in the Southern Uplands has grown well beyond the Wildwood's borders.

As restoration work at Carrifran progressed and flourished, opportunities arose for BFT to acquire two other significant sites in the Southern Uplands. First, in 2009 BFT purchased Corehead & Devil's Beef Tub. This property, of a similar size to Carrifran but with different geologic and topographic features, is located north of Moffat and removed from Carrifran by only 3km as the raven flies. Then in 2013 Talla & Gameshope (T&G) a large and imposing site on Carrifran's northern border, was secured by BFT. Purchasing this site more than doubled BFT's land holdings, increasing our ability to recreate self-sustaining natural ecologies and allowing the charity, for the first time, to begin thinking on a truly landscape scale.

To work effectively on this scale meant that BFT stopped thinking of these ecological restoration sites as separate projects, instead treating them as a joined up programme of work – Reviving the Wild Heart of Southern Scotland. Thinking about the Wild Heart also helped the Trust to move beyond a singular focus on woodland restoration. Although restoring native woodlands in appropriate locations within the project area is a cornerstone of this work, woodlands are not in themselves sufficient for these sites to return to a truly natural condition. Therefore this project will enable the return of thriving and varied habitats including native broadleaved woodlands, heathlands, moorlands, wetlands, deep peat and montane scrub.

Each of these habitats belongs in the areas where we work and each contributes to the return of 'wild' to Southern Scotland. Wildness, in a healthy condition, is now so rare that most people do not even recognize its absence. We are accustomed to describing as 'wild' the beautiful but barren uplands of Scotland. However, true wildness is abundant, not empty. 'Wild' should describe spaces that are ecologically vibrant and self-sustaining, with a profusion of native species present in numbers appropriate to the habitat.

While each of the BFT sites is at a different stage of ecological restoration, has unique characteristics and retains distinct work plans (such as continuing to farm at Corehead),

*Carrifran valley in October 2019*

together they enable the Trust to move forward with the landscape scale vision of work. The differing geology, soils and conditions across the sites means that there will be variation in the habitats that will thrive, however, a joined up approach can still provide the strongest outcomes for all three.

In developing our thinking for the Wild Heart the Trust agreed on several key ecological principles:

- The development of the Wild Heart should be 'nature led' as much as possible;
- The sites will not be managed for the benefit of any one species;
- We are not necessarily aiming for the maximum number of species possible.

Much of this is based on our understanding that, due to 'shifting baseline syndrome', we no longer have a clear concept of what our uplands could look and feel like. This was nicely summed up by a visitor to the Wildwood who wrote in *The Guardian* "There is a real sense here of what the glens, cwms and valleys of the British Isles would be like if they were let off the leash…I am grateful to everyone involved for this glimpse of a world I have missed for most of my life without knowing it." (*Across the Invisible Threshhold*, 7/9/15).

By nature led we mean that, rather than putting in place a set idea of what belongs there – possibly including habitats that do not fit the local conditions, which in turn might mean intervening in perpetuity in order to maintain an artificial system – we aspire to establish viable sources of seed of the species that research suggests were originally there, then stepping back to allow nature to take its course. As conditions change locally – possibly through climate change – the habitats will also change and we will not work against that process.

However, we still need to be active in managing the sites for years, probably decades. This is partly because overgrazing, for instance by deer, can occur as there is no longer any

*The Borders Forest Trust Field Group at 700m on Gameshope, June 2018.*
*A 'green desert' offering a clean slate for ecological restoration*

## GETTING GOOD ADVICE

During the early stages of Carrifran Wildwood, there was a very active but informal Ecological Planning Group, an offshoot of the Wildwood Group. It met in a Peebles pub or at Carrifran, and sometimes over 20 people turned up, some with other roles in BFT or academia and others from organisations such the John Muir Trust, the Southern Uplands Partnership and the Royal Botanic Garden Edinburgh (RBGE). It was chaired by Adrian Newton, then an Ecology lecturer at Edinburgh University and now at Bournemouth University. Over a period of 18 months this group drew up a very professional Environmental Statement without which the project could not have proceeded. Once these documents were complete, the Ecological Planning Group, then chaired by Crinan Alexander, turned its attention to assessing the progress of the young trees, and to recording the changing flora and fauna through field meetings at Carrifran. The accuracy of these records was greatly enhanced by the expertise of Roy Watling (fungi), David Long (mosses and liverworts), Brian Coppins (lichens) and Douglas McKean (higher plants), at that time all staff members of RBGE. More detailed surveys by John Savory (birds) and Stuart Adair (vegetation) have resulted in influential publications on changes in the bird populations and vegetation of Carrifran. This group has now evolved into an informal Field Group, meeting annually at one of the three major BFT sites, and reporting to the BFT Ecological Committee. The latter, chaired by John Thomas, meets about twice a year and provides expert advice to BFT Trustees and the Site Operations Team.

**Crinan Alexander**

natural check on deer numbers in Scotland. New woodland cannot establish successfully in these conditions. Our work is also not purely nature led in that we have decided to 'kick start' the return of native woodlands, and the repair of peatlands, rather than waiting many years for seed sources to arrive at the sites naturally. Furthermore, some of the missing native habitats, such as montane scrub, have been removed and absent from the area for so long that there is no remaining seed source in the region to replenish those populations. After much discussion, rather than taking a passive wait-and-see-what-arrives approach, the Trust agreed to bring back and establish seed sources in the Wild Heart that are as near as possible to what was there when it was last a self-sustaining ecosystem.

By not managing it for the benefit of any one species, the Trust is addressing two potentially difficult decisions in ecological restoration. The first is that we acknowledge there will be some species currently present in the area that will decline with this approach. The ecologically unnatural state of these sites when we first acquired them means that some species are clinging on because of – or despite – the management regime required to rear sheep on these hills. If bringing back healthy natural habitats means that the balance for some of the extant species shifts, that is a trade off we are willing to make. Secondly, we are not focused on creating a habitat suitable for the return or reintroduction of any one missing native species. Although there are important reintroduction projects taking place across Scotland, the Trust does not manage its ecological restoration work with specific reintroductions in mind. Instead, with nature leading and on a landscape scale, we will re-create healthy native habitats that can ultimately benefit all of Scotland's native upland residents.

Additionally, while BFT acknowledges that on-going land management and input by humans can sometimes result in increased biodiversity,

## TALLA-HARTFELL ECONOMIC PROJECT

The Southern Uplands Partnership and Borders Forest Trust are undertaking a study of the current economy and future opportunities in the valleys around the Scottish Natural Heritage 'Talla-Hart Fell Wild Land Area' in the Moffat and Tweedsmuir Hills, which covers about 10,000 hectares stretching from the Megget dam to the Crown of Scotland, the source of the Tweed (see map p.106). This landscape has the potential to teem with abundant, thriving wildlife, to sustain the local community with livelihoods connected to improving natural processes, and inspiring visitors to enjoy a world-class destination for nature. The project aims to create a community-led partnership to combat the risk of rural decline, celebrating the natural assets of the area, restoring natural ecosystems and wildlife and addressing climate change through tree planting. It seeks to develop a nature-based economy moving from single species management to multiple land use with productive woodland, farming and natural habitats.

The first step has been to establish a baseline of the existing economy of the area, which largely depends on hill sheep and commercial forestry, generating an annual turnover of around £10m including subsidies. Secondly a small team has been looking at the potential of alternative economic scenarios focused on the natural and cultural heritage of the area in the event of changes to the current grants and subsidies regime. This stage, when completed in early 2020, will be followed by consultations on the findings with all the different interests in the study area in order to develop an achievable and sustainable long-term strategy for the Wild Land Area and the local economy associated with it.

**John Thomas**

we do not aim to achieve simply the maximum number of species possible on our land. The Trust's goal is not the greatest biodiversity that can be maintained on a given area, but the level of biodiversity that best fits that area in a natural state.

Other crucial aspects to BFT's work in and around the Wild Heart include educational work with schools and the public and partnerships with other landowners. This work ranges

*The surviving ancient birch by the Gameshope bothy now has some growing company*

from speaking at group events to hosting school visits at our sites to providing practical advice encouraging and enabling restoration projects on other properties. Through these activities we broaden and deepen the impact of our approach to ecological restoration.

Hand in hand with environmental goals for the Wild Heart, the Trust holds an aspiration for the area to benefit people, whether that be local communities or visitors. Wildness does not, in and of itself, require an absence of human presence. For millenia humans thrived both within and on the edges of wild areas. BFT believes that engaging communities, and particularly young people, in the restoration of these spaces will benefit individuals, communities and the habitats we seek to restore. Only through personally experiencing the vibrancy of such sites, and contributing to their welfare, will people understand that this heritage is an essential part of our countryside. Currently, many people are engaged in our work in the Wild Heart, including: numerous volunteers carrying out vital work in the field, school groups participating in educational activities, youth groups contributing to the sites in practical ways, colleges and universities carrying out helpful research and a volunteer advisory group ensuring a consistent ecological rationale is employed across the project.

Furthermore, this project aims to demonstrate that meaningful economic activity and thoughtful land use can thrive in harmony with wild areas. It is BFT's hope that local communities will develop ways of benefiting economically from the return of biodiversity to these landscapes, enhancing communities and embedding restored habitats as productive and appreciated aspects of life in Southern Scotland. For example, communities that neighbour the Wild Heart may reap economic rewards in terms of ecotourism opportunities. Schools and colleges will visit and contribute to the care of these areas in ways that teach new skills and offer new experiences and connections to their own local world. If Southern Scotland can harness the economic opportunities that other countries have seen from nature-based economies, ecologically restored landscapes can become a new pillar of rural economies, diversifying opportunities for young people to stay and thrive in rural areas.

Over time, and with continued commitment from the many volunteers and supporters of the Wild Heart, we can recreate a healthy wild area that has not existed in Southern Scotland for centuries. Equally exciting will be if this can be well-integrated with human needs so that the presence of wild land can also contribute to sustainable human communities.

*Strata of the Ordovician-Silurian boundary at Dobs Linn, Grey Mare's Tail (NTS).*
*Inset; unusual exposure of fossil beach in greywacke on Firthhope Rig*

*Grey Mare's Tail, White Coomb and Loch Skeen, contiguous with Carrifran and*
*Talla & Gameshope in the Moffat Hills SSSI and Special Area of Conservation*

# THE NATURE OF THE WILD HEART

*Stuart Adair*

The 'Wild Heart of Southern Scotland' consists of the large upland massif centred on the Moffat and Tweedsmuir Hills which dominate the central Southern Uplands. Together, these hills form the largest area of montane plateau in the south of Scotland. This glacial landscape is formed from the sedimentary rocks comprising greywacke (mud-rich sandstone, shales, mudstones and siltstones) which were laid down during the Ordovician and Silurian periods. Dob's Linn in the Moffat Hills, made famous by the geologist Charles

## REBUILDING THE EAGLE POPULATION IN THE SOUTH OF SCOTLAND

The South of Scotland Golden Eagle Project, launched in 2017, aims to reinforce the small, isolated and vulnerable population of golden eagles in the South of Scotland. https://www.goldeneaglessouthofscotland.co.uk

Golden eagles have a long history in Southern Scotland, from east to west, populations were once healthy with the golden eagle playing an important part as an apex predator in the ecosystem. Over the last couple of centuries, human activity and changes in land use have caused the population in the south to fall as low as three breeding pairs.

Through a series of translocations over a period of five years and greater cooperation between stakeholders, the South of Scotland Golden Eagle Project aims to increase numbers and prevent the loss of this wonderful species from southern skies.

From their release base in the Moffat Hills the translocated eagles have begun to explore and interact with resident breeding pairs and locally fledged young. It is hoped that in time the eagles will rediscover long forgotten eyries and become a more familiar sight in the hills and valleys of southern Scotland.

The project is an opportunity to inspire local people and rebuild a sense of pride and guardianship in a southern population of golden eagles.

**Cat Barlow**

*Manorhead, a denuded valley northwest of St Mary's Loch, with a tiny patch of Juniper scrub surviving on the steep slope (where we twice collected cuttings) towards bottom left*

Lapworth in 1878, contains the best example of the Ordovician-Silurian boundary in the Southern Uplands.

The craggy, ripped and steep-sided U or V-shaped valleys (e.g. Carrifran, Black Hope and Talla), the high corries and hanging valleys (e.g. Loch Skeen-Grey Mare's Tail, Firthhope Linn, Devil's Beef Tub, Cramalt) and small ravines (e.g. Holly Gill, Dob's Linn) that dominate the area were carved out by the retreating ice-sheet around 12,000 years ago. The most visible evidence of the activity of the ice is the hummocky moraine (small hillocks formed of glacial debris) deposited by the retreating ice along the valley floors, especially around Loch Skeen and in Talla and Gameshope valleys. Glaciofluvial deposits of sands and gravels, formed by melting ice-water, mark out former meltwater channels between these little hillocks. Hummocky moraine is a relatively rare feature in the region and reminiscent of the western Highlands.

Exposed bedrock is evident throughout the area, especially at Raven Craig, Talla Craigs, Rough Craigs, Coomb Craigs and on valley floors and in watercourses marked by glacial striations left by rocks scraped over the bedrock by the movement of the ice. Deposits of colluvium (talus, scree) formed by rock-shatter, frost-heave and solifluction (downhill movement) are frequent in places such as lower Gameshope and on some of the higher summits. Some of the more gently sloping and level ground is capped by a thin layer of drift deposits (boulder clay, till, large boulders, sand, gravel and clay). The summits and higher ground are rounded and often near-level and form the remains of the original vast plateau, a kind of tableland, which dominated the scene before the glaciations of the Pleistocene. The altitudinal range of the area is wide, ranging from *c.* 120-840m a.s.l. and it contains some of the highest hills in the south of Scotland (e.g. Broad Law; Cramalt Craig; White Coomb; Hart Fell).

The soils of the area vary from surprisingly good, worm-rich and fertile brown earths on steeper, freely-draining slopes through poorer iron and peaty podzols on gentler slopes around the shoulders of the higher ground, gleyed (water-logged) silty alluvial soils along the haughs (floodplains) and peats of varying depth wherever drainage is impeded on level ground and the saddles between summits (e.g. Rotten Bottom, Brad Moss) to thin, weathered and stony skeletal soils on the summits.

The River Annan-Tweed watershed divides these hills along a north-south axis, and the River Clyde also rises within a mere stone's throw of the sources of the Annan and Tweed. The waters to the north and east of the massif drain into the North Sea via the Tweed Valley; the waters to the south and west drain into the Irish Sea via the River Annan and the Solway Firth. Feeding these river systems are waters from the highest natural lochs in the south of Scotland: Gameshope Loch (c.560m), which drains into the Tweed, and Loch Skeen (c.510m) which drains into the River Annan.

The climate of the area is also, to some extent, divided along the watershed. The Tweedsmuir Hills have the coolest climate, with the heaviest and longest snow-fall/lie, highest number of days of frost and coldest, driest and harshest north-easterlies south of the Highlands and are somewhat Continental in character. The climate of the Moffat Hills, in contrast, is milder, warmed as it is by the prevailing south-westerlies, with less snow-fall/lie and fewer days of frost, and is more oceanic or Atlantic in character. Rainfall is high across the entire massif with an annual average of c.2250mm on the higher ground, which is comparable with parts of the Highlands. The hottest month is July and the coldest is January.

The plant life of the hills consists of the open, short-cropped grassy and heathy vegetation so typical of the long-term pasturing of sheep, cattle and feral goats. Taller vegetation in general and trees in particular are very scarce indeed and confined to a handful of inaccessible cliffs and ledges. The white tails of cotton-grass and brightly coloured bog-mosses mark-out stretches of blanket bog formed over deep peats. Cushion mosses and small herbs mark-out the myriad springs and flushes that pepper the landscape.

Golden eagles can be glimpsed rarely, soaring high above the hills. Buzzard, peregrine and osprey are more common sightings, with owls mainly in wooded areas. Red grouse are managed for shooting on a few estates and occur in small numbers elsewhere, while black grouse are seen or heard in only a few places. A few pairs of ring ouzel breed in the area, and dotterel are noted on passage and breed on rare occasions, while other upland waders are now rare. The raven is widespread and carrion crow abundant, but woodland birds are scarce, although chaffinches are widespread and wood pigeon, mistle thrush and sometimes crossbills are present in conifer plantations.

Roe deer are common wherever there is woodland cover and Sika deer are well established in some of the post-war exotic conifer plantations that dot the area. Red fox and badger are common, and both these predators patrol even the highest hills; pine marten are present locally and probably spreading. On the Tweedsmuir side of the hills there is a healthy population of mountain hare, while brown hare are widespread at lower levels. Smaller mammals are well represented, with field voles sometimes extremely abundant.

The fish fauna of running water and the deeper lochs is dominated by Salmon and Brown/Sea Trout, but the numbers of these migratory fish are now very low. Three-spined Stickleback, Lamprey and Common Eel lurk in silty, deep, sluggish pools and in Gameshope

*Regenerating woodland at Craigdilly beside Megget reservoir, where a tiny fragment
of surviving woodland at about 370m was fenced but not planted in about 1973,
and where a Rowan-dominated wood has slowly spread uphill to about 550m*

Loch. Vendace, the rarest freshwater fish in the UK, was re-introduced to Loch Skeen in the
1990s. Arctic Char was introduced to Talla and Megget Reservoirs in the 1980s.

The Wild Heart of Southern Scotland has not always been like this. Using data from
the pollen record and from historical sources, as well as the evidence gleaned from the tiny
fragments of more natural plant communities that survive in some cleuchs and on cliffs out
of the reach of feral goats, we can gain an idea of the nature of the ecosystem in its more
natural state. Richard Tipping, the palynologist who has analysed the peat core from Rotten
Bottom, has suggested that Scottish woodlands would have been in their richest and most
extensive state about 6000 years ago. Direct evidence on the fauna is scarce, but reasonable
guesses can be made.

After the end of the last glaciation around 10,000 years ago in northern Britain, the very
gradual process began of colonisation by pioneer shrub and tree species that could disperse
rapidly and exploit the skeletal soils left behind by the ice sheets. They were accompanied by a
suite of associated plants and animals, some of which, such as beetles, left behind evidence of
their presence in the form of fossils. By 6000 years ago the major players in this slow-running
drama had entered the stage, and it is clear that a mature and biodiverse ecosystem was in
place in the Southern Uplands. This date coincides with the age of the ancient longbow from
Rotten Bottom, so that it was natural for the Wildwood Group, back in the 1990s, to decide
that it would be appropriate to try to recreate at Carrifran an ecosystem analogous to that

which existed at that time, around the end of the Mesolithic period (Middle Stone Age). Human presence during the Mesolithic consisted of only scattered hunter-gatherers who had altered their environment very little, so that 6000 years ago Carrifran would have looked very different from how it did at the turn of the 21st century.

Bear, wolf, lynx and wildcat would have prowled around the ancient gnarly Oaks and through the trembling Aspens and the tangled, twisted and contorted Holly, Hazel and Honeysuckle-rich undergrowth while both Roe and Red Deer used the latter to conceal themselves while browsing on the abundant and rich foliage beneath the canopy of wildwood. During the warmer summer months, the deer would have ventured out of the cover of the trees and mountain shrubs and up onto the open summits to graze on the heaths, alpine flowers and reindeer mosses and to join the elk and wild boar wallowing in the

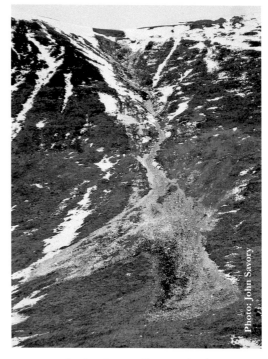

*Avalanches are frequent in the Southern Uplands in snowy winters: this was on Carrifran Gans in January 2010*

deep peats of Rotten Bottom. It was in this situation, perhaps, that the ancient hunter broke his longbow while trying to pick off an elk or boar or grouse, and the eagles and foxes joined the ravens looking on and waiting for the rich pickings left behind. Wetlands along the river valleys would have been maintained by beavers, and there would have been major spawning runs of Salmon and Sea Trout.

So, what did the woodland in this virgin landscape consist of? Hazel seems to have been dominant species on the better, freely draining soils, along with Oak, Birch, Holly and, to a lesser extent, Elm. Where soil conditions were suitable, the latter would have been joined by Ash. Rowan, Aspen, Hawthorn, Blackthorn and Wild Cherry were consistent throughout, especially on the better soils with Ash and Elm. Alder, Birch, Bird Cherry and Willow were abundant on damper soils and the narrow alluvial haughs. Although Pine forest had largely been ousted from the area by 7000 BP, it is likely that some individual Scots Pines survived in cooler, northeast facing locations. The woodland was probably quite open and scrubby for the most part, only occasionally thickening-up into closed canopy high forest along the valley floor over more productive soils. Moving upslope, the growth would have become more open, scrubby and low growing with Juniper and various species of stunted Willow and Dwarf Birch sharing the ground with dwarf-shrubs such as Heather, Blaeberry, Crowberry and Cowberry and eventually giving way to tree-less, wind-clipped summit heaths with Dwarf Willow, Woolly Fringe-moss and Lichens.

*Loch Skeen and Mid Craig, with Donald's Cleuch Head behind*

*Morainic deposits below Raven Craig, Carrifran*

# NEW DISCOVERIES OF BRYOPHYTES (MOSSES AND THEIR RELATIVES) IN THE MOFFAT AND TWEEDSMUIR HILLS

*David G. Long & Elizabeth M. Kungu*

Bryophytes are the most ancient land plants on earth and are thought to have arisen before or during the Ordovician Period over 440 million years ago, long before the flowering plants and the dinosaurs of the Triassic to Cretaceous Periods. Thus, as a group, they have survived numerous epochs of climate change in the past, and their tenacity may be due partly to their small size, their ability to evolve to occupy diverse ecological niches and their highly sophisticated chemical defences against pathogens. Worldwide, bryophytes comprise about 5,000 species of liverworts, 13,000 mosses and 150 hornworts. The three groups differ in their reproductive structures, but all share 'alternation of generations' with a green photosynthetic gametophyte stage (leafy or thallose plant) and simple sporophyte (capsule) which produces tiny spores for dispersal.

Bryophytes, though individually often inconspicuous, are collectively very important in providing ecosystem services. They have a remarkably high water retention capacity (up to 15,000 % of their dry weight), crucially important in mossy forests and peatlands where the water that they hold maintains moisture levels through dry periods and reduces runoff and flooding. Physically, woodland, peatland and aquatic species provide shelter for invertebrates and other small organisms, in turn food for birds, fish, etc. Many species are ecological colonists and pioneers, leading to rapid stabilisation of rock surfaces, soil and peat, reducing erosion and soil loss. Perhaps their biggest service is in locking up carbon, especially in bogs and peatlands (peat is largely the decaying remains of the peat-moss *Sphagnum*), which globally locks up 320 billion tonnes of carbon, about 44% of the amount held in the atmosphere as carbon dioxide.

In Scotland there are about 950 species of bryophytes, significant on a global scale. Over one third of this total (339 taxa) have so far

*Talla Moss, an important peatland habitat*

Photo: David Long

Photo: David Long

*Bryophyte-rich flushes in Donald's Cleuch,
Talla & Gameshope*

been recorded in the three large sites in the Moffat and Tweedsmuir Hills owned by Borders Forest Trust, mostly during a series of surveys over the past two decades. With a total area of over 3,100 hectares, an altitudinal range of 175 to 821m, and a total annual rainfall (in nearby Ettrick Valley) of over 1,500mm, the scene is set for a rich bryophyte flora. Geology is an important factor and though the bedrock is uniformly of Silurian Greywacke (typically quite acidic in nature), in many places there is evidence of more localised calcareous outcrops and lime-rich spring water welling up to give rise to base-rich flushes. The area has a good diversity of habitats, including crags, screes and other rock outcrops, streams, flushes, blanket bog, dwarf shrub heaths and very large areas of rough mostly acidic grassland.

For bryophytes, the most significant missing component is any extensive area of ancient or native woodland, an omission which is at the heart of BFT's plans for ecological restoration. The most extensive (but still small) area of older native woodland is at Corehead & Devil's Beef Tub, whilst at Carrifran and Talla & Gameshope are found only fragmentary relict stands of older native trees along the streams including Birch, Rowan, Ash, Hazel, Aspen, Holly and others. This deficit is thought to be largely the result of long-term grazing pressure, as is the degraded nature of much of the grassland, blanket bog and montane heaths. Thus the present bryophyte richness is highly localised and fragmentary, mostly concentrated in refugia which have survived against the odds. This is expected to change in future, particularly in the new woodland, which at Carrifran in under two decades is already showing signs of new colonisation by incoming epiphytes and woodland floor species.

Symers Macvicar, a GP who was born in Moffat in 1857, later became one of the greatest British bryologists and author of the *Student's Handbook of British Hepatics*. In July 1907 he visited Talla Linns (just outside the BFT Talla & Gameshope site) and first discovered that some of the oceanic liverworts common in his adopted home in the West Highlands of Scotland, could also be found in the Southern Uplands. As this area is closer to the Solway than the North Sea, this is perhaps not surprising, but only very recently have some of his discoveries been added to our checklist. Some of these have been found in the gullies on Garelet Hill overlooking Talla Reservoir, in the wonderful ravine of March Sike in Gameshope and on the cliff ledges and rocky gullies of Raven Craig and Firthhope in Carrifran. In some of these places oceanic liverworts grow along with the diminutive oceanic Wilson's Filmy Fern, *Hymenophyllum wilsonii*.

Of the oceanic liverworts, most welcome is the recent discovery that Orkney Notchwort *Anastrepta orcadensis* is found in Priest Gill, Talla Craigs, Garelet Hill, and quite abundantly in March Sike. Other oceanic liverworts are Lesser Whipwort *Bazzania tricrenata*, Waxy Earwort *Douinia ovata*, Western Frostwort *Gymnomitrion crenulatum,* Pointed Pouncewort *Harpalejeunea molleri*, Pearl Pouncewort *Lejeunea patens,* Pearson's Fingerwort *Lepidozia pearsonii*, Hooded Veilwort *Metzgeria leptoneura*, Taylor's Flapwort *Mylia taylorii*, Prickly Featherwort *Plagiochila spinulosa* and Western Earwort *Scapania gracilis*. Most of these have been found in Talla & Gameshope and Carrifran, though fewer in Corehead. Less well-known perhaps are the oceanic mosses, of which Bristly Swan-Neck Moss *Campylopus atrovirens* is quite a common shiny black moss on wet rock ledges, while the much more local species Irish Crisp-moss *Oxystegus hibernicus* (Carrifran) and the related *O. daldinanus* (Corehead) have been recorded only in small patches, and the very rare Welsh Pocket-moss *Fissidens celticus,* also at Corehead.

Montane bryophytes, so characteristic of the Scottish Highlands, are rare in the Southern Uplands. In the BFT sites they are concentrated in two habitats - in montane flushes and on crags and screes. Good flush communities are quite widespread, but those in the headwaters of Donald's Cleuch in Gameshope are particularly rich and include two Nationally Scarce (NS) mosses, the beautiful bright pink Duval's Thread-moss *Bryum weigelii* and green Rugged Collar-moss *Splachnum vasculosum*. The former also grows on the higher slopes at Carrifran. Elsewhere, a very special NS flush species is River Thyme-moss *Pseudobryum cinclidioides* growing beside Gameshope Loch at 565 metres. On the high-altitude crags, such as Raven Craig and Talla Craigs, are found several local montane mosses, Lapland Yoke-moss *Amphidium lapponicum*, River Thread-moss *Bryum riparium* (NS), Alpine Ditrichum *Ditrichum zonatum,* Black Grimmia *Grimmia incurva*, Long-fruited Thread-moss *Pohlia elongata*, Slender Fringe-moss *Racomitrium sudeticum* and the diminutive liverwort White Frostwort *Gymnomitrion obtusum*. On loose stones in high-level screes are Spruce's Rustwort *Marsupella sprucei*, Bristle-leaf *Brachydontium trichodes* (NS) and Blytt's Fork-moss *Kiaeria blyttii*. A few of the crags have some outcrops rich in lime, where a number of calcicolous montane bryophytes grow, notable being Lesser Rough Earwort *Scapania aequiloba* (NS), String Grimmia *Grimmia funalis*, Twisted Grimmia *Grimmia torquata*, Upright Brown Grimmia *Schistidium strictum* and Oeder's Apple-moss *Plagiopus oederianus.*

On the fine, but partially degraded, blanket bogs such as Talla Moss, Crunklie Moss, Rotten Bottom and at the head of Firthhope, *Sphagnum* mosses predominate and no fewer than 20 out of the 35 British species have been recorded, some only in small quantity. The two most interesting are Slender Cow-horn Bog-moss *Sphagnum subsecundum* in Crunklie Moss, and Flat-leaved Bog-moss *Sphagnum platyphyllum* in Carrifran and under Stirk Craig. The on-going peatland restoration work should improve the quality of these habitats for bryophytes, particularly by retaining water through blocking up ditches and eroded gullies. A sign of former degradation is the local abundance on disturbed peat of the invasive southern hemisphere Heath Star Moss *Campylopus introflexus*.

As explained above, native woodland is planned to expand greatly in coming years, and few special woodland species are yet recorded. Noteworthy is the fact that at Corehead more epiphytes have been noted than in the other two sites, due to the greater number of

SOME NOTABLE MOSSES
OF THE WILD HEART:
*Photos: David Long*

*Ostrich-plume Feather-moss*
Ptilium crista-castrensis

*Rugged Collar-moss*
Splachnum vasculosum
*in Donald's Cleuch*

*Wilson's Filmy-fern*
Hymenophyllum wilsonii
*a tiny oceanic fern*

*Long-fruited Thread-moss*
Pohlia elongata
*in Gameshope*

*Pendulous Wing-moss*
Antitrichia curtipendula
*a local and declining*
*species on Raven Craig;*

*Orkney Notchwort*
Anastrepta orcadensis
*an oceanic liverwort*

**SOME NOTABLE MOSSES OF THE WILD HEART:**
*(continued)*

*Duval's Thread-moss*
Bryum weigelii
*in Donald's Cleuch*

*White Frostwort*
Gymnomitrion obtusum
*on Talla Craigs*

*Marble Screw-moss*
Syntrichia papillosa
*on old tree at Corehead*

*Slender Cruet-moss*
Tetraplodon mnioides
*growing on old bird pellet in Carrifran*

*Upright Brown Grimmia*
Schistidium strictum
*a montane calcicole moss*

older trees, including five epiphytic Bristle-mosses *Orthotrichum* species, Small Hairy Screw-moss *Syntrichia laevipila* and Marble Screw-moss *S. papillosa*. In vascular plants, a number of 'ancient woodland indicator' species have managed to cling on throughout these hills in the herb layer far from any trees, such as Wood Anemone *Anemone nemorosa*, but in the bryophytes only one ancient woodland indicator moss, the elegant Ostrich-plume Feather-moss *Ptilium crista-castrensis* has been seen, in Carrifran at Rispie Lairs at 590 m and below Raven Craig at 500 m altitude. This species is typical of native Pine forests in the Scottish Highlands – which poses the intriguing thought that Scots Pine could again flourish here as it did several millennia ago.

Colonisation of new habitats by bryophytes can be slow, particularly if there are no nearby sources of propagules to facilitate spread. However, the new plantings of trees make Carrifran a good place to monitor arrival of new epiphytes by spore dispersal – any epiphytes on trees and branches must have come in within the past two decades. The young trees on the main valley floor still have almost no specialist epiphytes, whereas in the extreme south-east of Carrifran, close to the adjacent mature conifer plantations (where humidity is high) a number of incoming epiphytes are now spreading, notably Forked Veilwort *Metzgeria furcata*, Even Scalewort *Radula complanata*, Wood Bristle-moss *Orthotrichum affine*, Elegant Bristle-moss *Orthotrichum pulchellum*, Bruch's Pincushion *Ulota bruchii* and Frizzled Pincushion *Ulota phyllantha*. Over the coming years as the trees mature, these and other species are likely to progress up the valley.

One neglected group of bryophytes which need more study are the rheophytes - species which cling to boulders in the streams, of which only a few are frequent: Claw Brook-moss *Hygrohypnum ochraceum*, River Grimmia *Schistidium rivulare* and notably Alpine Water-moss *Fontinalis squamosa* which as its common name suggests, is a characteristically montane species.

Apart from the epiphytes mentioned above, the three sites are remarkably similar in their bryophyte flora, and the differences recorded (Carrifran 185 mosses, 66 liverworts, Corehead 200 mosses, 62 liverworts and Talla & Gameshope 187 mosses, 66 liverworts) suggest that differences reflect less the total land areas but more likely the differing levels of recording activity between the sites and perhaps a greater variety of habitats at Corehead. Further field work in all sites will undoubtedly push these totals higher.

As described above, the history of past land management has probably contributed to the rarity of some bryophyte species, and the total absence of others which might have been expected. In terms of bryophyte conservation, most of the actions needed to halt and reverse this trend have already been instigated by Borders Forest Trust, such as reduction of grazing pressure, increasing broadleaf tree cover, restoration of montane dwarf shrub heaths and peatland restoration. Some of the oceanic species which are only just hanging on, as in March Sike, should flourish better with some tree and shrub protection, which will increase humidity. It is possible that some of the flush species will face competition from taller vegetation under reduced grazing pressure, but in Carrifran the flush communities are on thin rocky substrates and seem to be holding up well. As much of the restoration work in the BFT parts of the Wild Heart is of an experimental nature, time will tell which species benefit from the new regime, and which may show a decline. The early signs at Carrifran are that the gains will greatly outnumber the losses in all fields of biodiversity, and bryophytes should be no different in this respect. However, for the future it is important that recording and monitoring of bryophytes, particularly the changes associated with increasing woody vegetation, should be continued indefinitely in years to come.

Photo: P. and A. Macdonald/Aerographica

*Devil's Beef Tub, Corehead farm and the hills towards Hart Fell*

# COREHEAD & DEVIL'S BEEF TUB: NATIVE WOODLANDS, FARMING AND COMMUNITY INVOLVEMENT

*John Thomas and Hugh Chalmers*

The 640ha hill farm of Corehead, situated just five miles north of Moffat, was purchased in 2009 for the sum of £700,000 after a vigorous fundraising campaign. Borders Forest Trust sees this as a great opportunity to show how farming and woodland restoration can come together, and the current vision for Corehead is that it 'will become an important resource in the south of Scotland demonstrating how biodiversity, ecosystem services and farming can thrive together.'

*Members of Reforesting Scotland learning about management of Corehead from Borders Forest Trust staff, with the Devil's Beef Tub in the background*

## COREHEAD AND THE LOCAL COMMUNITY

Community engagement got off on a good footing at Corehead and Devil's Beef Tub. Local individuals and Moffat Academy assisted with fundraising for the land purchase by selling trees to local families for planting on site. We could not have asked for a better start. Within the first year a Site Officer was employed and Borders Forest Trust established a firm presence in the local community. The early days of educational work involved pupils assisting with practical site maintenance and management tasks such as drystone walling and meadow management. This provided great benefits on site, whilst also providing the young people with a Rural Skills National Vocational Qualification (NVQ). BFT's education officer hosted one-off curricular linked field trips, including school Biology department visits to investigate a variety of habitats; small groups of young people took part in Forest School themed activities to build their interpersonal, team and problem solving skills. Interest and opportunities continued to grow.

As demand for activities and projects continued to increase, Borders Forest Trust successfully secured funding to employ a Community and Education Officer based in Moffat. This was when things went from strength to strength. With more capacity and more presence, more community focused initiatives were possible. A fortnightly community volunteer project was established, community events were organised and the number, frequency and themes of school visits increased.

Over the last few years a particularly successful John Muir Award focused project has become an annual school partnership project. Staff fondly call it 'The 44', with an average of forty four children in Primary 7 from Moffat and other primary schools coming to visit. Exploring the Corehead site they develop new skills and make new friends and bonds in preparation for moving on to High School together. Over a few weeks, the children take part in a variety of activities following the John Muir Award themes of 'Discover' (treks around site); 'Explore' (wildlife investigations, team challenges); 'Conserve' (e.g. bracken bashing) and 'Share' – the children keep journals, create photo displays and presentations to showcase at a Certificate Ceremony to which parents, school staff and local VIPs are invited. The evident benefits achieved in the delivery of this project provided positive recognition for Corehead. Word travelled far, parents and the wider community became involved and this in turn led to the development of even more projects and facilities, for instance the Corehead Log Cabin (a new base and venue for local groups and activities) and our very successful Junior Rangers out of school club working in partnership with staff from the National Trust for Scotland (NTS).

**Anna Craigen**

The farm runs across south facing hills from the Devil's Beef Tub to the top of Hart Fell, looking towards the Solway. The northern boundary runs along the watershed at about 450m a.s.l. between the catchment of the Tweed to the north and the multiple sources of the River Annan flowing southwards past Moffat. Furthermore, the source of the River Clyde is only a mile or so to the west, suggesting a reason for a nearby hill being named 'The Crown of Scotland'.

*This planting at Corehead is very successful, but removal of the plastic tubes is going to be a long job*

Corehead has strong historical associations. It includes Broad Tae, the remains of an ancient settlement and now a scheduled monument (which the Trust has to protect) and has strong associations with William Wallace, whose sister married the farm tenant around the end of the thirteenth century. During the following three hundred years the Beef Tub was a favourite place for Border Reivers to hide their stolen cattle, and in the 17th century it was the scene of the celebrated death of a prominent covenanter at the hands of the dragoons.

A decade after the purchase of Corehead by BFT, it has 195ha of native woodland, with 230,000 trees planted up Tweed Hope, Whitehope and Lochan Burn valleys including Ash, Oak, Elm, Aspen, Birch, Bird Cherry, Alder, Hazel, Juniper, Blackthorn, Hawthorn and a variety of willows. When Corehead was bought there was only one small but rich fragment of woodland, in the steep gully of Tweed Hope.

BFT's Site Officer has overall responsibility for Corehead along with Carrifran Wildwood and Talla & Gameshope. The Trust has retained 300 Blackface ewes and followers which are managed by a local farmer contractor. There are areas of wetland, wild bird cover, flower rich meadows, protected and planted riparian zones, an orchard and recently planted small areas of montane scrub, including Juniper and Dwarf Birch.

There is now a sturdy log cabin for use by volunteers, constructed largely from our own larch logs, and over the years a series of community activities has taken place, including a Junior Rangers' programme, drystone dyke building courses and a chair-making course. Our new car park and signage welcomes visitors, many of whom are walking the Annandale Way, as Corehead is at the head of the Annan Water.

*Surviving native woodland in Tweed Hope, adjacent to one of the conifer plantation at Corehead*

Making a success of all this activity – both on the ground and financially – is no easy task, especially with the low earnings and rising costs of upland sheep farming. The farming and woodland components of the site will continue to be managed, for as long as it is financially viable, as a small scale working example of the potential for combining low intensity stock farming with the development of native woodland habitats; but with farming subsidies under scrutiny, BFT will be subject to the same pressures as other hill farmers.

In 2019 Corehead reached its 10th anniversary, so now is a good time to assess where we are and to consider the future for the site. An important aspect of Corehead, not least because of its proximity to the substantial town of Moffat, is the use of the site for community engagement, education, information and volunteering, and BFT has already done much work in this context.

Other opportunities which may come up in future include establishing an area of restored wetland, setting up a native tree nursery, extending the orchard and fencing off an allotment site for vegetables. Recently, Reforesting Scotland, a national charity with the aim of restoring the land and the people especially in a forested landscape, has been working on a Thousand Huts campaign. This has succeeded in changing the planning system so that it is easier for people to build a modest hut in woodlands for recreational use. Being able to stay overnight in woodland brings many benefits, and could perhaps bring a ground rent to BFT, and bring people back into the valley.

BFT is keen to have more involvement from the local community and we recently set up a 'Woodlot Scotland' agreement to let the four conifer shelterbelts (6ha), described by one senior Scottish Forestry manager as 'carbuncles from the 1970s', to three local Foresters for management as woodlots. Large trucks cannot reach the site to get timber out, as the access to Corehead is along a narrow, rough farm track twisting tightly through our neighbours' steading and crossing two narrow bridges over the river. In a way this is fine, as it encourages us to work at a smaller scale and over a longer period, with benefits being derived locally. The woodsmen will slowly thin and fell the trees, making the most of the logs locally, and the 6ha could be replanted. But a more attractive option which we will be exploring with Scottish Forestry and the woodlots team is to plant productive broadleaves rather than conifers over the same or a larger area elsewhere on the site.

*Riggit Galloway cattle, perhaps an appropriate breed for the Devil's Beef Tub*

One of the unsatisfactory features of current forestry procedures is the practice of replacing felled conifer plantations with new plantations on much the same footprint. Although a percentage of broadleaf trees is normally included, there is rarely much planting of shrubs, and the result is perpetuation of hard-edged blocks with little biodiversity benefit. At Corehead we will include planting shrubs in a broad band around the edges and encouraging natural spread of scrubby habitats into the grassland further out.

There is also potential to bring back beef to the Beef Tub! It would be possible to bring cattle to Corehead during the summer. Cattle would break up the sward that has become dominated by Bracken over the last decade, and which is very difficult to treat on steep ground without recourse to chemicals. The heavy feet of cattle also break up grassy areas and allow wildflowers to return. The way cattle eat with their tongue wrapped around grasses, as opposed to the selective nibbling of sheep, means that more diversity returns to the upland rough grazings.

The effect of seasonal cattle trampling on the Beef Tub might encourage thorny scrub and trees, as it probably appeared to the Reivers who kept stolen cattle there, hidden prior to driving them elsewhere for sale or slaughter. This process is similar to what has been happening recently on the Knepp estate in Sussex, where cattle and other herbivores at low density are allowed to range over large areas. An account of this process is given in Isabella Tree's book 'Wilding'.

*Gameshope Loch on Talla & Gameshope, the highest substantial loch in the Southern Uplands*

Photo: John Thomas

*First day of planting at Talla & Gameshope, 30th April 2016*

# TALLA & GAMESHOPE: RESTORING OUR WILDEST HILLS

*Jane Rosegrant and John Thomas*

It's too high, steep and rocky for commercial forestry and best for sheep or cattle only in July and August, but it will make a rich landscape of upland woods and montane habitats full of plants and wildlife fed by the tumbling waters of the Gameshope Burn, one of the finest hill burns in the Borders. What better place for restoration – a blank canvas denuded and impoverished by past use?

This is Talla & Gameshope, BFT's most recent acquisition, over 4,500 acres (1,832 ha), connected to Carrifran Wildwood and the largest of BFT's sites. It is an especially diverse and dramatic landscape, from the stunning Gameshope Burn, to the more rolling glacial features of the Talla valley, to the boggy Talla Moss and to the high tops of the encircling hills. In fact, it is such an enticing place that early on it was considered by the Wildwood Group as a potential site for BFT's first property. However, it was not for sale at the time and the Carrifran valley turned out to be a wonderful alternative.

## HOW WE BOUGHT OUR LARGEST SITE

Finding funds for charities is always an interesting process but when someone comes along and suggests that you could buy one of your top-list most-wanted potential conservation properties then it really concentrates the mind! Particularly when the offer comes with a (realistic) price tag in the 'who wants to be a millionaire' category and you have just six weeks to raise the funds before it goes on the open market. Talla & Gameshope was too good to lose, it led on naturally from Carrifran while offering different conservation opportunities, and would also make us serious players with a needed and justifiable voice in conservation plans for the Southern Uplands. So it had to be done. It offered another challenge, however, because it meant a coming together of quite different cultures. The culture of big business representing the seller: deadlines, targets, key indicators, along with the rather softer, more considered and longer term approach of a small Scottish conservation charity. Where to begin? The best place is always to begin with people. What do they want, what are their ambitions and what do they see as the future? And that applies to both the seller and the buyer but also to those generous people who would become our donors. It is easy to assume that the drive within those three sides could be different, just because those people come from different experiences. But truly it wasn't and perhaps that is the beauty of the conservation world. There was passion on all sides to make the right thing happen. Gradually we built a vision that encouraged the flexibility and conservation commitment of the seller and embraced the generosity and engagement of some quite remarkable donors for whom Talla & Gameshope is a true legacy. And the money was raised, to many people's astonishment, in six weeks. For me it was possibly one of the most enjoyable, rewarding and nerve-racking fundraising events of my career.

**Steve Sloan**

*Talla Reservoir and Gameshope valley from the air, May 1996*

*Talla Craigs (750m), already home to relict populations of several rare plants, is the primary site on Talla & Gameshope for restoration of montane scrub*

Years later, in 2011, Talla & Gameshope was offered for sale. BFT and the John Muir Trust joined forces and made an offer to purchase the land. We missed out on being the highest bidders and it went to a private owner. Happily, he had a strong interest in conservation and woodland restoration and was an interested neighbour for Carrifran. In late 2013 he decided to sell most of the estate and offered BFT the prospect of purchase.

It was much too important an opportunity to miss out on, though we knew it would be a challenge to raise the agreed £900K. Even more challenging, we had only a brief window of a matter of weeks to complete the purchase. Through a focused effort on the part of Trustees and staff, £400K was raised through a few large donations from individuals and one Trust. The remaining £500K was provided by an interest-free loan made by a small number of very supportive BFT donors. In November 2013 the purchase was finalised and BFT set out on the twin tasks of raising money to repay the loan and planning the ecological restoration of the site.

The fundraising lasted for a period of 5 years, with the loan fully paid off in October 2018. The money came from a wide variety of generous donations including 320 individuals, 20 trusts and foundations and an especially generous legacy. The willingness and commitment of people to make it possible for a small organisation to achieve this ambitious purchase was testament to the growing importance of ecological restoration in the public consciousness.

Planning for ecological restoration at Talla & Gameshope began as soon as the purchase was final. The previous owner had asked for 12 months to continue running his sheep there

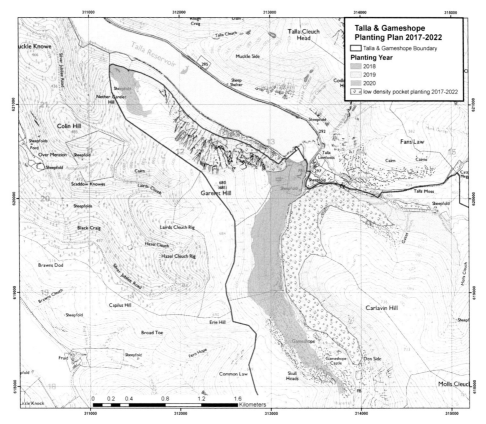

The main planting areas at Talla and Gameshope Ordnance Survey
© Crown Copyright 2019. All rights reserved. Licence number 100022432

*Nickie's Knowe on the east side of the upper Talla valley, where erosion has exposed mineral soil, providing a rare – and difficult – opportunity to establish an extensive area of montane scrub*

and BFT agreed. This allowed us the chance to carry out ecological surveying while grazing was on-going. In the summer of 2014 a National Vegetation Classification (NVC) survey was completed, setting a baseline from which to measure future changes, as well as giving us information vital to applying for future woodland planting grants.

## MONTANE SCRUB ESTABLISHMENT AT TALLA & GAMESHOPE

*Planted Downy Willow, a key species for re-establishment in the Wild Heart*

*The first Dwarf Birch saplings planted at Talla & Gameshope, bringing back a species lost to the Southern Uplands several decades ago*

The montane character at this site (with over 60% of the ground at 600m [2000 ft] a.s.l or over) lends itself readily to the establishment of high-altitude tree-line woodland and montane scrub. Montane (or simply mountain) scrub is a form of high-altitude tree-line woodland. The habitat occurs at the very highest limits of woodland growth and consists of low, stunted and dwarfed species of trees, shrubs, dwarf-shrubs and alpine wild flowers. In Scotland, montane scrub is now a very rare, fragmented and isolated habitat. Centuries of burning and grazing have reduced this precious habitat to a handful of tiny scattered remnants mainly located in the Highlands with just a couple of very restricted examples in the Southern Uplands (e.g. Moffat and Galloway Hills).

Montane scrub establishment at Talla and Gameshope began in 2016 on the high, steep, rocky and northeast facing crags of Talla Craigs. Downy, Tea-leaved, Dark-leaved, Eared, Grey and Montane Goat Willows, Dwarf Birch and Juniper have joined the naturally occurring Dwarf Willow and one solitary Dark-leaved Willow and the suite of Alpine herbs such as Alpine Saw-wort, Alpine Meadow-rue, Alpine Clubmoss, Alpine Bistort and Mossy Saxifrage and the Boreal and Low Alpine heaths of Blaeberry, Crowberry, Cowberry and Heather. Some Aspen has been established on the lower crags. The flora of this area is already rich and diverse in character and the re-introduction of montane scrub – an important and all but completely missing habitat in the Southern Uplands – will enhance the biodiversity and landscape value of the area greatly. The re-establishment of Dwarf Birch in particular – a plant which was locally extinct in the area – has been especially uplifting and goes right to the very heart of what ecological restoration is aiming to do – restore lost habitats and species.

Directly opposite Talla Craigs immediately below the summit of Nickies Knowe there is an extensive area of hill slope failure (landslip) which will be planted with a similar mixture of montane scrub species as above in the spring of 2020. This area of landslip (which has removed

the poor podzol soils right down to the original parent material) offers a rare opportunity to establish montane scrub on substrates very similar to those that prevailed during the immediate post-glacial conditions with very little in the way of weed competition. These bare areas are already being colonized naturally by Willow and Rowan seedlings. The regionally rare dwarf-shrub species Bearberry and its close companion, Petty Whin, will also be tanslocated here in the future as will the equally rare calcicole Stone Bramble. Stirk Craig and Rough Craig are also earmarked for montane scrub restoration. The latter includes a direct habitat link to Carrifran via the established montane scrub in Firthhope and on Gamesgill Crags.

A summary of all the montane scrub species established to date at Talla and Gameshope is listed below along with a list of typical montane plants found at these sites and potential species to be established in the future.

### Montane scrub species re-established to date

Downy Willow, Tea-leaved Willow, Eared Willow, Grey Willow, Montane Goat Willow, Dwarf Birch

### Species already occurring in montane zone

Dwarf Willow, Dark-leaved Willow, Rowan, Ling-heather, Blaeberry, Cowberry, Crowberry, Great Wood-rush, Alpine Meadow-rue, Alpine Saw-wort, Alpine Bistort, Mountain Sorrel, Roseroot, Mossy Saxifrage, Lady's-mantle, Moonwort, Dwarf Cornel, Aspen (at lower level)

### Species to be re-established later

Bearberry, Petty Whin, Stone Bramble, Raspberry, Broom, Whin, Burnet Rose, Ivy, Honeysuckle, Mountain Birch, Hazel, Hawthorn, Bird Cherry, Scots Pine, Rockrose

*Left: Three montane species that had survived on Talla Craigs (from top) Dwarf Cornel, Dwarf Willow, Roseroot*

**Stuart Adair**

*Any extension of the wood northwards faces destruction by avalanches*

Photo: John Thomas

*Volunteers dealing with Norway Spruce that prevent any extension of the wood westwards*

BFT was aware that some woodland planting would be required as too many of the species needed for a healthy upland wood were missing from the site. However, we hoped that the character of the site with its screes, rocky faces and remnant vegetation along the Gameshope Burn would lead to some natural regeneration more quickly than at Carrifran or Corehead. Five years on from the removal of grazing, Rowan and several upland willows have already taken off along the burn with many young shoots, some on old stems, appearing. Aspen has also begun to spread naturally and we are watching to see what else may appear.

While observing the natural regeneration we have also moved forward with actively planting on the site. As of the end of May 2020 170,000 trees have been planted, spread across 140ha of the site. The species mix varies depending on soil type and other conditions but includes Sessile Oak, Hazel, Aspen, Downy Birch, Bird Cherry, Alder, Holly, Juniper, six species of willow, but sadly no Ash because of dieback. But high up above everything else almost on the wind scoured plateau itself we have been able to plant Dwarf Birch because, unlike Carrifran, Talla & Gameshope is not a designated site. Scottish Natural Heritage does not permit the planting of Dwarf Birch at Carrifran because of the designations. The densest areas of planting have been paid for through grants from Scottish Forestry but other areas have been planted – and will continue to be planted – by dedicated, hardy, enthusiastic volunteers.

Volunteers have been especially instrumental in the planting of montane scrub species at the higher elevations on site. One of Talla & Gameshope's special characteristics is the opportunity afforded

*Surviving Aspens on cliff and forest of regenerating suckers at top right*

Photo: Stuart Adair

*Gameshope Dean      Above - 2014      Below - 2019*

Photo: Stuart Adair

*Bitter Vetch; Common Dog Violet;*
*Dog's Mercury; Globeflower, Wood*
*Anemone and Honeysuckle*

## GAMESHOPE DEAN: A RELICT FRAGMENT OF THE WILDWOOD

A tiny (0.4ha) fragment of the old native forest has survived on the steep flushed banks and cliffs in the narrow ravine of Gameshope Dean, near the mouth of the Gameshope valley. Although tiny, this remnant is incredibly species-rich and luxuriant and illustrates clearly both what has been lost from our hills and what we are trying to restore. An old iron fence may have been erected in Victorian times to prevent sheep falling down the cliff, and at some point in the 1970s or 1980s, this remnant of native woodland was fenced and framed-in by the exotic conifer, Norway Spruce. The spruces have been ring-barked by BFT and are now either dead or dying.

The remnant woodland itself consists of low growing, tangled mixtures of Ash, Downy Birch, Rowan, Hazel, willows, Dog Rose and Honeysuckle over various ferns such as Male-fern, Scaly Male-fern, Lady-fern and Common Polypody, tall-herbs such as Great Wood-rush, Marsh Hawksbeard and Dog's Mercury and other typical woodland herbs including Common Dog Violet, Primrose, Herb Robert, Wild Strawberry, Barren Strawberry, Sanicle, Wood Sorrel and Wood False-brome and a rich suite of mosses including Common Tamarisk-moss, Big Shaggy-moss, Lesser Pocket-moss, Swan's-neck Thyme-moss and Common Feather-moss. Among the more notable and regionally rare plants occurring here are Stone Bramble and Hard Shield-fern, both species typical of base-rich Ash-Elm woodland.

Where the ground is wetter and more heavily flushed, the woodland resembles riparian Alder woodland with Wild Angelica, Meadowsweet, Water Avens, Yellow Pimpernel, Opposite-leaved Golden Saxifrage and Lady's Mantle among the field layer. At the other end of the extreme on drier and more freely draining soils, the stand takes on the character of heathy upland Oak-Birch woodland with Heather, Blaeberry, Wood Anemone and frequent Downy Birch seedlings joining the flora. Downy Birch is the most abundant form of natural regeneration closely followed by Rowan, Ash and various species of Willow including Eared Willow, Montane Goat Willow, Grey Willow, Tea-leaved Willow, Dark-leaved Willow and their various hybrids. Aspen is not present within the wood but there is a good surviving stand a few hundred metres upstream.

This tiny relict woodland played a key role in the origin of the Wildwood project. It was a visit here by Philip at the start of a walk up Gameshope valley in May 1993, followed by the sight of tiny native trees growing on an islet in Loch Skene (but nowhere else in the surrounding landscape) which provided the inspiration for a large scale ecological restoration project driven by a grassroots community group. The first trees in the Wildwood were not planted until 1st January 2000, and were in Carrifran rather than Gameshope, but in 2013 Borders Forest Trust purchased Talla & Gameshope, soon starting its restoration and bringing the wheel full circle.

**Stuart Adair and Philip Ashmole**

*Gameshope Dean, the precipitous gorge in which native trees and ground flora have survived*

*Alpine meadow below Talla Craigs
after removal of grazing stock; inset
Moonwort and Alpine Meadow-rue*

*Gameshope in 1993*

for large scale restoration of montane woodland, a very rare but once common habitat in Scotland. 80% of the site is over 550 metres, making it unsuitable for much low level woodland planting, but ideal for bringing back the rarer montane species such as Downy Willow *Salix lapponum*, Tea-leaved and Dark-leaved Willow *Salix phylicifolia and Salix myrsinifolia*. Especially exciting has been the volunteer planting of a 30ha area of montane scrub that runs across the boundary between Carrifran and Talla & Gameshope – creating the first natural ecological connection in centuries between these two special sites.

As well as the wealth of opportunity that Talla & Gameshope offers for ecological restoration within and across its boundaries, it was evident from the start that it also provides a wider link, connecting the Moffat Hills SSSI with the Tweedsmuir Hills SSSI. In this way it offers a rare opportunity to enable the restoration of a large area of hills and valleys to their natural state, providing habitats extensive enough to be truly sustainable, in contrast to many isolated areas under conservation management elsewhere.

Furthermore, in recognition of the special nature of land in this region, in 2014 Scottish Natural Heritage named a section of the locality, the Talla – Hartfell Wild Land Area (WLA). It is one of only two such areas of officially recognised Wild Land in the Southern Uplands. About a third of the named area falls within BFT's ownership, spread across Carrifran, Corehead and Talla & Gameshope. This recognition of the special nature of each of these sites led BFT to build upon the inspiration of Talla & Gameshope and begin developing our idea of 'Reviving the Wild Heart of southern Scotland'.

# MAKING RESTORATION HAPPEN: WORKING WITH AUTHORITIES, FUNDERS, PARTNERS AND PEOPLE

*Nicola Hunt*

When a new major piece of land is bought and ideally also paid for, there is little time to stop and celebrate as the focus turns immediately to developing plans of what to do and how to fund it. Making this happen involves much planning, working with funders, authorities, partner organisations and local people. It is imperative to work out what is already on the site and sometimes in it – 'in' in an archaeological sense – before developing plans and quantifying the projected outputs and outcomes for activities that are required to source funds for work.

A primary component of restoration in our local hills is the establishment of native woodland on predominantly treeless ground that has been without trees for millennia. Many habitats, such as montane heath and heather moorland, can regenerate naturally if released from grazing pressures but diverse native woodland cannot develop if there are no parent trees producing seed, and no 'seed bank' in the soil from which young trees can grow. BFT's preference for ecological restoration is to leave it largely to nature, but when circumstances prevent natural processes from achieving this, then a more interventionist approach is taken. On large denuded sites, planting is essential to bring back native woodland of diverse species to the land.

The first step is surveying the land to establish what is there and to inform management decisions of what to do. An ecologist is employed to carry out a National Vegetation Classification (NVC) survey, a method of classifying natural habitats according to the vegetation they contain. This survey provides information on the habitats that exist on the site and a general indication of health is also obtained at this stage. The survey is used to determine which habitats would be potentially suitable for woodland restoration as well as providing information on habitats of conservation interest that should not be planted. The sites identified as suitable are then surveyed at a more detailed level including assessment of soils and existing vegetation to work out what type of native woodland would be suitable for the specific areas, matching trees to appropriate site conditions. Alongside the field survey work-desk based surveys are also carried out to look at archaeology, species records and other features of interest.

Once areas considered suitable for planting have been identified, work begins on the development of woodland plans, working with the local Scottish Forestry team. Scottish Forestry (previously the Forestry Commission) is the Scottish Government agency responsible

## INSPIRING STUDENTS

*Stuart Adair explaining the wildwood project to students from*
*Bangor university, who arrived at the same time as a major snowstorm*

For many of our students, both at undergraduate and at Masters level, and both from the UK and from overseas, the visit to Carrifran Wildwood is the highlight of our study tour of south Scotland. The students leave the site inspired by seeing what is possible through dedication, hard work, and a vision of what is possible. On top of this, the Wildwood itself gives our students a glimpse of what a true Scottish wilderness would be like. The contrast between the Wildwood and the commercial forestry that we visit in Eskdalemuir on the same day illustrates profoundly the rich variety of ways in which the landscape can benefit all stakeholders. We will keep coming back! From a personal perspective, I love my annual visit back to Carrifran and post-visit report back to my now-grown son who did a sponsored walk from Traquair to St Mary's Loch when he was about 6 years old in order to raise funds for Carrifran. He wouldn't recognise the valley now that Mother Nature's protective coat is growing back. One day he will bring his own son here and they will see with their eyes what we have seen only in our imagination.

**Mark Rayment**

for forestry policy, grants, support and regulations. With ambitious targets for woodland creation, Scottish Forestry provides grants to fund new native woodland planting and BFT works closely with it in the development of schemes which form the primary source of income for most of the woodland planting on BFT's large sites.

The application process while considerable is fairly straight forward – develop woodland planting plans from the site surveys, identifying areas to leave unplanted, map the areas using Geographical Information Systems (GIS) and calculate areas, consult with stakeholders to ensure that there are no issues with the proposed planting plans, modify plans if necessary following consultation, work out species composition, planting density, tree protection and ongoing management programme, complete application process and wait for the outcome.

Consultation is a major part of the development of plans for the restoration of woodland on site and the process for applying for planting grant. Those consulted come from a wide range of interest areas relating to access, cultural heritage, landscape, biodiversity and ecology and water quality. Consultees include organisations such as Ramblers Association, Mountain Bothy Association and local authority ranger services, who are concerned with walking and enjoyment of the land, and wish to ensure that planting does not affect access and walking routes. There are also those concerned with the history and archaeological interests of the site including local authority archaeologists, Royal Commission on the Ancient and Historical Monuments of Scotland and local community archaeological interest groups, all working to ensure that planting does not impact on archaeological features.

Organisations with interest in ecology focus on finding out more about wildlife and species on the sites, since they wish to minimise the impact of planting on species or habitats of conservation interest; they include Butterfly Conservation, RSPB, Wildlife Recording Centres, local authority ecology officers and private individuals.

Talla & Gameshope, unlike the other two large BFT sites, sits within a Drinking Water Protected Area as the ground water flowing through the site feeds the Talla Reservoir, a major water supply for Edinburgh. This has led us to consulting and working with Scottish Water to ensure that none of the habitat restoration work being carried out (such as tree planting or peatland restoration activities) impact on water quality.

Conventional forestry grants provide most of the funds for the main planting work, but they are only part of the funding jigsaw as the grant alone is not sufficient to cover the costs associated with planting, fencing and the ongoing management to establish the woodland. The remote and inaccessible locations of the sites in the Wild Heart adds substantially to the cost of the works, resulting in a significant shortfall between the actual cost and the associated grant income. For example, the approved Forestry Grant Scheme grant for a deer fence was just £6.80/m, while the actual deer fence cost was in the region of £15/m. Without additional funding, this planting would not be possible. To fill the gap BFT worked with Forest Carbon to sell the carbon associated with the creation of this woodland. Working with Forest Carbon was a straightforward process and has enabled this shortfall to be covered and the planting work to proceed at Corehead and Talla & Gameshope.

Not all of the plantable ground on the Wild Heart sites is suitable for conventional forestry grant-funded planting activity, so funding to support other planting work needs to be found elsewhere. Conventional forestry grants have prescriptive requirements including high densities of trees (ie number of trees/hectare) to be planted and requirements for tree growth to reach establishment in a relatively short period. Unfortunately this is not always deliverable on the large BFT sites as much of the ground is high (above 250m) with less fertile soil so that tree growth is slow. Furthermore, places suitable for planting are often intermixed with lots of rock, scree and non-woodland habitats of conservation interest, so planting at high density is not possible. In these circumstances when trees will grow but not within the scope of the forestry grants, funding must be sourced elsewhere.

A particular area of woodland restoration that is not suitable for conventional forestry grants is montane scrub, also known as mountain woodland, a nationally rare and almost extinct community in southern Scotland. Thankfully the conservation and restoration importance of this community nationally is considered a worthy cause and has attracted a number of different funders and support, including organisations such as the Woodland Trust and Scottish Natural Heritage's Biodiversity Challenge Fund and individual donors, as well as volunteers to actually plant the trees. BFT is fortunate in having committed volunteers who are willing to walk long distances to reach high planting ground and often to camp in extreme winter conditions in order to plant and restore this important habitat.

Volunteer involvement is an integral part of BFT's mission, as implied by our slogan 'Rooted in the Community'. Volunteers come to realise that they are central to BFT's work, and are rewarded with a sense of achievement in making a difference to our natural environment, while also receiving benefits to health and well being and in learning new skills and more about nature. BFT is rewarded with the achievement of facilitating the engagement of people in improving our native woodland heritage and connecting them with nature, while also helping to minimise planting costs through volunteers carrying out work that would otherwise need to be done by contractors. We are continually aware, however, that volunteers need support, and funding is needed for staff and resources to run volunteering activities.

In an ever changing world of funding, BFT needs to be proactive in seeking out new grants and funding opportunities as they become available, and to be reactive to changes in the priorities of funders. We must be ready to grasp opportunities when they arise, but must always remain aware of the danger of becoming 'funding led' and allowing our vision to be compromised by tempting avenues for funding.

Scottish Natural Heritage (SNH), the government funded body responsible for nature conservation in Scotland, is one such funder, whose funding priorities change

## ON WORKING FOR BORDERS FOREST TRUST

My time as Site Officer with BFT began in April 2014. I arrived fresh from a Ranger post down in England and was drawn to the work of this pioneering organisation in ecological restoration – a phrase and concept completely new to me. From early on, I was taken aback by the achievements of such a small charity with a bold vision and an army of committed volunteers. I had to adapt to working in one of the harshest and challenging environments. I would spend days moving trees by foot or by quad bike into crags and gullies and up onto hill tops. I would have groups of impassioned volunteers join me weekly or more sporadically, keen to get going and get these trees into the ground. And why? Because we all believed it was the right thing to do and because we could all see it working. In a relatively short period, the valleys at Carrifran and Corehead were becoming wooded once more. The summer birdsong was a welcome companion on an early morning walk. We could all see that given the chance, the trees would grow again and nature would return in abundance. My time at BFT has certainly inspired me to follow a life path dedicated to creating more space for nature.

**Lynn Cassells**

constantly and which has been a major funder of work at Carrifran, Corehead and Talla & Gameshope as well as of BFT core work over the years. Initially SNH funded the Carrifran site officer for five years to support work with volunteers and improve the condition of this designated site. SNH then supported the Corehead staff team to engage local people in conservation work and deliver education work, and latterly the SNH Peatland Action Grant has funded a number of peatland restoration activities on both Carrifran and Talla & Gameshope and montane scrub restoration on all three sites in the Wild Heart. The future direction of SNH's funding priorities and availability of grants is uncertain and BFT must keep looking to other sources to continue this work.

European funded LEADER programmes for rural development have also been a major funder of the people engagement activities and small scale habitat restoration work at Corehead. These funds were administered through local authorities and have been some of the most challenging of grants to administer due to the stringent and changing European conditions and requirements. In securing funding, the administration of grant reporting on the delivery of the work is something not to be overlooked and is often a significant commitment for which there is seldom financial support. Looking to a future outwith Europe, this type of funding will cease to exist and it is unknown whether other sources of funding for rural development will be available that BFT can access.

Charitable Trusts have become an increasingly important funder of the work on the large sites over the years. Different funders have different funding priorities so matching the work to these priorities is essential to secure funds for the work on site and the staff costs associated with its management. One of the major attributes of BFT's 'Reviving the Wild Heart' programme is that it is not just about wild land for wildlife but it is wild land for people too. A place where people can explore, appreciate and learn about the returning wildlife and regenerating habitats, a place where people can contribute to habitat restoration through planting, surveying and carrying out conservation activities. This inclusion of people is a fundamental component of the aims of BFT and has the added benefit of helping to open up more funding streams for engagement, participation and education work. Both large and small charitable trusts such as Tubney Charitable Trust, Garfield Weston and the Brown Forbes Memorial Fund have supported and continue to support both the ecological restoration and people engagement activities across the sites. Growing and nurturing relationships with funders through developing good track records for delivery of targets is important and often leads to continued support of projects.

It is important also not to overlook the individuals who contribute financially to the work at our major sites. While these donations are often small, they demonstrate the support that individuals have for the restoration of lost habitats in southern Scotland and the value they place on it.

Owning land gives a degree of entitlement to government subsidies such as its rural payments scheme. However, the nature of the work on our major sites is not conventional and as a result entitlements were lost from sites that are no longer grazed despite being kept in good environmental condition. Unfortunately BFT's interpretation of 'good environmental condition' is not the same as that of the rural payments division of the Scottish Government which stipulates that the land has to be grazed or surveyed annually using an overly elaborate and complex methodology that is unsuitable for upland environments. This was a real

## CARRIFRAN AS AN EXEMPLAR: INFLUENCING THE PROFESSIONALS

When we wrote the Carrifran Wildwood Mission Statement, we included a final sentence: "Access will be open to all, and it is hoped that the Wildwood will be used throughout the next millennium as an inspiration and an educational resource." A year or so later, at the start of our fundraising to buy Carrifran, we began to receive not only generous donations but also feedback showing that our ambitious vision of a revived landscape touched a deep chord in many people. Now, the key word that we hear in the reaction of visitors and from student parties is 'inspiration'. We hadn't realised that this would happen so soon.

Throughout the last two decades, we have been impressed by the number of requests we get from organisations engaged in conservation, restoration ecology or explicit 'rewilding' – in addition to those from educational institutions – for someone to guide groups of their professional land managers, trustees or members round Carrifran (and now our other sites). We are especially pleased to interact with people from government agencies, who may be in a position to influence interpretation of rules and the targeting of grant support. Such occasions, of course, involve learning on both sides, and they often lead to reciprocal visits by BFT people to sites owned or managed by the organisations concerned. It all helps to spread the word.

At Carrifran it is easy to give visitors a general feel for what our work is achieving, but we are often frustrated by our inability to show them – on a short visit – the most unusual and perhaps most exciting aspect of our work: the attempt to establish montane scrub between 600m and 800m, well above the usual limits of woodland planting schemes. Montane scrub on a significant scale is extremely rare in Britain, and there is little knowledge of its extent and composition in the past. However, in the Southern Uplands as well as the Highlands of Scotland, there are vast areas of high land, which may be mainly anthropogenic, kept treeless by the grazing sheep, cattle and feral goats. These areas – like the slopes and valleys below – can be transformed into diverse and beautiful habitats.

**Philip Ashmole**

frustration as the subsidies for Talla & Gameshope could have been put to good use financing activities that are extremely difficult to fund such as continual repairs of the perimeter stock fences to ensure neighbouring stock is excluded from the sites. We live in hope that support from the Government eventually will be forthcoming in recognition of the multi-benefits for our environment of restored and cared for areas of wild land.

Securing funding is a continual challenge and casting the funding net as widely as possible and avoiding reliance on a small number of funders is essential to continue to finance work on our major sites. Through considerable planning, engagement and fundraising effort, an elaborate jigsaw of funding pulls together finances to allow the Trust to work towards restoring lost habitats and creating a wild haven where both people and wildlife have a place.

Borders Forest Trust is a small organisation but despite its size achieves a tremendous amount. These achievements are due to working with others, volunteers, partnership organisations, government. Being a partnership organisation always ready to work with others builds the capacity of the Trust enabling it to punch above its weight at a time of uncertainty and change in upland land use.

# CONSERVATION, ECOLOGICAL RESTORATION AND AGRICULTURE

## Testing the bars of the conservation prison
### Philip Ashmole

George Monbiot, in 'The Conservation Prison' chapter in his book 'Feral', challenged environmentalists and the authorities to focus on a fundamental question 'Does our current management of protected sites represent the best that we can do for nature?' Monbiot clearly thinks that the answer is 'No'.

Sites of Special Scientific Interest (SSSIs) and other protected areas are chosen as examples of the best that nature has to offer in Britain, with the aim of maintaining them 'in favourable condition' which roughly equates to keeping them as they are. Many of them, however, have already been degraded by human activities, and Monbiot makes an impassioned plea for us to focus less on preserving what they now offer, and more on what nature could re-create if given the chance.

In the last years of the 1990s activists in Borders Forest Trust raised the money to buy Carrifran valley, a magnificent but degraded site in the heart of the Southern Uplands of Scotland. Carrifran offered an extraordinary opportunity for ecological restoration. We wanted to remove the man-made obstacles – mainly hundreds of sheep and feral goats – that prevented natural ecological processes from operating in the valley, and to lay the foundations for the gradual re-establishment of the habitats and most of the plants, animals and other organisms that would once have graced these upland hills and valleys.

There was one obvious hurdle to overcome. Carrifran formed about one fifth of the Moffat Hills SSSI, and the designation could potentially inhibit restoration of a more natural ecosystem, leaving the site as an example of Monbiot's 'conservation prison'. Instead, two decades on, Carrifran is widely

*Staff of Scottish Natural Heritage with members of the Wildwood Group in 2009 at 700m in the denuded corrie of Firth Hope as planting of montane scrub was getting under way*

viewed as a prime demonstration of "What rewilding looks like". It is worth considering how we got from there to here.

Over several years in the late 1990s we negotiated with Scottish Natural Heritage (SNH) custodians of the SSSI, over our desire to hand Carrifran back to nature. We explained that we wanted to set in motion fundamental changes at Carrifran, transforming it gradually into 'self-willed land' in which only minimal human intervention would be necessary. We got away with it, by a combination of luck, goodwill, and of course homework. The luck was that the primary reason for the SSSI status of this part of the Moffat Hills was the presence on the crags and the surrounding high plateau of 'the richest assemblage of montane and sub-montane plant species in the Southern Uplands'. Since these special plants were confined largely to places inaccessible to grazing stock, we were able to argue successfully that our interventions – primarily removal of sheep and feral goats and establishment of a first generation of native trees at lower levels – would not adversely affect them. (As explained earlier in the book, there is actually a more exciting story to tell about the special plants.)

The goodwill, enthusiasm and practical support shown by staff at all levels within SNH, at that time and over the next two decades, has been key to the success of the Wildwood project. Nonetheless, we have sometimes had to accept that since Carrifran is part of an SSSI, SNH have a veto on what we do. We still do not understand their reluctance to allow riparian planting along our hill burns – it may be a legacy of acidification caused by the crowding of conifers in plantations of the 1970s right up to the edges of burns. SNH also asked us not to plant on some large flushed areas near the mouth of the valley, because they were home to plants dependent on open areas with some degree of enrichment. While it is understandable that conservationists may be reluctant to accept change to a habitat that currently harbours scarce species, ecological restoration requires the establishment of natural ecosystem processes – in this case succession to a wet woodland habitat of a kind that is now entirely absent from the Moffat Hills.

Two other episodes have brought into focus for us the complex nature of the conservation prison. The first followed a chance opportunity for an SNH staff member to read the manuscript of the paper by Stuart Adair on his resurvey of the open-ground vegetation of Carrifran after about a decade of absence of sheep, cattle and feral goats. The result was a visit to Carrifran in 2015 by about 20 SNH staff from all parts of Scotland, to see for themselves the effects of release from centuries of intensive grazing by domestic animals. As Stuart explains in Part II of this book, these effects were strikingly positive, and the interest shown by SNH staff demonstrates their awareness of the desirability of some rethinking of the rules relating to designated sites.

The second – and to us depressing – episode was an off-the-record remark by an SNH person, suggesting that the flexibility shown by SNH in the 1990s in relation to our plans for the transformation of Carrifran might not have been possible if the Moffat Hills SSSI had already been designated as a Special Area of Conservation (SAC) under the European Commission Habitats Directive. If this assessment is correct, it implies that the bars of the conservation prison may still be firmly in place.

The Habitats Directive focuses on the preservation of specific habitats that are considered to be under threat in the European Union, and if an area is designated as an SAC, particular habitats within it are specified for strict preservation. In 2004, when the Moffat Hills SSSI had been accepted as a Candidate SAC, SNH wrote that:

> *"The conservation objective for the site is that there should not be deterioration or significant disturbance of the qualifying features based upon their condition at time of formal identification. This should also ensure that the integrity of the site is maintained and that the site continues to make a full contribution to achieving Favourable Conservation Status."*

In March 2005 the SSSI was formally designated as a Special Area of Conservation, and a list of the 'Qualifying Interests' was provided. This set the scene for the denial by SNH – in 2008 – of our request for permission to plant Dwarf Birch (*Betula nana*) at Carrifran. We had put forward a considered case for inclusion of this species in planting high up on the site, on the basis of historical records nearby and the discovery by Wildwood Group member Crinan Alexander of a specimen of Dwarf Birch in the herbarium of the Royal Botanic Garden Edinburgh (where he worked) which had been collected in 1857 near Innerleithen, less than 20 miles from Carrifran. However, SNH responded that planting of *Betula nana* at Carrifran 'could be damaging to the interests of the SSSI and could compromise the integrity of the SAC'. Here, surely, was a strengthening of the bars.

Intriguingly, Borders Forest Trust has recently been awarded funding from SNH for high level planting of montane willows and Dwarf Birch on Talla & Gameshope, which is contiguous with Carrifran but is not a designated site.

## Carrifran: habitat restoration in a protected landscape
### Chris Miles

The Wildwood project came to my attention in the late 1990s when Scottish Natural Heritage were first engaged in discussions with Borders Forest Trust. They came to SNH because Carrifran lies in the Moffat Hills Site of Special Scientific Interest, notified for their geological interest and an assemblage of upland habitats and plant species that are unique in the south of Scotland.

SSSI management is guided so that it maintains the notified features through consents and management agreement with the land managers. However BFT wanted to transform Carrifran from what it was to a native woodland by removing the graziers and planting trees. This was a unique proposal in an SSSI and we needed to decide whether the important notified features in the area could be maintained while accommodating such a transformation. Otherwise there was no point in BFT acquiring the site. We decided that they could be sustained and probably enhanced with an appropriate management plan.

In 2005 the Moffat Hills became an SAC, an even higher level of protection for the habitats and species. There is a higher level of presumption against change in management for SACs and so it is unlikely we could have agreed the project once this was in place. So the timing was good and 20 years later we are seeing the benefits of expanding populations of the rarer plants as well as new biodiversity complementing the features of the site.

## Agri-environment schemes and nature
### Hugh Chalmers

For over 30 years there have been 'agri-environment' schemes, where government subsidies are paid to farmers to protect or enhance semi-natural wildlife habitats on farms in Scotland. The kind of thing available to farmers include keeping artificial fertilisers off species rich grassland, maintaining wetlands, fencing off water margins, reducing sheep numbers on heather moorland (to reduce overgrazing) and fencing off small patches of ancient woodland, usually situated in steep gulleys (also known as cleuchs). Some might say that farmers should have been looking after these habitats in any case, but that is a discussion for another day.

*The old trees in Raking Gill will survive, but the ground flora is almost non-existent*

The schemes were initially targeted in sensitive areas, for instance the Central Southern Uplands, and were largely welcomed by slightly suspicious farmers, some of whom were reluctant to reveal what was on their farm. As a FWAG Advisor in the 1990s I helped to arrange schemes on behalf of farmers. I can now look back at the legacy of the considerable amount of money which was spent and I am not impressed. It was always going to be difficult to measure the benefit of reducing sheep numbers on a heather hill, and one farmer actually mentioned that since he had taken 300 ewes off the hill (which he was compensated for annually) his lambing percentage had gone up, so he was effectively being paid twice, with no measurable benefits to the environment.

Another shortcoming of the scheme was that many of the options were very short lived, with annual payments for five years on water margin management. On a memorable occasion, during a FWAG evening site visit with farmers, the host insisted that he would remove the fencing from the water margin if the payments did not continue.

However, the most frustrating aspect was that farmers were paid to fence off areas for woodland regeneration. These were vitally important tiny remnants of native woodlands hanging off steep slopes as refugia, away from browsing by sheep, goats and deer. They were the last genetic remains of the original wild wood, with species such as aspen and hazel, and by fencing in a wider area around them, the intention was that they would survive, regenerate and increase, providing a seed source for future native woodland restoration.

The schemes have largely failed. Neglect of the fences by farmers, and allowing livestock to continue to graze, has resulted in the continued loss of biodiversity. The government department concerned was not interested when informed of what was happening. Later, when Borders Forest Trust worked with the Forestry Commission, doing similar woodland conservation, we were obliged to make things work, with FC Woodland Officers policing the schemes with the threat of reclaiming funds.

However, we live in times when the government, farmers and environmentalists are striving to grow more and better food while maintaining soil health and biodiversity and also minimising release of greenhouse gases. Government financial support for these efforts is surely appropriate, but ensuring that the outcome is 'public money for public good' is easier said than done. Our experience has made two things clear to us: that support schemes must be long term, and that effective enforcement or checking needs to be carried out to ensure that the planned environmental outcomes are realised, in the medium and longer term. The current Forestry Grant Scheme contracts available in Scotland now (in 2020) do have a 'pay back with interest if it fails' condition, and require the new woodlands contract to be there for at least 20 years. That is the sort of contract that may provide real benefits, and could also be used in relation to grant-aid to farmers as well as in forestry.

Photo: Philip Ashmole

*Raking Gill; a cleuch precipitous enough for trees (but hardly any woodland flora) to have survived through centuries of intensive grazing. Fencing as part of an Ecologically Sensitive Area scheme promised renewal, but was breached a few years ago so all the benefit was lost. Inset: goats inside the broken fence at the top of the cleuch*

# In place of monoculture: diversity and multiple land use
## John Thomas

Much of the Uplands of Southern Scotland is capable of being more productive, not necessarily in terms of cash, than is the case at the moment. Under monocultures of cash crops such as conifers, sheep or grouse or where a site is frozen in a 'conservation prison' the land is not contributing all that it could for public benefit nor for a flourishing environment. Well planned habitat restoration shows how rich and diverse the uplands can be, not just for biodiversity but for natural flood management, providing air and water quality, carbon storage, leisure and recreation and public health and well being. When an area is restored for nature as part of a well thought out mosaic of woodland, heath and scrub, productive forest of conifers and hardwoods, farmland, flood management and recreation it will be more sustainable, supporting much greater species diversity, many more jobs and small businesses and a thriving diverse community. Multiple benefits flow from multiple land use. All of these outcomes can be addressed in all but the smallest pockets of land if there is a commitment to multiple land use rather than monoculture. That commitment has to be reflected in a support system which values each of these outcomes as equal. When one outcome is valued above all others there is a rush to that outcome resulting in an unsustainable monoculture impoverishing the land.

John Wright

6 Ring Ouzels Feeding on Rowan
berries – Moffat Hills
8·10·19

*These ring ouzels were feeding on Rowan berries, but we have seen them feeding in mature stands of Junipers, when they tend to emerge suddenly from the inside of one bush and fly low and fast into the base of another*

# WORKING WITH LANDOWNERS

*Nicky Hume*

Borders Forest Trust does not have the means nor desire to own and manage an ever-increasing area of land and yet we know that, valuable as our sites are, they are not enough. Not big enough to reverse the alarming crash in biodiversity, not big enough to ensure every local person has a wild space in which to relax and connect with nature, not big enough to absorb the amount of $CO_2$ our Borders population is producing, not big enough to intercept all the heavy rain to prevent downstream flooding and not diverse enough to provide us with all that we need from our land. We cannot achieve all of these things on our own and that's why engaging with others and working with local landowners to promote, advise and assist with native woodland creation and management has always been a key part of our work. By extending our reach in this way we can truly achieve landscape scale ecological restoration.

## DRIVERS FOR LANDOWNERS

What makes a landowner decide to plant native trees? For some, it's a selfless act: a gift to wildlife for which they expect to see no profit or reward other than the satisfaction of watching the woods grow and fill with life. Others are keen to tap in to the benefits that native trees can bring to their business, quality of life and wider landscape. Native trees have something to offer everyone:

- By absorbing carbon dioxide trees help to mitigate climate change.
- Trees can provide shade and shelter for livestock. This can dramatcally increase lamb survival rates, bringing significant financial and animal welfare benefits.
- Soil quality is improved thanks to reduced erosion and rich leaf litter.
- Trees intercept runoff. This can prevent fertilisers, herbicides, pesticides, slurry or animal waste from entering waterways. The benefits of this to the river system are clear but these are also things that can result in significant fines and so, once again, trees can be good for business.
- Increased tree coverage reduces flood risk: roots stabilise riverbanks and trees intercept and absorb water helping to reduce peak river flow after heavy rain.
- Trees can provide winter fodder for animals and a sustainable source of fuel for people.
- Native woodlands increase biodiversity which is essential for a healthy landscape.
- Trees are good for our health; they improve air quality and shield us from road pollution. Time outdoors and surrounded by nature benefits both our mental and physical health.

*This Rowan is epiphytic on an ancient and decaying Alder, and has sent a major root down the Alder trunk from the original settlement point; it may outlive the host, and become fully independent*

- Native woodlands provide great spaces for recreation and relaxation: something that can be a big asset to landowners running leisure and hospitality businesses.

Those are the practical reasons to plant trees and each of them has been a contributing factor in the decision to do so for many of the landowners we have worked with. Then there are the more personal, thoughtful and sometimes completely unexpected reasons, which in many cases are the main drivers behind woodland creation and management projects. These are the ones that matter the most. After all we are emotional animals and a woodland that means something to someone is a woodland that survives.

Here are just a few examples: the farmer who, inspired by volunteering at Carrifran, decided to set aside an area of unproductive land for a wild woodland of his own; another farmer, young, excited to take on the family land and acutely aware of environmental issues, who was quick to set about filling odd corners, gullies and field margins with trees. There are those who have expressed a sense of duty in their decision to plant native woodland, feeling that their generation's lifestyle is partly to blame for the condition of our natural world today; those who are inspired by tales of the Ettrick Forest to bring back a fragment of this once magnificent, sprawling habitat; one farmer who wanted to slow the erosion of a river bank to protect her track, and a group of school children who wanted to leave a legacy for future pupils. We've worked to help people plant or manage trees as: a memorial woodland, a place for holiday guests to enjoy, a woodland to bring in more visitors, shelter for racehorses, shelter for a house, a screen for an unsightly development, a WWI memorial, a wild food project, a place to hang hammocks, a woodland for birds, a gift to the local community, another step in a lifetime's work, a woodland to be planted by friends, a woodland to remember a friend…the list goes on.

Photo: Nicky Hume

*A collaborative project between Borders Forest Trust, a local farmer and Traquair Estate where volunteers helped us to plant trees to supplement the surviving old ones in an ancient wood pasture. The work will ensure that the next generation of wildlife, farmers and other people will continue to benefit from this oasis of biodiversity and valuable shelter for livestock*

## BARRIERS

With so many good reasons to plant native trees, why isn't it more common? The answer lies in a complex web of costs, grazing animals, a lack of knowledge and headache-inducing grant applications. The biggest of these however has to be the grazing animals, whether that is deer, sheep, goats, voles or rabbits; if it wasn't for them, we wouldn't need to plant woodlands in the first place and this book would never have been written.

In the Scottish Borders we have a long history of sheep farming. Sheep have grazed here since at least the 12th century; the Cistercian monks at Melrose Abbey had one of the largest flocks in the UK and traded wool across northern Europe. As an industry, sheep farming is not only important in feeding and (historically) clothing our population but also as one of the few ways of earning a living in rural areas. It is well and truly ingrained in our landscape and culture. And yet we cannot shy away from the fact that as sheep farming has expanded, our woodlands have receded. It's no mystery: sheep eat trees. Wolves and lynx, which used to roam freely here, were a threat to livestock and so were heavily persecuted. This, along with habitat destruction, led to their eventual extinction from Scotland in 1680 when the last wolf was reportedly killed. The problem here is that those predators also ate wild animals, and now they are not here to do so. This means that as well as domestic sheep, we now have huge numbers of wild herbivores, especially deer, since their population now goes largely uncontrolled. All those hungry mouths are preventing our last remaining woodlands from regenerating and make it very difficult to establish new ones.

Extract from Ordnance Gazetteer of Scotland 1882 – about Ettrick forest and James V in 1528. *The second day of June the King past out of Edinburgh to the hunting, with many of the*

*'Wood pasture' established by Borders
Forest Trust near St. Mary's Loch*

*nobles and gentlemen of Scotland with him, to the number of twelve thousand men; and then past to Meggitland, and hounded and hawked all the country and bounds; that is to say, Pappert-law, St Mary-laws, Car-lav-irick, Chapel, Ewindoores, and Longhope. I heard say, he slew, in these bounds, eighteen score of harts. After this stately hunting, James... in order to increase his revenues, turned 10,000 sheep into Ettrick Forest, to graze there under the tending of a thrifty keeper... and by this act he led the way to such a conversion of the entire forest into sheep-pasture, as occasioned a rapid and almost total destruction of the trees. The last sovereign of Scotland who visited it for the sake of the chase was the beautiful Mary. Excepting a few straggling thorns, and some solitary birches, no traces of 'Ettricke foreste feir' now remain, although, wherever protected from the sheep, copses soon arise without any planting.*

This leads us to the problem of cost. Until we either control deer numbers more effectively ourselves or bring back apex predators to Scotland, we're stuck with forking out thousands of pounds for deer fences or plastic tubes to let young trees grow. This is a huge barrier for landowners. Trees themselves are cheap: at less than £1 each, many landowners could afford to regularly buy small quantities to plant themselves when time allows. In some places, natural regeneration would do the job for them, for free! The costs of protection are, however, prohibitive and so most are forced to seek grant funding.

Grant funding is the next big challenge. We're lucky enough to live in a country where some of our taxes are used to fund woodland creation and management projects and so in theory cost shouldn't be a barrier. The problem lies in applying for the funding. Long, complex application forms requiring expert knowledge, in-depth surveys, digital mapping skills and detailed planning are something that most landowners have neither the time nor experience to complete. The level of detail required is, quite rightly, intended to prevent the planting of inappropriately-designed forests or those that will have a detrimental impact on the environment. Those who plant purely commercial forests can expect to make a profit from their timber sales and so can better afford to pay an experienced agent to complete funding applications for them. For those wishing to plant more natural, multi-purpose woodlands that will enhance the landscape and environment, it is usually not feasible to pay an agent since the associated benefits are not always monetary. As a result, very few of these projects go ahead without some sort of additional support or funding.

The final major barrier is a lack of knowledge about woodlands and how to look after them. It's been so long since trees blanketed our landscapes that we have lost our woodland culture. We no longer forage in the woods for wild foods, shelter our animals among trees during bad weather, coppice trees for renewable timber or rely on trees for building materials, and traditional woodland crafts have almost completely died out. Most people don't realise how much healthier our lives, wildlife and landscapes could be with more trees.

In other parts of the world, guard animals such as dogs or even llamas (http://www.sprucelane.com/guardllamas.pdf) are used to protect livestock from predators, allowing them to coexist. In parts of mainland Europe and North America predators are gradually retuning or being reintroduced, bringing with them huge benefits from increased tourism revenue and biodiversity and even a reduction in flooding (learn about the Yellowstone Wolves here: http://www.bbc.com/future/story/20140128-how-wolves-saved-a-famous-park). Businesses aimed at environmentally conscious customers that donate some of their profits to tree planting, are springing up everywhere (check out *ecosia.com* for forest friendly internet browsing!). Action and awareness of the importance of trees and restoring ecological processes is continually growing. We hope in the future we will see a system where landowners are paid to provide ecosystem services such as carbon sequestration, natural flood management, air purification, biodiversity and soil fertility (in some of these areas it's already happening slowly) but until then organisations like Borders Forest Trust will continue to support land owners in their work to plant and care for native woodland, and strive to take the edge off some of the biggest barriers they face.

### How does Borders Forest Trust help?

It's clear from the list of complex barriers and persisting bare hillsides that help is needed to support those who want to plant and restore native woodlands in the Borders, and that's where BFT comes in. The initial idea and drive needs to come from the landowner but BFT is often the catalyst required to kick-start a project, and to ensure it is a success. Over the years we've provided advice, attended site visits, carried out ecological surveys, created planting designs, offered funding guidance, completed grant applications, consulted stakeholders, carried out practical works and always strived to help people overcome the unexpected challenges along the way. Thanks to our many generous funders we have often been able to offer some of these services for free, removing one of the main barriers.

Working with others brings its own challenges and we have occasionally found ourselves gently persuading people that planting dense Leyland cypress, killing all the moles in preparation for planting, letting the sheep in when the trees are still tiny or keeping the rhododendrons for the pretty flowers may not be the best approaches. However those are insignificant hurdles compared to the rewards of working with local people who share our passion for woodlands. It's inspiring to hear peoples' reasons for planting trees and to see the determination and work they put in. Every landowner we work with tells a few of their friends, family or neighbours about their project and so knowledge of BFT and enthusiasm for native woodlands amongst the community gradually spreads.

Over our first 20 years BFT has worked with 45 landowners to assist with the management of over 1800ha of land, 1150ha of which were new native woodland habitat creation projects. At the time of writing this book we are working with a further 18 land owners to plan the planting or management of a further 150ha of woodland.

*The Argo ATV on Cocklaw Knowe*

*Temporary bothy at Lochan Burn erected in May as a refuge from extreme conditions during planting in winter*

*Planter at Lochan Burn one minute after an an avalanche brought rocks and snow down the slopes of Hartfell Shoulder*

# GETTING TREES IN THE GROUND: A CONTRACTOR'S VIEW

*Paul Short*

Shortly after the purchase of Corehead & Devil's Beef Tub by Borders Forest Trust in 2009, Treesurv were awarded the contract for the main native woodland planting on the site, which was to be in three successive years, in separate valleys with burns which – with the one from the Beef Tub itself – comprise the source of the River Annan.

Treesurv had been established in 2003 as a partnership between the father and son team of Paul and James Short. We wanted to cover a broad base of woodland management activities and moreover, lead the way with the reestablishment of native woodland. Our close working partnership with BFT began with Corehead. This became a benchmark project for Treesurv and led to further work for BFT in various parts of Talla & Gameshope. The experience and acknowledgement we gained from our work on Corehead has also provided the business with a lead into work for the Forestry Commission, the Woodland Trust, the National Trust for Scotland and the River Annan Trust to name but a few.

The key for us as a business when taking on projects such as Corehead is to find the right people to carry out the work to our exacting standard. We are proud to have built a strong team of experienced women and men who not only understand the environment and what we are trying to achieve but who can cope with the sometimes extreme conditions and always with a positive attitude.

Our first challenge on beginning in autumn 2010 was the sheer number of trees to be planted during the first planting season at Corehead. The area to be planted was the whole valley containing the Tweedhope Burn. In total 128,000 plants, stakes and tree shelters had to be taken into Tweedhope and planted in a way that looked as natural as possible. Trees came from the nursery as 40 to 60 cm root plugs, all native species; in effect perfect miniature trees. Each one needed to be planted with individual protection; for this project that meant one wooden stake and one 60cm tree shelter, per tree. That first planting season at Corehead was straightforward hard work but very enjoyable, as slowly but surely things started to take shape. By the end of the planting season it was finished, all 128,000 trees, stakes and shelters were installed and all that was left to do, was for the trees to grow. This they have done.

The second planting season was a very different project from year one in Tweedhope. The Whitehope Burn runs from below Whitehope Heights, along the western base of Middlefield Rig; very straightforward planting when you get there – it is just the getting there that causes the problems. The only way to get the planting team with trees, stakes and shelters onto site, was to come over the top of the hill just north of Cocklaw summit using an All Terrain Vehicle (ATV). This season's numbers were much smaller than Tweedhope, only 49,000, but

*Members of the Montane Scrub Action Group with Forestry Commission staff on the Bennan in the Galloway Forest park where Treesurv planters are at work on ground previously mounded*

the routes into the planting area were much harder and it felt like the weather this second season was not going to be as kind as in the previous one.

We use an eight wheeled ATV, an 8x8, for this kind of terrain. The problem with accessing this kind of site is the sheer number of times you have to travel to it over the winter period when no vegetation is growing. Wet, steep ground with no growing vegetation gets very slippery and on this part of the hill we had very few options to change our route to the planting area. The answer came when it was decided to reinstate the old track over this part of the hill; the diggers appeared on site one day and work started. Work on the track progressed well and eventually we could start to use it for our journey over the hill into Whitehope. We did have some spells of very poor weather that season but the day did come when all 49,000 trees were planted and again all that was left to do was for the trees to grow. Again they have.

We then came to year three of the main planting at Corehead. This season's planting was to be undertaken in the area beyond Whitehope, in the valley running between Middlefield Knowe to the west and Hartfell Shoulder to the east, following the line of the Lochan Burn.

With 50,000 trees to be planted, all native species, using the same method as the two previous years: stake, tree shelter etc.

This season's planting introduced a new problem: approximately thirty tons of materials needed to be taken to the new planting area. Accessing the site by 8x8 ATV took almost a one-hour drive. This was fine for the planting team, tools, plants etc, but the problem was getting wooden tree stakes and tree shelters to site. ATV capacity for moving so many tons of materials was very limited. The answer was a helicopter!

For the day of the helicopter lift, everything had to be in place and to that end a team of BFT and Treesurv staff worked hard to make sure that the many bulk bags of stakes and shelters needed for the coming planting were in one of the lower fields by the Black Barn ready for the airlift. They were lifted over to Lochan Burn and dropped in pre-planned locations across the site ready for work to commence. On the day of the helicopter lift the weather was perfect and everything went smoothly. The helicopter took just six minutes per return trip to site. Half a day and all the stakes and shelters were where they needed to be. It was just a case of taking up plants as we needed them.

A planting site so far away from the Black Barn and road, in the winter months, requires Plan B in the event of a sudden change in weather conditions and to that end we felt that some shelter was needed. The only thing to do was to build a temporary wooden bothy, complete with homemade wood stove. Again this required the moving of materials, but on a scale that could be undertaken by our ATV. As things turned out we did have to use the bothy on many occasions. It was a great help during some of the coldest weather, to be able to get a little bit of warmth and shelter. The drive to and from Lochan Burn could be cold and miserable, the route going over the track at Cocklaw and beyond up to Whitehope Heights, then Whitehope Knowe and The Gyle to enter Lochan Burn below Strong Cleuch on Hartfell Shoulder.

However one of the most vivid memories we have was from the last week we worked before Christmas. We had high pressure and it was getting dark by late afternoon; the drive back from site was amazing, everything white with the developing frost and as soon as we topped Whitehope Heights, the view to the south was spectacular, the sky was clear and we could see for miles: We could see the ribbon of lights from the traffic on the M74 and dozens of lights from buildings as far as the Solway.

The work that third season progressed steadily, stopped only by the occasional fall of snow. One of which left us with very large deposits of snow build up along the upper slope of Hartfell Shoulder. Although it did not take long for the snow on the lower slopes to melt, the higher craggy slopes remained covered. On one seemingly routine planting day, a section of this mass of snow started to move and we had an avalanche. The first thing we were aware of was the rumble, as the snow started to collapse, then the spray of powdered snow filling the air above the falling snow and then the loosened stones bouncing down the hill like great footballs. It only took minutes for that wall of snow to fall, but it gave us a reminder of the forces of nature.

We had no more problems with snow that winter and the planting went well. We got to the end of that planting season with a certain regret that it was all over. The three main planting seasons at Corehead had been an enjoyable challenge and all the trees appear to be growing well. We knew more things were in the pipeline for Corehead and further afield but we were sorry this planting was finished.

*Even stock fences have difficulty surviving in winter conditions, although foxes still manage to travel, sometimes leaving very strange tracks*

*Carrifran, Black Hope amd Moffatdale in the Wild Heart of Southern Scotland - 2015*

# GETTING TREES TO GROW

## Herbicides, screefing and physical protection
### Hugh Chalmers

At Borders Forest Trust we have recently decided on a moratorium on the use of herbicides. This is a change to the agreed position we took at Carrifran during the Ecological Planning Group phase from 1998-2000. Then, we decided that we would use only two kinds of silvicultural herbicide, whose side effects on health and the environment appeared then to be acceptably low.

The first, 'Roundup' (active ingredient glyphosate) was used in summer months to create a small circle of around 50-70cm diameter of dead vegetation where we could plant a sapling during the following tree planting season (November to April). Independent trials had shown that this treatment increased the survival rate and growth rate of small saplings. The second herbicide, 'Kerb' (active ingredient propyzamide) was used where grasses became dominant around a sapling (despite the Roundup treatment) and was used between December and January. We stopped using Kerb around 2006 as new evidence showed that it adversely affected amphibians. We had also found it difficult to apply effectively within the necessary cold weather (but snow-free) window.

*Andy Wilson and Tuesday volunteers compressing vole guards in the skip*

*Vole guards and herbicide circles*

*Removing thousands of tubes from trees on steep ground is a non-trivial task*

*Roebucks scent-marking their territory target thumb-thick unbranched vertical stems*

*Damage to Aspen caused when the fence erected to protect surviving native trees in Black Cleuch at Fruid was breached by feral goats. This tree won't die soon, but long-term survival of the stand seems doubtful without further intervention*

The evidence against Roundup is now developing and has resulted in successful (but currently under appeal) actions against the current licence-holder, Bayer chemicals, in the USA. The evidence points to glyphosate being a possible cancer-causing agent in the same risk category as red meat and shift work (which disrupts circadian rhythms) and a possible disruptor of bee behaviour (in a trial involving 30 bees).

Using Roundup in our woodland planting was very effective, and we still have concerns about how to ensure survival and strong growth of delicate saplings in a pretty hostile environment, with most places we plant having vigorous and competitive vegetation cover. There are various ways to reduce the competition from other vegetation for space, light and nutrients. Ground preparation can take many forms, such as ploughing, mounding or screefing. The latter involves scraping back a thin layer of vegetation about 50cm x 50cm, with a hand mattock, and planting the tree there. Ploughing and mounding (hinge or inverted mound) are more drastic, and involve heavy machinery on land not too steep and rocky. Cutting the grass around the saplings simply makes things worse, and simply endangers the trees. We hope that in future screefing followed by planting with more robust and sturdy saplings with well-developed roots will allow trees to get off to a good start, and to satisfy the contract requirements of Scottish Forestry when grant aid is involved.

At Carrifran, our seven year planting programme relied on small saplings generally less than one year old, having been sown in spring and planted the following November to April. One reason was that these saplings are much cheaper than two-year-old saplings as they spend less time in a nursery, and don't need to be potted on. On our newer BFT sites, if we can source saplings of correct provenance which are more robust with well-developed root collar (say 10mm diameter) and bushy roots, then perhaps these trees will out-compete vigorous vegetation.

In the UK, most planting of native trees involves the use of some kind of protective guard. At Carrifran, we have been working hard over the last few years to remove 60cm tree tubes and 20cm vole guards. We originally decided that we would use only vole guards, which over the years have come in various types of plastic but which are all springy enough to wrap around a sapling and short cane, thus providing support. They provide minimum protection from short-tailed field-voles, which can appear in plague numbers when grazing is removed in preparation for planting, and which can cause major damage to trees, especially when there is long-lying snow. They still allow low branching of the developing saplings, making them a more natural and stable shape on the exposed hillsides.

However, in some areas we capitulated to the demands of the Forestry Commission – apparently our trees were not establishing quickly enough to satisfy the terms of the Woodland Grant Scheme contract. As a result, 10,000 green plastic tubes, 60cm high and supported by a wooden stake, were used to protect existing small saplings and several thousand new trees, especially Sessile Oak planted in areas with bracken, which we had found were often swamped when bracken died and collapsed in the winter. This involved considerable cost, but was a very visible demonstration of our commitment to satisfying the contract.

The tubes worked reasonably well, and encouraged growth of trees in gappy areas. However, we try to remove them as soon as possible, as they do affect the growth form and can cause trees to be shocked as they pop their heads out of the tube (or when we remove the tube), and they seem to be a magnet for deer. The task of removing them and disposing of them responsibly should not be underestimated., and it would be interesting to weigh up the effort and cost of using tree tubes in comparison to just planting more and larger saplings in vole guards. At Corehead, where 280,000 trees were planted between 2009 and 2012 using 60cm tubes, we have a major task on our hands to remove the plastic.

## Controlling the browsing
### John Thomas, Hugh Chalmers and Scott Speed

"You'll have to put up a deer fence." "Will we?" The Wildwooders dared to challenge the conventional wisdom of the day back in the 1990s. Yet Carrifran Wildwood has grown from scratch to tall trees up to 9m high with less browsing than in many a fenced broadleaved wood, and this without a deer fence in sight. We had decided not to erect a deer fence – unpopular with hillwalkers and vulnerable to extreme weather conditions – and instead to exclude sheep and feral goats with a high stock fence, 1.4m high and with seven line wires, and to control the roe deer by shooting. Red deer were not present nearby, although Sika deer were viewed as a potential future problem (as they are now in Talla & Gameshope).

Deer are a natural component of Scottish open country ecosystems, and we welcome them to all our sites in the Wild Heart of Southern Scotland. However, knowing the devastation caused by high populations of red deer in the Highlands, and the dramatic effect of fencing plots in areas heavily browsed by deer, we established two deer-fenced control plots at Carrifran to assess the impact of deer on our growing trees. We removed the lower one when it became clear that the trees outside it were growing well, and brought forward the date for removal of the higher one (enclosing Holly Gill) after a greyhen (female black grouse) was killed on the wire – something we had always worried about. After two decades, it is clear that the deer fences had little long term effect on growth of trees in those compartments, planted at a time when most of the valley was still denuded and unattractive to deer.

However, this is not the whole story and there were lessons to be learned. Our continued annual planting of tens of thousands of tiny broadleaved saplings made the valley increasingly

*Volunteers repairing an old fence at 680m on Speir Gairs above Gameshope Loch*

attractive to roe deer, and we were not protecting our trees with tree tubes. We had always realised that in the absence of a perimeter deer fence, we would have to resort to control by shooting. Initial hunting effort was low, and lack of serious browsing damage in the first few years made us a little complacent. However, we did keep an eye on our vulnerable trees, both opportunistically and by using volunteers to make formal assessments of the damage in each compartment in the years after planting.

By 2004 it became clear that browsing damage was at an unacceptable level, and after consultation with the Deer Commission for Scotland we decided to change the culling regime. Deer control is closely regulated by Scottish Natural Heritage, and close seasons apply to protect females with calves. We obtained licences for out of season and night shooting, and arranged weekly visits by a very capable professional stalker, Scott Speed. We had already bought a rifle and organised training for our Project Officer Hugh Chalmers, and recruited some well qualified volunteer stalkers to make occasional visits. Shooting deer is a skilled and demanding task; it is difficult to spot the deer, and more so to get within a range of 200m for a safe and effective shot. We look forward to the time when lynx can do at least part of the job for us.

At Carrifran the annual cull of roe deer since 2005 has run at an average of around 20 per year, but with a sharp increase to 32 in 2019, probably as a result of the felling of the adjacent Polmoodie plantation. Red deer have not been seen, and are scarce in the Southern Uplands. Only one Sika deer has been shot, but more will come in future. Deer damage is limited to smaller trees, but our avoidance of the use of tree tubes except in bracken patches, coupled with slow growth at high elevations, leaves trees within reach of deer for many years. However, impact on Downy Birch and Alder, two of the most numerous species, rarely has serious effects, though Ash tends to suffer. While leading shoots of Sessile Oak are often removed in the higher parts of the valley, the bushy, multiple-stemmed form of oaks protected only with short voleguards ensures that growth continues, eventually producing trees well adapted to the exposed conditions.

At Carrifran only about one in four stalking visits results in a kill, but the frequency of visits keeps deer moving and reduces their opportunity to settle and establish territories in the valley. Nonetheless, the size of the site means that deer can do some damage undisturbed, and this is especially true of the plateau around the valley and the heads of the side valleys. Here, browsing and also 'fraying' by bucks of stems of willows or other species in the montane scrub can cause significant – though normally non-lethal – effects. Also in these areas mountain hares sometimes nip off many twigs of willows, doubtless slowing increase in biomass of the plants.

At Corehead & Devil's Beef Tub BFT has put less effort into deer control, since it was decided at an early stage to protect planted trees by using tree tubes, and also by deer-fencing two of the main planting areas; Tweed Hope, the third area, is not deer fenced. The result of this protection has been rapid woodland establishment. However, the necessary annual repairs to the deer fences are a drain on resources, and there is an unwelcome legacy of several hundred thousand plastic tree tubes that must be removed in the near future – a large task for which dedicated funds are not available. Furthermore, an initial small-scale planting of montane scrub suffered serious damage since it was not within the deer-fenced enclosures and was close to the boundary stock fence, which is old and does not effectively exclude our

*Black and white trailcam image of stalker Scott Speed in snow camouflage*

neighbour's sheep. Current planting of montane scrub at Corehead is within the deer fenced area.

Controlling browsing by deer at Talla & Gameshope, extending over 1800ha of land (more than half of it above 600m) presents major challenges. The 18km perimeter stock fence was in a poor state when BFT purchased the site, and one substantial length of it had to be replaced. Keeping the rest of it proof against sheep requires continual effort, and the threat of damage by deer and drifting snow is a continual worry. In 2020 BFT is planning to build a deer fence high up along the west side of Gameshope valley from near Talla Reservoir to just south of the bothy. The need for deer fencing in this part of Gameshope is mainly because browsing is not just from roe deer but also from the large herd of Sika deer in the Tweedsmuir-Menzion plantations, where felling is under way. Sika are trickier to stalk than roe, having a number of strategies to escape detection.

A rota of wonderful volunteer boundary wardens, set up in 2001 by Myrtle Ashmole and currently organised by John Thomas, checks 14km of the fence monthly; the rest is checked intermittently by the Site Officer and volunteers. Repairs and maintenance on the Talla & Gameshope and Carrifran fencing is undertaken by a small squad of tough volunteers with the aid of the Site Officer who takes responsibility for repairs and maintenance of the fencing at Corehead. New fencing and replacing fencing beyond repair is done by contractors when affordable.

Protecting the woodland from browsing by deer and livestock is very demanding for volunteers who are often working in unpredictable weather, and very time consuming for the Site Officer and costly for the Trust, especially when new fencing is required.  As funding for all maintenance and renewals comes from donated funds the Trust is very dependent on and highly indebted to both the donors who cover the cost of materials and the volunteers who give up their time. The only fencing that is grant-aided is for protecting new woodland, but the current rates for funding by Scottish Forestry are well below the full cost for fencing over the ridges and across the high plateaux to the tops across steep, stony ground, through bogs and mires and over cleuchs and screes. These fences, installed by expert contractors, also have to be funded in part from donations.

Whilst deer fences are undesirable and expensive but sometimes necessary, stock fences are essential for as long as there are cattle, sheep or goats grazing next door. All three of BFT's sites in the Wild Heart are adjacent to areas grazed by domestic livestock, thus requiring over 42km (26 miles) altogether of stock fencing to be checked and maintained, most of it on the ridges and over the tops up to 800m.

Taking a long term view, we are confident that restored native woodland will largely look after itself in the decades to come, but browsing by deer will still need to be controlled, by hunters if not by

*Winter repairs to fence across Rotten Bottom. BFT now owns the land on each side of the watershed, so this fence can eventually be removed.*

natural predators. Domestic livestock are a different matter. It is often lost sight of that the necessity to install and maintain these miles of fencing results from the livestock damaging trees, not vice versa. Stock should be controlled by their owners, just as it is dog owners' responsibility to prevent their dogs from worrying sheep. But in immediate practical terms we are also aware in BFT that where fencing is concerned, there are enormous economies of scale. Two areas that are both free of large herbivores do not need a fence between them to protect the trees from browsing. Ecological restoration is best done on a landscape scale!

# *Some lessons learned*
## *Andy Wilson*

During the 20 years of planting with Borders Forest Trust, we have had great success in creating new woodlands, the legacy of which can now be seen at Carrifran, which in 2017 won the Scotlands Finest Woods award jointly with Mar Lodge. However, in the process of this woodland creation, and the woodlands on our other sites we have gone through an evolving process as we revaluated how we manage our young forests. One of the main issues, when planting vulnerable young trees, is finding the right kind of protection from all the creatures that want to eat them. Most of the plants that we use come from the nurseries cell-grown; these are plants that are grown individually, so that the roots develop in a cylinder of compost, making planting, handling and storage very much easier. Having been regularly fed with fertiliser, cell grown plants are nutritious and attractive to any passing herbivore. We could just use bare rooted plants, but these dry out very quickly, can drown, and need much more care when planting, hence we generally go for cell grown plants, which are very tough when they are dormant.

To protect these young trees we have gone through quite a journey! At Corehead and Talla & Gameshope we have generally used 60cm or even 120cm tree tubes. These tubes protect trees from voles, rabbits, hares, sheep (and with the 120cm) deer. The 60cm tubes are very popular and are used all over the country for woodland restoration. However, we found that at the heights we are planting (300-700m) the trees were doing well within the tubes, but then getting wind burnt as they left the tubes, leaving them stunted. We also found that in many tubes the trees were becoming swamped with moss, which sometimes rotted them.

*Juniper grown in tree tubes are healthy but problematic when the tube is removed*

The species that really doesn't like these tubes is Juniper. These would form into a top heavy lollypop shape, losing all their lower growth. Due to these problems, we moved onto mesh netting for Juniper. This stopped the lollypop effect but the plant tended to become wrapped up in the mesh and then had to be carefully freed. Given these problems, we moved onto using small vole guards for Juniper. Voles are the greatest threat to our young trees, and they are so prevalent on the open hillsides where we are planting, protection of the junipers seemed totally necessary, and we started to wrap them in vole guards. This seemed satisfactory in protecting the trees and allowing them to grow naturally. Then one day we noticed a group of Junipers in a densely populated vole area that had no protection and had not been eaten. This was a game changer, as it meant that the voles had little interest in the juniper and we could move away from any protection altogether.

For other trees, voles are a major threat, so although we have moved away from using 60cm tubes at Talla & Gameshope, we have had to continue using vole guards. The vole population is cyclical, with populations showing strong highs and lows. Outside the bird breeding season I can use my collie Jess as my vole indicator, since she is skilled at

*Fi Martynoga looking at low growing well branched oaks on an exposed slope at Carrifran*

*Volunteering wth Borders Forest Trust is hard work*

catching them! If she isn't finding any, then it's a good sign that the population is low, allowing us to plant without any protection at all and to use the money saved to increase the tree density. It is a risk and there will be losses, but it is a far more sustainable solution. The big problem with using any form of protection is the management of it after about eight years, when the tree ceases to need it. With the 60cm tubes this is a big issue, getting them off the hill, then finding a sustainable way to deal with them. There is the thought that they are degradable. They are, but only in strong sunlight, and they are not bio-degradable, so they have to come off the hill. The same is true with the vole guards, which are easier to clear from the trees, but still present the problem of finding a way to deal with them once they are removed. We are trying hard to find fully bio-degradable vole guards, but as yet with very limited success; fingers crossed that this will change soon. But for now we have moved from loads of protection on our trees to as little as possible, through watching vole populations and hopefully in the near future using a fully bio-degradable tree protection solution.

## *Reaching volunteers in new ways*
## *John Thomas*

The combination of social media and rising concern about climate change has stimulated a welcome tsunami of enthusiastic volunteers. When 60 or more people, most of them new to us, signed up for a planting weekend work party in Autumn 2018 and all turned up we wondered how long it would last. When many of them came back again with some new faces on a cold, wet and miserable Sunday at the end of November the same year, planted all day fortified by some hot soup, and then said how much they had enjoyed it we knew we had tapped into a new and dependable source of help. And so it has proved; Adrian, our capable volunteer coordinator now has almost 250 volunteers regularly circulated on social media.

These new volunteers range in age from 20 to 80 years, many of them in their 20s and 30s, all very committed to what we are trying to achieve and quick to grasp the principles of the right tree in the right place. It has been immensely encouraging for all of us involved from the early days in reviving the Wild Heart, knowing that there is a new generation ready to follow on restoring habitats in the Moffat Hills and Tweedsmuir Hills.

A strong and committed body of volunteers is always likely to be essential to this work. Volunteers often provide continuity over many years, well beyond the length of time most employees remain with a small, local charitable organisation such as BFT. That continuity and commitment, exemplified by the Carrifran Tuesday volunteers, sustains the long term vision and goals of the work.

BFT's Facebook page has become a major channel of communication with information being relayed on to many others using Twitter, Instagram and whatever is the preferred channel of communication of the day. However social media is not a substitute for other established channels both digital such as the website and e News and BFT's printed quarterly newsletter.

Key to this level of engagement has been the appointment of a volunteer coordinator. The proximity of the Wild Heart to Edinburgh, Glasgow, Newcastle and Carlisle has also helped. They are all within less than a couple of hours travel as our sites are just 20 minutes off the M74, not that you would notice once you were in the Wild Heart. This has enabled us to hold regular volunteering days as well as weekend work parties. The weekend events have always been based around camping on site with volunteers being self sufficient, although at the Gameshope good use has been made of the excellent bothy. It's surprising how many tired but happy volunteers you can get into a single-roomed bothy on a wet and windy night!

# REVIVING PEATLANDS IN THE MOFFAT AND TWEEDSMUIR HILLS

*Hugh Chalmers*

*Feral goats at Rotten Bottom in 2004, shortly before their removal*

*Eroding peat at Rotten Bottom before removal of goats*

Deep peat forms in cold, wet and flat areas of the Southern Uplands, starting in some places as the glaciers retreated. At Rotten Bottom on the watershed between Carrifran and the head of the Gameshope valley, it accumulated over ten millennia at an average rate of around 1cm in every 30 years. The pollen grains of trees, shrubs and other plants captured in the layers of peat provide a continuous record of vegetation in that area.

Peat can also hide secrets. At Rotten Bottom about 6000 years ago, someone left their broken yew bow on the peat bog. The acid peat preserved the finely crafted weapon, which is now in the National Museum of Scotland in Edinburgh. The bow would not have been found by Dan Jones, a local Psychiatrist, if the 3m deep peat bog at Rotten Bottom had not been eroding, probably as a result of damage caused by grazing sheep and feral goats over the centuries, leaving the bow sticking out from a peat hag.

*Rotten Bottom in August 2019 with some healing of the bog surface*

*Volunteers at work on eroded peat*

*Jute netting showing only a little success*

*Dams in deep gullies have little effect*

The exposed hags of deep peat at Rotten Bottom are gradually revegetating now that the area has been free of grazing for 15 years. However, higher up at the source of the Little Firthhope Burn, just below the summit of White Coomb, an area of deep peat was still eroding badly when BFT bought Carrifran, threatening our one and only bog pool, complete with dragonflies and surrounded by a mosaic of dwarf shrubs including Cloudberry, Blaeberry and the rare Bog Bilberry. The Wildwood Steering Group agreed on the need to take remedial action, but no funding for the work was available in the early years.

However, restoring peat bogs is now recognised as an essential tool in the fight against climate chaos, and during the past five years BFT has obtained several tranches of funding through the Peatland Action project administered by Scottish Natural Heritage for the Scottish Government as part of their commitment to tackle climate change. In 2019 it had a budget of £14m and it is supporting work all over Scotland to restore damaged peatlands.

In the early phases of the restoration work at Carrifran, BFT was encouraged by SNH to do informal trials of several low-tech approaches. The initial efforts involved a high camp on a very wet summer weekend, as well as some single volunteer days, to place jute mesh and later sisal mats on bare peat, as well as coir rolls, small wooden dams and bags of peat to impede runoff in developing gullies.

This work was fairly effective in halting erosion in the shallow gullies, but had little effect where gullies were deep and bare peat surfaces were nearly vertical. Problems included decay of the netting before vegetation was re-established, and failure of the steel fixing staples to hold the netting and mats in position in such exposed situations.

Strikingly successful, however, was the use of long coir rolls fixed with posts across shallow gullies near the head of the eroding area. Shallow pools floored by peat fragments were often formed above the rolls, and these were quickly colonised by vegetation, especially Bog Cotton. Even in areas where flowing water had removed all the peat, leaving rock and mineral soil exposed, coir rolls had significant effects, allowing some plants to become established.

Manual techniques using jute mesh were also employed to a limited extent at Talla & Gameshope, to try to halt erosion of small areas of bare peat low down in the upper Talla valley, close to places where remains of trees have been found preserved in the peat; this work also was rather unsuccessful.

Mechanical techniques, however, have generally proved to be effective. Additional government funding has enabled more extensive remedial action to be undertaken elsewhere at Talla & Gameshope. At Talla Moss historic damage to the almost level surface of the raised bog was caused mainly by the digging of drainage ditches that led to drying out of the peat. To reverse this, 300 peat dams were created over 5.7km of ditches which have successfully helped to raise the water level, re-wet the blanket bog and create conditions for bog mosses and other vegetation to recover.

At Crunklie Moss in the Gameshope valley, at over 500m, an area of around 17ha (2,600m$^2$ of hags) of badly hagged and eroding peat has been reprofiled using low-ground-pressure diggers in the hands of very experienced operators. The machines delicately strip back a layer of vegetation at the top of the peat hag, re-profile the vertical edge to a 30 degree slope, then gently place back the turf, sometimes supplemented with some heathery turfs borrowed from nearby. The result is an intact blanket bog surface, where sphagnum moss will re-grow and carbon will again be captured. .This technique has recently been

*Dave Bone fixing coir rolls across shallow gullies*

*Natural England visitors looking at regeneration of bog vegetation promoted by coir*

*Gully transformed into live bog*

Photo: David Long

*Crunklie Moss, an important peatland habitat rich in Sphagnum species, where reprofiling is being used to heal eroding peat hags*

Photos: Rachael Coyle

*Low ground pressure digger reprofiling a steep peat hag*

*The same site six months later*

178

*Talla Moss showing drain blocked with*
*peat in the restoration programme*

*Stump of ancient birch tree preserved in the*
*peat bank of the upper Talla burn*

## THE BODY IN THE BOG!

Somewhere in Talla Moss lies a body, once disturbed but never removed. Peter Hedley worked and lived alongside the head shepherd and his family and four other under-shepherds in the small farmhouse in the steading at Talla Linnfoots. Peter was an apprentice shepherd on the Talla & Gameshope estate as a teenager in the 1940s. His job was to look after the sheep that were hefted on the eastern side of the Gameshope Valley and twice a day he would set out from the steading and walk up the bottom of the Gameshope Valley towards Carrifran, climb to the top and return back towards Talla before descending down the face. Another shepherd looked after the sheep on the western side of the valley. Peter remembers one day when one of the other shepherds was sent with the horse and sledge up to Talla Moss to dig some peat for the fire. He returned to the farmhouse sooner than expected looking very pale and without any peat! He claimed he had uncovered a body in the bog, but once realising what it was, had quickly re-covered it and left in a hurry. He never gave an exact location and the body has never been re-found. Who it could be we shall still have to wonder.

**Tim Frost**

used on Winterhope Moss east of Loch Skeen, and BFT plans to employ it further at Talla & Gameshope on 53ha of Brad Moss, and also to complete the work at the head of the Little Firthhope Burn at Carrifran, where manual efforts have not succeeded in halting erosion in the places with the deepest gullying and most substantial areas of bare peat.

There are big issues in southwest Scotland regarding peat, as mentioned by Mary-Ann Smyth below. Where peat is eroding into watercourses, this can cause acidification, especially where underlying rock is acidic, for example around the Merrick in Galloway. Loch Grannoch is surrounded by conifers on peaty soils underlain by granite; in the past it scavenged 'acid rain' caused by pollution from industry in England, and as a result it can no longer support fish life. Galloway Fisheries Trust is experimenting with adding crushed limestone into watercourses to reverse the acidification.

*Carrifran volunteer Sunday, August 2000. Notice new deer-fenced exclosure around surviving trees in gully*

*Wildwood supporters celebrate the purchase of Carrifran on*
*Millennium Day by planting the first trees in the valley*

# WORKING WITH COMMUNITIES: WOODLANDS FOR LOCAL PEOPLE

*Anna Craigen*

Borders Forest Trust is a small organisation with great aspirations. These aspirations are dependent on the continued interest, support, passion and hard work of individuals, local communities and communities of interest, i.e. people power. Growing and maintaining relationships is a crucial component of our work.

Our Wild Heart vision is inspirational, attracting interest, support and involvement from people near and far. After many years of hard work, the visual, physical and scientific evidence of ecological restoration at Carrifran is tangible. The then and now site photographs never fail to receive gasps of amazement in any given audience. There could not be a more powerful showcase of what is possible when promoting opportunities for community involvement in other sites in the Wild Heart.

We take every opportunity to share our achievements and vision – staff, trustees and volunteers all play their part in this, whether it is manning a promotional stand at local and national events, hosting a site visit for a visiting group; sharing our news on social media or, standing in front of a TV camera on a windy hillside in driving rain. Sustaining this level of promotion is a commitment for us to ensure our continued success.

Photo: Anna Craigen

The process of new site acquisitions and ecological restoration in the Wild Heart has involved many community consultations. It is very important in the early stages of a project's inception to share the vision with local people, avoiding jargon to explain the overall aims at the site. This facilitates constructive and positive dialogue amongst a range of local participants and enables clear feedback on our proposals. Findings from these events inform the content, direction and development of the site strategy and accompanying grant applications to meet our aims and vision, whilst at the same time addressing the needs and interests of the local community.

Once things get off the ground local interest needs to be maintained whilst ensuring there is sufficient BFT staffing, funding and capacity (an ongoing challenge!). Community engagement has a cyclical nature. During our years of project delivery there are peaks and troughs in community activity. These are attributable to changes such as local enthusiasts who are passionate project promoters moving to other areas; changes in social trends; changes in the capacity and agendas of local service providers, e.g. NHS, Councils and Schools, to name but a few. Demand for projects come in surges depending on the direction and impetus for change within a given community. Borders Forest Trust aspires to meet these demands and work in partnership with local community focussed projects that suit delivery in the outdoors.

Meaningful engagement takes time. BFT has a strong commitment to establishing relationships with local individuals, groups, organisations and schools in the Wild Heart area. We have learned that it is very fruitful to identify key people within a community to enhance our outreach potential. By growing connections and befriending local people with strong local knowledge and presence, more of our opportunities, news and project information is shared. Following this up with good quality activities and projects leads to return visits, more word of mouth, wider outreach and community involvement, new ideas, increased opportunities and even bigger projects.

In the Wild Heart sites it is crucial for us to create practical opportunities for communities to get involved. In spite of our growing presence and all of the communication mechanisms available today it is still difficult to reach everyone to promote the opportunities available. Having a local presence, a staff member, is the most productive way of encouraging and building wider community engagement and keeping communities informed. A proactive and accessible member of staff in the Wild Heart is vital to its ongoing success.

*"If you want to have a look, have a go, or you want to help out, yes please, we value your involvement!"* By listening to local demand and needs, following changes in national policy, and devising and delivering a varied programme of events and training opportunities we continue to attract a diverse range of people with different interests, needs and abilities to the Wild Heart. If someone is not keen or able to remove vole guards, are they happier conducting a butterfly survey? We never like to turn away an offer from a volunteer, even if they would like to help with something we do not really need at that time. Once you get a volunteer on board, it is amazing how their services and skills fall into place and become a real asset at some point.

The health benefits of the great outdoors are well evidenced nowadays. More and more people with mental and physical health issues are being prescribed time outdoors to take part in outdoor activities, and more support agencies are looking for outdoor opportunities for their clients. The Trust aims to increase its capacity in the Wild Heart to deliver projects that address the 'Outdoor Therapy' trend. As well as experiencing an increase in demand for 'therapeutic' outdoor opportunities to promote Health and Wellbeing we regularly hear that climate change or environmental concerns are the main driving factor for individuals getting involved.

We are witnessing a growing army of keen and willing helpers keen to: reconnect with nature, take more responsibility for the environment and do something to mitigate their impact on it. Many simply desire to play a part and see positive change in large scale ecological restoration on their own turf – this is very good news for us! Without the thousands of dedicated passionate volunteers that have helped us over the last 20 years our work and achievements would quite simply not have been possible. They are our muscles, brains, eyes, dirty hands and the true heart of the Wild Heart.

*Volunteers taking a break at the car park in 2003*

*Challenging conditions!*

# A PLACE FOR PEOPLE IN ECOLOGICAL RESTORATION

*Anna Lawrence*

One of the most emotive questions associated with ecological restoration concerns the role of people: what is their place in restored ecosystems, in the activities of restoring them, in deciding what is restored and how? And which people are to be involved? The discussion becomes even more intense when the related but more ambiguous term 'rewilding' is used. For some, it is frustrating that the arguments are still raised; they feel rewilding should not drive a wedge between people and nature. But others feel that humans have caused so much damage, the only way to protect nature is for us to keep out.

Underpinning any discussion about the role of people in ecological restoration, is the fundamental question of whether people are part of the ecosystem, or not. Those old philosophical debates about 'nature vs. culture' shaping our land are highly relevant. It might seem like progress that we now have official designations of land as 'wild', for example, or 'natural', but many are critical: what is labelled 'wild' in the Scottish context often seems to echo longstanding ideas that our empty landscapes are romantic because (supposedly) untouched by humans. This romantic ideal applies particularly to the Highlands but is also celebrated in tourist literature for southern Scotland. But these landscapes are very far from natural or untouched. If these unpeopled lands are unnatural, are more peopled lands more natural? Or, if people don't belong in the landscape, what place is there for them in ecological restoration?

These issues are particularly meaningful when viewed through the lens of 'community'. Much is made of the distinction between 'communities of place' (the people who live in or near the land being restored) and 'communities of interest' (groups of people who care about the land, but may live anywhere). In practice, the two terms overlap and entangle. We can say that communities are groups of people who share an attachment to a place; and that those who live there are particularly informed and involved. The economics and the ecology of place directly affect the people who live in that place. Both communities of place and of interest are important for the values they share and the stories they tell about the land and its condition, history and meanings. These attachments, and the knowledge, experiences and livelihoods, make communities important in ecological restoration.

The organisation Rewilding Britain, which works '*to reverse ecological decline and help tackle climate breakdown*' defines four principles of rewilding. First among them is 'Rewilding embraces the role of people – and their cultural and economic connections to the land – working within a wider, healthy ecosystem.' They continue: 'Rewilding is a choice of land management. It relies on people making a collective decision to explore an alternative future for the land.'

## TUESDAY VOLUNTEERS AT CARRIFRAN

Why would a rope exactly 5.64 metres long be essential to a Tuesday Volunteer? Do the maths, and you find this is the radius of a circle enclosing 100 square metres – or 1% of a hectare. One of the jobs of the Tuesday squad was to survey the compartments – planted in an anti-clockwise sequence round the valley – as they approached their 'five-plus' inspection by a Forestry Commission Woodland Officer. Trees grow slowly on poor soils in the uplands, and final payment under the Woodland Grant Scheme depended on a certain density per hectare of trees thriving after five years. We spent many days surveying compartments, two volunteers to a rope length, categorising trees as Thriving, Struggling or Dead; and from this, decisions could be made to do additional planting or to use a granular herbicide to give the young trees a better chance, and so then qualify for the full payment. We were never convinced that the use of herbicides was effective or desirable, and chemical control of vegetation at Carrifran stopped many years ago. Poorer survival and slow growth of trees were issues mainly on the west side of the valley, compartments 4C and 4D in particular, where the ground is generally stonier and wetter than on the east. In a few doubtful cases, the Forestry Commission reasonably suggested a repeat inspection after another two years, and eventually with further and more varied planting, those compartments were signed off.

Under guidance of the site managers, Tuesday Volunteers have proved useful in a number of ways. Our core activity has been planting trees and shrubs for species enrichment. Oaks, planted after the infrequent 'mast years' when we could collect plentiful acorns reasonably close to Carrifran, have gone into drier ground, often where bracken has taken hold. We enjoy planting aspen, not quite needing to be belayed, but putting them in steep gullies was fun; the more inaccessible the sites, the more rewarding it was to get trees established. Lots of willows have gone in all over Carrifran, though we would prefer not to be quizzed on which varieties.

Remove the high Rylock fences round our temporary deer exclosures? – the Tuesday volunteers can do it, and help remove the posts and wire off site, although strainers and watergates were beyond us. Make the Paddock path easier to walk round? – volunteers will build some steps. Carry out a small mammal survey? – we can manage that and appreciate the value of s**t ('scat' of course) in identifying the residents.

And if there's nothing to build or plant, we will say yes to removing plastic tree tubes and voleguards, though with less enthusiasm. We look forward to affordable products being developed which are genuinely biodegradable at our latitude.

Over the twelve years I have been a regular at Carrifran, I have seen the valley transformed from a bald U-shaped valley with young saplings just beginning to form tree cover, to a definite

woodland habitat rising towards the skyline. We all feel pride in having been part of this transformation but it's also been very satisfying to share the camaraderie of the regular volunteers under the guidance of Hugh, George, Lynn, Phil, occasionally Ali and Keith, and now Andy. They've all been good leaders, but only one took us swimming on a hot summers' day in 2014!

**Robin Sloan**

How then can communities contribute to the choices and decisions that must be made in relation to restoring ecosystems? Conventionally, the words 'participation' and 'engagement' offer us a spectrum of ways to involve ourselves and others – with a key issue being the definition of who is taking the initiative, and who are the 'others'. The mode of engagement that gives communities (of whatever type) the most direct power over land management decisions is ownership. The mode that offers the most opportunities to the widest range of people is volunteering. In between lie questions of who is deciding, how does the law shape opportunities for deciding, and how are others involved?

The scope for communities to lead or participate in ecological restoration in Scotland is profoundly shaped by our history and policy on land ownership. Scotland has the most unequal distribution of land ownership among all the countries of Europe. That was the conclusion of a study in 2001, and despite all the land reform legislation since then, it is still the conclusion in a study carried out for the Land Commission in 2019.

Nevertheless the opportunities for community involvement have changed beyond recognition in that time. The way was pioneered by major headline-catching buyouts, many of them in the north-west and the islands, often led by communities demanding change long before they had policy on their side. Following devolution and the creation of the Scottish Parliament in 1999, new attention was turned to fairer ownership, and the first Land Reform Act was passed in 2003, creating the Community Right to Buy. Further legislation has expanded the opportunities, notably through the Community Empowerment Act which opens the way for transfer of assets from public bodies (such as local authorities) to community ownership. Neither path to ownership is easy – both buyers and sellers find the process quite challenging, and many successful purchases have avoided these legislative formalities by negotiating with a willing seller. The net effect is that, through community efforts helped at times by legislation and government funding such as the Scottish Land Fund, more than half a million acres of Scottish land are now in community ownership. It is the policy of the Scottish Government that this should be a million acres by 2020. Organisations to support them have also grown up in the lifetime of Carrifran, including membership associations (such as the Community Woodlands Association, and Community Land Scotland) and advisory services (such as the Community Ownership Support Service). So what happens when communities own land? One of the drivers of land reform is social justice, but for many this is deeply connected with environmental restoration and healing of centuries of extractive land management. The rewilding debate attracts passionate debates about the place of people in restored ecosystems. In Scotland, there is much evidence that the two go hand in hand. Community Land Scotland has produced a position paper on the subject, which reflects that community owners don't look out over a 'wild' landscape, but rather a deserted place that supports far less biodiversity than in earlier times. Far from being 'unspoiled', CLS point out, it is a spoiled landscape.

This is a powerful and interesting statement. CLS relates this situation particularly to the Highlands and Islands of Scotland, and in the context of this book, it is worth giving consideration to its application in the south of Scotland, where the loss of people from the landscape is a contemporary sore point. So far, the shift of ownership to communities has been much slower in the south, but it is fair to say that ecological restoration has been driven more by local people than by landowners. And of course, by communities of interest with a strong attachment to the place.

## WORKING WITH THE NEW WAVE OF VOLUNTEERS

Volunteering has always been the bedrock for the expansion and progression of restoration on the large sites owned by Borders Forest Trust in the Wild Heart of Southern Scotland. The amazing bunch of volunteers who have given their time and energy over the years, have allowed us to progress and move on in so many aspects of management activities across the sites; ranging from planting trees, removing plastic tree protection, repairing fences, pathwork and removing internal fences.

Around the three sites in the Wild Heart the volunteer activities vary as much as the volunteers do. For many years we have had a rock steady and very supportive regular group of volunteers at Wildwood, who know the site like the back of their hands. The work there is easing back with an average of 4000 trees going in through the winter planning season. The focus of the weekly volunteer work is now tree guard removal, and with over 600,000 trees this is not a small job! Once a year we have a high camp where we focus upon the montane planting at over 600m, which we are committed to for quite a few more years yet.

At Corehead we gather volunteers mainly from around the Moffat area. The work at this site is constant and varied: one week we may be repairing dykes, the next planting trees, removing tubes, repairing the track, the list goes on and on! This site has so much potential, due to its location, its in-bye land and perfect aspect for reforesting, it's like a flower waiting to bloom!

Talla & Gameshope is new, exciting and huge, and it is here where we are attracting large numbers of young and enthusiastic volunteers. All of a sudden the emphasis from our volunteers is not simply ecological restoration, but it has become a planetary movement, planting trees to mitigate climate change, and so many of the new wave of volunteers are now planting for the planet. Of course that goes hand in hand with our ethos for ecological restoration, though the primary motivation with many volunteers has changed. This new hunger to plant trees

brings in a lot of young volunteers, from many different backgrounds, all united in the simple act of wanting to plant a tree.

It's so exciting to see everyone from all ages, backgrounds and interests getting involved in our sites. Each person who comes out volunteering is so valuable, bringing in their energy, enthusiasm and desire to make the project work, helping us to recreate our lost landscapes and ancient woodlands once more.

**Andy Wilson**

Which brings us to other ways in which communities can take part in ecological restoration. Many see ecological restoration as an opportunity to restore the connection between people and nature. Experiences of Borders Forest Trust, and similar organisations such as Trees for Life, reflect this: the process of bringing trees and life back to the desert hillsides of the Highlands, and of the Southern Uplands, is inspiring. People who spend weekends in the cold, wet and windy hills, or even in the snow, planting trees or removing plastic tree tubes or maintaining fences, often express great joy and optimism. A modern malady of our affluent comfortable lifestyles is a lack of purpose; in confronting the devastated hillsides of the Scottish hills, volunteers from a wide range of backgrounds can

## EXTINCTION REBELLION AND TREE PLANTING

Extinction Rebellion (XR) is a newly formed world-wide organisation committed to reducing the threat of climate change. In September 2019, 70 members based in Glasgow asked if they could help BFT plant trees, as part of a 'regenerative action'. The terminology was new to us, but we are very familiar with the 'regenerative power' of planting trees; it makes you feel good! The number of volunteers was a bit daunting, but we are always up for a challenge, and we have a lot of trees to plant on our land.

At Gameshope, we are restoring a large area of upland sheepwalk to montane scrub. A mixture of birch, juniper, downy willow and dwarf birch is being planted on some of our steepest and highest land, and this sounded ideal for a large group of young and enthusiastic tree planters. We are lucky to have a bothy at Gameshope, a mile or so up the steep track from the roadhead at Talla reservoir. This is the converted byre of Gameshope cottage, where the shepherd lived, and they would have kept a house cow. The Mountain Bothy Association re-roofed and refurbished the byre, and it now has 8 bunks. This proved an ideal location to base the tree planting event, and Andy put up our massive ex-army bell tent, complete with wood-burning stove; this was to prove an invaluable warm and dry haven.

On the Friday, XR volunteers started arriving, and with the help of the quad bike and trailer, a massive amount of fresh food (all vegan), cooking pots, and tents (including a latrine tent) were taken up the track. Tents were erected, and cooking started on an open fire, whilst a pit was dug for the latrine tent some distance away. The meal was shared along with stories of what XR were trying to achieve, including the forthcoming 'Action' in London, where some were planning to be arrested, so that they could explain publicly in court what they were doing. As the chat went on late, stars appeared, and then the Milky Way, in a spectacular show of the heavens, impossible to see in light polluted cities.

Saturday dawned bright and cold, and volunteers were soon geared up and shown how and where to plant trees, with a catering team left at base. Saturday night was another bright night, and guitars were produced and songs sung. Sunday was cold and rainy, but everyone seemed to survive the night, and groups were soon back up the hill with packs of trees and planting spears. By mid afternoon, we were crowded in the shed, tent and bothy, sheltering from the hard rain and eating a fantastic risotto, produced in the camp kitchen. We planted 5,500 trees that weekend. A truly regenerative action for all concerned.

We look forward to welcoming XR and other well organised and all similarly committed volunteers back to the Wild Heart.

**Hugh Chalmers**

discover unexpected meaning. Older studies on the usefulness of volunteers seem to see them as a sort of transaction: how to get the best from free labour. But the focus now is much more on these transformative experiences. Yes, Carrifran would not exist without the tens of thousands of volunteer hours put in. But also yes, the experience of planting *Betula nana* on the high ridges of Gameshope, when you have carried in those seedlings, climbed the hills with them, and dug the holes while trying to cling to the rocky hillside with one hand, is never forgotten. That experience, that sense of contributing, and the new awareness of what is possible, is just as important as the dwarf birches finding their feet at the newly rediscovered treeline.

*Extinction Rebellion campers relaxing by the Gameshope bothy*

So communities can be involved by taking control, and they can be involved by immersing themselves in the landscape and in the experiences of restoring the ecosystems. Members of the community include those who live on that land, visit that land to work with it, have specialist knowledge to share about that land. The outer transformation, the restoration of the ecosystem that we inhabit, is mirrored by an inner ecological restoration, of meaning and connection. A restored ecology is a human ecology; we plan to be part of the future, and we gain immeasurably from the processes of making that future.

# SOME THINGS GOING ON AROUND US

## Kielderhead Wildwood and the Carrifran connection
### Adrian Manning

As a native of Northumberland, I grew up in landscapes very similar to, indeed contiguous with, those of the Southern Uplands. These 'Borderlands', dotted with rural towns and villages in the river valleys, and fells, moorland and plantation forest in the uplands between, are also defined by another feature; they are almost completely denuded of their native woodland. As a child I would often dream of hiking though the vast, wild upland woodlands that no longer existed, full of exciting animals that are now extinct and I wondered: *could we ever bring those woodlands back?*

*Ancient Scots pine tree at Kielder with an embryonic new wildwood behind it.*
*Inset: recently planted Alders by the Scaup burn*

While studying at the University of Edinburgh in the early 1990s, I was hugely influenced by the pioneering thinking about ecological restoration happening in Scotland at the time. Most notably the work and long-term vision of Alan Watson Featherstone and Trees for Life. Back then, what has become more commonly termed 'rewilding', seemed far off in the future, and only possible in the distant Scottish Highlands. I yearned for rewilding closer to home, but it seemed impossible.

It was around this time that Philip and Myrtle Ashmole and colleagues held the visionary *Restoring Borders Woodlands* conference in 1993. This ultimately led to the creation of the Carrifran Wildwood. I remember being hugely inspired by the articles in the proceedings of that conference, and the subsequent journey of Borders Forest Trust towards ownership of Carrifran on 1st January 2000. In particular, two things really struck me about the project. First, that my seemingly impossible dream of wild upland woodlands in the Borderlands might actually be possible. Second, that university academics, expert practitioners and the community could bring about profound change on the ground if they worked together towards a common vision. I took these ideas with me as I departed for New Zealand in 1996, and when I ultimately became an academic at the Australian National University (ANU) in Canberra.

While developing my research agenda in conservation biology and restoration ecology in Australia, I retained my interest in ecological restoration in the uplands of the UK, and I followed the progress at Carrifran closely. Philip Ashmole and I corresponded about the project, and also about the potentially native Scots pines at Williams Cleugh, in Kielder Forest – just over the border in England. I had been interested in these almost mythical pines since the 1990s, but only learned the bioclimatic modelling techniques needed to better understand them when I joined the Australian National University. In a collaboration between Australian colleagues and those in northern England and Scotland, we were able to provide insights into the potential nativeness of the pines. We were also able to identify potentially suitable sites for pines in future wildwoods in southern Scotland and northern England; these included areas within Carrifran and Talla & Gameshope. Our findings also led to Philip and his colleagues collecting seed from the old Kielder trees over many seasons, planting the progeny near treeline at Carrifran.

Through the discussions that Philip and I had, which included our friend and colleague Angus Lunn of the Northumberland Wildlife Trust (NWT), we wrote a proposal for the creation of the 'Kielderhead Wildwood' – which would include native pine woodlands like those found in the Scottish Highlands. The NWT and Forestry Commission liked the proposal (and there were a number of visits of staff to Carrifran), and it was developed by NWT into a successful National Lottery Heritage Fund bid for £354,000. The project is now well under way, led by Project Coordinator Heinz Traut, and is gaining a lot of support from volunteers, along with growing multi-disciplinary research interest from universities in the region. Thus the development of the Kielderhead Wildwood is very much following the path of, and is inspired by, Carrifran. I would argue Carrifran is as much an idea, or way of thinking about ecological restoration, as it is a geographic location. In the future, we hope to see the realisation of an even broader landscape vision beyond Kielderhead. So, thanks to the catalytic effect of Carrifran, hiking through vast upland wildwood in the Borderlands may be more than a dream in the future.

# Mountain woodland in the Galloway Forest Park
## Rob Soutar

Photo: Andrew Jarrott

## INTRODUCTION

Galloway Forest Park extends to 70,000 hectares. Just over half of this area is productive conifer forest. The rest is mountain, moorland & grassland, a third of which is designated for nature conservation. There is only about 600 hectares of ancient and long established woodland, including the iconic Glentrool oakwoods. But there is already as much as 2,200 hectares of new native woodland which has largely been initiated following clearance of timber crops. Let me explain…….

Forest Enterprise Scotland (now Forestry and Land Scotland) has been restructuring the forest to diversify its age structure and species composition and improve upon a range of environmental objectives. This will permit a sustainable timber harvest in the future and has already opened up watercourses and created a new habitat network that runs through and interlocks with the conifer forest. Stands of planted broadleaved trees are embedded amongst areas that were deliberately left unplanted when adjacent timber crops were restocked. The network links existing native woodlands and follows watercourses from the treeline down to sea level. Natural regeneration of trees and shrubs is transforming much of this into an open form of new native woodland. This is assisted by the periodic culling of intruding conifers near watercourses in keeping with The Forests and Water Guidelines.

In this chapter I explore the further plans in place to double the extent of this new native woodland. This is to meet public expectations of the Galloway Forest Park in terms of landscape, biodiversity and tourism. It follows at least two decades of advocacy and support for further diversification of this type. The focus is now on transforming the upper forest edge into an open woodland of broadly natural character.

## SOME PEOPLE

The zone of climatically dwarfed trees and shrubs that once linked forest and open mountaintops has almost vanished from Scotland. Happily the early trail blazers, including the legendary Dr Derek Ratcliffe, established that fragments had survived in Galloway. This later inspired a generation of volunteer naturalists including Ian Murgatroyd, Peter Harrison, Peter Norman and Richard Mearns, as well as me. This enriched my day job as the Forest District Manager at the time. And in our spare time, we free climbed, scoured the cliffs and crags and some of us even swam to islands in the hill lochs in search of juniper, willows and other woody plants, in a phenomenon sometimes called 'Extreme Botany'.

In the first decade of this century the conservation and community organisations on the Galloway Forest District Advisory Panel energetically advocated the expansion of native woodlands. The Cree Valley Community Woodlands Trust, led then by Peter Hopkins (later by Peter Robinson and Linda Moorhouse) was on the ground planting with the aim of creating and connecting native woods from the treeline to the coast. Scottish Natural Heritage and the Montane Scrub Action Group also influenced strategy and provided specialist support.

*Ian Murgatroyd collecting samples of willows for identification from Craiglee*

Photo: Rob Soutar

This atmosphere of 'extreme botany' and commitment to conserve and expand native woods inspired our participation in the Action for Mountain Woodland project (2005 -2010). 'AMWood' recruited volunteers to assess the state of Scotland's threatened mountain woodlands and involved the wider public in practical restoration work. In the Galloway Forest Park volunteers surveyed and studied self-sown native trees and shrubs and gathered seed and cuttings to grow on new planting stock, particularly of downy willow *Salix lapponum* and juniper *Juniperus communis*.

## MOUNTAIN WOODLAND REMNANTS

Our expectations of supplementing the few existing records of remnants of treeline and montane scrub were initially modest, but as the work progressed remarkable new examples were found on cliffs, crags and islands in lochs above the modern forest. Treeline communities, now restricted to tiny fragments, include species such as Juniper, Rowan (*Sorbus aucuparia*), Downy Birch (*Betula pubescens*), Aspen (*Populus tremula*), willows (*Salix* spp.) and roses (*Rosa* spp.) especially the Burnet Rose (*Rosa spinosissima*) and stretch out to the scrubline where we found additional species often regarded as high altitude specialists; Downy Willow and above that Dwarf Willow (*Salix herbacea*) in the so-called 'bare hilltops'.

These montane species may seem out of place in the relatively low lying Southern Uplands (Merrick, which is the highest peak, is only 843m a.s.l.). However, the climatic

*Forestry Commission staff and members of the Montane Scrub
Action Group inspecting newly discovered prostrate Juniper
in a rocky cleft at the Bennan demonstration site*

limitations to the growth of trees and shrubs cannot be forecast by altitude alone. The natural treeline may in places reflect exposure to winter gales, but the AMWood surveys suggest that summer drought can be more influential in limiting the stature of trees and shrubs. We found treeline and scrub communities at lower altitudes on sites with minimal soil depth and year-round exposure. In such places, the tallest trees recorded are only a few metres high, allowing light demanding shrubs to co-exist with trees that would otherwise shade them out. We found the vast majority of Galloway's juniper on cliffs and bluffs, most commonly between 300 and 400 m asl. – all of this is of an obligate ground hugging form of *Juniperus communis* ssp *communis* (it is not *J.c.* ssp *nana*) that would be shaded out by vigorous grasses and dwarf shrubs, never mind trees.

## NEW MOUNTAIN WOODLAND

Over the years, charismatic wildlife such as black grouse and dense flocks of bullfinches were often observed along the edges between moorland and planted forest. This started us thinking about creating a forest edge of open woodland and scrub as a means to broaden the edge habitat for wildlife and improve the landscape.

The original intention was that this 'moorland fringe' would be created largely through natural regeneration, mainly on sites disturbed by timber harvesting. This seems to work at high elevation on modest slopes with peaty soils and a suitable seed source nearby. Following felling of the conifer crops 25 to 50% of suitable sites have regenerated with Eared Willow (*Salix aurita*), Grey Willow (*Salix cinerea*) and their hybrids (*Salix* x *multinervis*). However, Sitka Spruce *Picea sitchensis* can also feature prominently.

Natural regeneration, often of downy birch, rowan and/or willows, can also be successful after felling on podsols, brown earths and rankers. Such sites, however, are more likely to revert to rushes and grassland which quickly becomes resistant to colonisation by trees. We do not as yet fully understand the processes involved, but we do know that success is dependent in large part on the size and fecundity of seed sources.

FCS, CVCWT and SNH worked together to test and improve the specification of this 'moorland fringe'. An SNH-funded project of the British Trust for Ornithology (BTO) found 59 bird species in patches of moorland fringe and tentatively concluded that the highest value to birds is when woodland cover extends to about 30%. Most of the survey examples were predominantly open Sitka Spruce scrub with only a few broadleaves.

However, project partners wanted to see a more reliable and quicker transition to woodland dominated by native species, so 'woodland fringe' was introduced; this describes the prescription of extensive planting of mainly Rowan and Birch where there is no adequate seed source nearby. On a smaller scale, enrichment planting of a wider range of native species is undertaken to act as seed sources in the future.

One of the biggest requirements in achieving this vision is the control of browsing by deer and in places, feral goats and sheep. Grazing pressure has to be low to permit the creation of continuous woodland of any species other than Sitka spruce and arguably two or three other resistant conifers. Currently we are able to achieve a scattered, clumped and very open type of scrub that meets our needs provided an adequate seed source exists nearby. As the level of browsing is reduced further, we hope to increase the level of natural regeneration of native species.

### THE DEMONSTRATION SITE AND GARDEN

Inspired by Borders Forest Trust at Carrifran and The National Trust for Scotland at Ben Lawers we have planted a 300 hectare new native woodland on the Bennan hill which can be experienced from the Merrick hill path. In addition to its educational purpose it is hoped that the Juniper and Downy Willow seed orchards established on the Bennan will enhance the distribution of seed over the Merrick range though bird and wind dispersal. Whilst the Bennan is deer fenced, mountain hares are damaging planted broadleaves, but there is no plan to cull this species due to its declining numbers in the Southern Uplands. Volunteers from the Cree Valley Community Woodlands Trust created a Mountain Woodland Garden in the car park of Glentrool Visitor Centre so that the visiting public can safely see species typical of the montane scrub found in Scotland.

### GENETIC VARIATION

Genetic conservation is at the core of our strategy to expand Mountain Woodland in the Galloway Forest Park. Andrew Jarrott has taken the lead in multiplying stock using clone banks, seed orchards and micro-propagation. The new supply chain produces many times more plants each year than remain in the native Galloway populations of Aspen, Juniper and Downy Willow. Unusually, all of the thousands of Juniper plants produced from about 60 separate clones retain the ground hugging form and so do all of the 120 or so plants grown from seed by CVCWT volunteers.

### POSTSCRIPT

Forestry and Land Scotland has shared our endeavours and experience in Galloway with several other Mountain Woodland projects under development in the Highlands. Richard Thompson (FLS Native Woodland Ecologist) now sits on the Montane Scrub Action Group and is co-ordinating FLS activity in partnership with The National Trust for Scotland, Trees for Life and The John Muir Trust.

# Reviving the Galloway hills: repairing peatlands
## Mas Smyth

Borders Forest Trust's work inspires and gives confidence to others. One example is the work of environmental charities in South West Scotland, where Crichton Carbon Centre and Galloway Fisheries Trust have been collaborating to restore ecosystems in the Galloway Hills. Using the collaborative ethos of the Galloway and Southern Ayrshire Biosphere partnership, we've begun to work out how to restore the peatland and bring back the wild salmon to the rivers.

Galloway rivers used to be rich in wild fish, but during the 1970s, the salmon and sea-trout numbers crashed. Since then, the Galloway rivers became famous as some of the most acidified catchments in the UK. We used to blame this on acid rain, hard rock, and the way that conifers capture atmospheric pollutants. Only recently have we realised that it's not just the conifers and the granite that are to blame, but the draining and deep ploughing of the peat on which the conifers had been planted.

The Galloway Hills are much wetter than Carrifran, and although woodland is natural on our slopes, a blanket of peat should cover our wildest, wettest and flattest ground. But Galloway has been subject to more than a century of efforts to drain the peat and create farmland, and latterly forest plantation. Luckily for the carbon, draining doesn't work properly on peat: the climate is too wet and the peat is too deep. Despite this, ditches and channels were dug across the moorland, and an even more intensive system of deep ploughing and ditching has been used to plant conifers. But conifers planted on deep peat don't thrive. Even the sheep prefer drier ground. The peatland ecosystem had been damaged, and for little benefit. And damaged peatland is not just ugly, it causes trouble. It's a triple whammy: firstly, man-made ditches flood much peatier water into the rivers than is natural, so the rivers become acidic, dirty and warm. Secondly, and bad for the climate, drained peat dries, erodes and loses its

*Eroding blanket bog*

*Peaty ditch in a conifer plantation*

carbon. Thirdly, after a rainstorm, the ditches sluice too rapidly into the rivers, flooding downstream towns.

Climate change means we need to keep the carbon in the ground; and our increasingly long droughts and heavy rainstorms mean we need to keep the ground soft and able to soak up and store the rainwater. Restored peatland can continue its natural function: storing carbon and soaking up rain.

Restoring blanket bog on drained moorland is relatively easy: first you map the ditches, then you block the ditches using low ground-pressure excavators, making hundreds of small peat dams at intervals along each ditch so that the water can no longer flow off the moor. More complicated, but even more important, is restoring the extensive areas of eroding bare peat we see across many of our hills, like up at Little Firthhope. Here, we aim to stop erosion and peat loss by revegetating bare peat badlands, gently smoothing peat haggs, and helping seal and heal eroding gullies.

Restoring blanket bog from beneath conifer plantations is surprisingly effective, as we now have a range of techniques we can use to block the drains, flatten out the ridges and furrows and allow the water table to behave more naturally.

## HOW IT CAME ABOUT

Back in 2008, after the RSPB had begun work in the Flow Country, and we had set up the Crichton Carbon Centre in Dumfries, I was asked to calculate roughly how much carbon could be saved by restoring bogs. This proved more difficult than I had expected, and took almost five years, with a team of scientists from Scotland, Wales and England. In the

*Peaty ditch on a moor*

*Blanket peat damaged by fire, cultivation and drainage*

end, we produced the metrics and protocols which underlie the Peatland Code, and proved that although peatlands sink as much carbon as woodlands, the main trick is to stop the peatbogs from losing their carbon.

Meanwhile, Jamie Ribbons and his team at Galloway Fisheries Trust were trying to bring back salmon to the Galloway rivers. Fish eggs and young salmon and seatrout were

Photo: Mas Smyth

*Restored Sphagnum bog*

dying, because many of the headwaters flush with acid during the first flood after the spring drought. Only the toughest brown trout could survive. Jamie's team had hatched and released salmonids into the rivers, and (with Cree Valley Community Woodlands) had restored native woodlands along the river banks to create dappled shade and habitat, but the river chemistry was still wrong.

It was only when the two teams got together that they realised they were looking at two ends of the same problem: the damaged peat on the Galloway hills. By around 2015, Clifton Bain and others at RSPB and IUCN had spot-lit the European-funded peatland restoration in the Flow Country and the Pennines, and created a political focus which galvanised the Scottish Government into funding their own peatland restoration. After all, much of Scotland's carbon emissions were coming from damaged peatlands. Through SNH's Peatland Action they provided funds and systems, and a network of peatland restoration advisors. Emily Taylor was a key player, she had worked on the peatland carbon metrics at Crichton Carbon Centre, so she connected Peatland Action with Galloway Fisheries Trust… and talked to the landowners, Forestry, and SNH, showing how it could make sense to restore the habitat, block the ditches, repair the peatlands, re-wild some of our wetlands … and the rest will be history, we hope.

By 2019, a number of projects have been undertaken to restore previously afforested ground which proved the work could be done. This has now paved the way for a much more

Photo: Mas Smyth

*Is the peat good and quaking healthy? (just checking)*

strategic, and ambitious, approach to prioritising peatland restoration in areas of poor water quality and timber growth on both private and publicly owned land. Most of the restored moorland is recovering well, as open blanket bogs and raised bogs, soft wet habitats of Sphagnum Moss and Heather, Bog-myrtle and Sundew, frogs and dragonflies. Windswept. Treacherous. Wild.

So BFT's dream of reviving the wild heart of southern Scotland is a dream of many parts… A dream of beauty, nature, global climate and local ecosystems. And people. People who work through rain and wind and sun, behind the scenes and on the hills, to help nature recover.

# Southwest Community Woodlands and Taliesin
## Ed Iglehart

1n 1995, the vision of a Millennium Forest stirred the enthusiasm of many people all over Scotland. There were two major ideas: first, to extend and improve native woodland areas throughout the country, and second, to re-establish and strengthen the connections between communities and their local natural history.

When Reforesting Scotland held its annual Gathering at Laurieston Hall in 1995, there was much talk of the Millennium Forest project, and Tim Stead, an old friend, pointedly noted that there were no proposals from Southwest Scotland, the most forested part of Scotland. He and Eoin Cox, stalwarts of Borders Community Woodlands (Wooplaw Community Woodland), bullied Alyne Jones and myself into trying to organise local interest. Alyne organised a meeting of potentially interested folk, and a local voluntary association, Southwest Community Woodlands (SCW) formed, its core being made up of folk whose interests in local environmental matters had come together earlier in response to proposals to bury nuclear waste in the granite hills at the heart of the Galloway Forest Park, the bulk of which lies in the west of the Stewartry of Kirkcudbright.

Southwest Community Woodlands Trust (SWCWT) was formed to provide the corporate identity required by funding bodies, most notably the Millennium Forest for Scotland Trust

*Taliesin provides opportunities for children of all ages*

*Trees provide a third dimension*

(MFST). The model constitution was identical to that of Borders Forest Trust (BFT). In our MFST project we planted trees from 'Watershed to Waterfoot', started a tree nursery and mounted two woodland festivals. We now own and manage 23 acres as a growing woodland and activity centre.

A divergence of priorities between MFST (countable trees and hectares) and SWCWT (people, plants, creatures, places and their relationships) resulted in a cordial separation. SWCWT continues to develop in association with a number of local initiatives, including riparian planting along the upper Urr and elsewhere, an 'Orchard and Wild Harvest' project and the continuing development of our community woodland centre at Taliesin where members and others gather for skill-sharing and good food, Forest Schools, semi-annual 'Kids Camps' (families) and summer 'Teen Camps' with minimal adult supervision. We seem to have taken the Millennium Forest's second aim to heart.

The trees we planted from watershed to waterfoot in the early days are now canopied woodland, and Taliesin has changed from bare grazings to a wooded landscape with at least twice as many self-sown trees as there are planted ones. There are ponds and wetlands too. And there is much of the music of birds and happy children.

We have good relations with Scottish Forestry, who manage the public forests adjoining Taliesin on three sides, and play a part in cooperative restoration of disused hazel coppicing on Potterland Hill, a 'Plantation on Ancient Woodland Site' (PAWS) undergoing transition towards native woodland in line with current policy.

The Wildwood idea (now Carrifran and the Wild Heart) has from the beginning, been a constant inspiration. We are in many ways a smaller sibling of the Wildwood and Borders Forest Trust. Children of Tim Stead. Small is also Good.

# Cree Valley Community Woodlands Trust
## Peter Robinson

The Cree Valley in Wigtownshire near Newton Stewart contains some beautiful remnants of the former extensive ancient broadleaf woodlands. Once important in local industries, these woodland remnants are today recognised for their value in contributing to biodiversity, recreation and tourism. Cree Valley Community Woodlands Trust (CVCWT) was established in 1999 with the aim of creating a mosaic of habitats to form corridors, linking these existing remnants from 'source to sea'.

Run by a Project Manager and an Administrator, CVCWT has always had a high reliance on invaluable volunteer involvement and has had many participating volunteers, always with a core of long-term volunteers.

In the early years CVCWT administered an EU LIFE project involved in 'Sustainable forestry to protect water quality and aquatic biodiversity'. This work was continued later when large tracts of riparian habitat bordering the River Cree and its tributaries were freed of invasive conifer regeneration and intermittently planted with native broadleaved trees. This will create varying levels of shade and light along the river banks and provide detritus for aquatic invertebrates. The recovery of the River Cree from acidification is still ongoing but the basis for recovery has been established.

*Cree Valley Community Woodlands Trust tree nursery*

*Downy Willow cuttings and other trees, many of them destined for Borders Forest Trust*

As formerly afforested areas have been cleared of conifers CVCWT has selectively planted these areas with locally appropriate native broadleaved tree species and along with natural regeneration, aimed to create a native broadleaved woodland of national importance and high conservation and landscape value, providing opportunities for species to colonise the new woodlands from established ancient and semi-natural habitats. Continued removal of conifer regeneration is a vital part of this process.

To help satisfy the need for local provenance trees for planting projects, CVCWT set up its own nursery in 2010. Volunteers collect seed from local woodlands and have established a productive organic tree nursery, producing some 10,000 or more trees per year, now also supplying trees to other woodland creation projects including Borders Forest Trust. Seed was also collected for the Millennium Seed Bank at Kew Gardens.

CVCWT`s tree nursery lies at the heart of Barclye, an extension of the RSPB`s Wood of Cree reserve, already the largest ancient oak woodland in southern Scotland. CVCWT volunteers have contributed to the planting of 200,000 trees in this area through providing and planting trees to extend this woodland and to create more woodland pasture.

CVCWT have also worked closely with Forest and Land Scotland (FLS) in establishing high elevation montane scrub and 'fringe' woodland. This type of high level scattered scrub and woodland would surely have been a common feature of the Galloway Hills before extensive grazing, and the return of this habitat will enhance the landscape, reduce acidification in the catchment zones and increase biodiversity, providing valuable habitat for endangered species such as Black Grouse. A clone bank of Downy Willow (*Salix lapponum*) growing at the nursery, obtained from the few remaining shrubs in the hills, has enabled CVCWT volunteers to take several thousand cuttings each year which are being used as the backbone of these plantings.

The promotion of native woodlands to the public and involving the local community have always been foremost with CVCWT and many projects have taken place involving schools, Newton Stewart Activity and Resource Centre, other groups and the general public. Woodland archaeology, provision of easy access paths, interpretation panels, publication of leaflets and newsletters and presentations have enabled public engagement.

# From Carrifran to the Lowther Hills
## Anjo Abelaira

Nested in the Lowther Hills, west of the Moffat Hills, are the former lead mining villages of Wanlockhead and Leadhills. At 400m over sea level, Scotland's Highest Villages are encircled by a similar, deforested landscape as Carrifran was not long ago.

In 2014 community land buyout initiatives were put forward in Leadhills and soon after in Wanlockhead. With spoil tips and post-industrial remains still blighting the local surroundings, the community placed ecological restoration as one of their core visions for a future community-owned land. Carrifran was used as a case example by the buyout group in Leadhills and Wanlockhead.

Buyout negotiations are still ongoing at the time of printing this book. However, in 2018 one of the local community groups, Lowther Hills Ski Club, secured 3ha of land to start a pilot planting scheme on Lowther Hill between 550m and 700m.

The initial planting scheme of 3,000 trees was completed in autumn 2019 with a selection of native species which largely followed the example of Carrifran. The new woodland, by the ski slopes of Lowther Hill and the Southern Upland Way, will provide a valuable improvement to a landscape that has been devoid of trees for centuries. It will now be enjoyed by thousands of visitors, hill walkers, skiers and outdoor enthusiasts for years to come. And in due course, once the local community land buyouts have been completed, the experience gained by the pilot planting at Lowther Hill will be key for a more extensive environmental regeneration around Scotland's Highest Villages.

*Planting at about 670m beside the ski slope on Lowther Hill,*
*with the club house below and Wanlockhead in the distance*

# Gorrenberry Jubilee Wood
## Jane Bower

Gorrenberry Farm is a 1000ha hill farm in the Hermitage Valley, Scottish Borders. Its lower boundary is Hermitage Water, at about 200m, and it runs up steep hills to 620m. It was mainly a heavily grazed sheep farm in 2011 when it was purchased from its previous owner. In 2008, 101ha of Sitka Spruce had been planted and 74ha of native broadleaves had been planted along the burns, but sheep and deer had inflicted considerable damage.

The sheep were then removed, an ecological survey undertaken and a further 366ha of native broadleaves were planted in 2012-13 with the help of a grant. The trees are not fenced but about 50 roe deer have been taken every year. Vole damage has necessitated some replanting with vole guards. Unfortunately the ash trees planted on the lower slopes are showing signs of ash dieback and are being monitored

*Golden-ringed Dragonfly*

closely. Otherwise the trees have generally done well, with strong growth at the lower levels and bushier, slower growth higher up the hills. Plenty of flowers, butterflies and birds in summer. Tilhill manage it and have taken great interest in this ecological restoration project. Signs indicate the easiest routes for walkers. More information is at www.gorrenberry.org.uk.

# Langholm Moor: community regeneration and ecological restoration
## Kevin Cumming

Langholm is a small town with a big history in the Scottish Borderlands. Previously a textile capital of Scotland with famous sons such as Thomas Telford, Hugh MacDiarmid and the family of astronaut Neil Armstrong, it seemed that Langholm's future was bright. However the demise of most of the textile industry has left empty buildings with only the echo of looms weaving, and has led to rural challenges similar to those seen throughout the rest of Scotland. The young generation move away for university education or to find jobs and the ageing population becomes more isolated. Although conifer plantations have sprung up all around and wind turbines appear on the horizons the benefit to the community is hard to see. Is Langholm about to receive the catalyst it needs to boost regeneration and the dawn of a new beginning for this special place?

In the Spring of 2019 a wonderful opportunity arose for reviving not only the community of Langholm but the biodiversity of the Southern Uplands with the sale of Langholm Moor by Buccleuch Estates. At around 25,000 acres (over 10,000ha), much of it is designated as a Site of Special Scientific Interest (SSSI) for its geological formations, upland breeding bird

*Langholm Moor, with riparian native woodland*

Photo: Kevin Cumming

Photo: Kevin Cumming

*Red Grouse and Blackcock*

assemblage and upland habitat, as well as being a nationally important Special Protection Area (SPA) for breeding hen harriers, the UK's most persecuted bird of prey. This was a once in a lifetime opportunity for the people of Langholm.

Up stepped the community of Langholm led by local development trust, The Langholm Initiative, seeking to buy by mutual agreement the western half of the moor for the benefit of both nature and the local economy. On the eastern half of the moor the town of Newcastleton investigated a purchase of their side and ultimately decided on a modest 700 acre project that they felt fulfilled their community needs.

Wisely securing early support from local and national political representatives regardless of party, the communities of Langholm and Newcastleton successfully negotiated a pause in the sale with Buccleuch Estates. It was then agreed that both communities would be given time to investigate the feasibility of community ownership of Langholm Moor.

In the months that followed, the Langholm Initiative engaged expert advice from SNH, RSPB, Borders Forest Trust and the John Muir Trust. They have begun developing ambitious plans to convert what was formerly one of Scotland's most well-known grouse moors into a community run nature reserve. After a rapid fund raising effort which saw donations from far and wide, a feasibility study has been commissioned. This will form the basis for the business case on which to secure support from the Scottish Government for the acquisition. It is anticipated that a fundraising campaign will be required to put the business case into practice. The results from the feasibility study are keenly anticipated.

Many people may be familiar with Langholm Moor, which has been the site of two scientific studies regarding land management for the purpose of driven grouse shooting. The latest of these studies, The Langholm Moor Demonstration Project, ran for nearly ten years and produced its final report in 2019. The overall aim of the study was to establish driven grouse shooting as the economic driver for conservation work on an SSSI and an SPA. It also hoped to bring some resolution to the issue of raptor persecution on grouse moors. Tactics

*Male Hen Harriers over Langholm Moor*

*Little Tarras valley, Langholm Moor, with dense birch regeneration in some places*

*Tarras Water, Langholm Moor*

such as diversionary feeding for hen harriers were deployed to reduce the perceived impact on grouse. In the end the project was brought to a close after there was an apparent failure in being able to get the grouse numbers to a level that could be shot economically.

Langholm Moor also holds immense cultural significance to local people. The annual Common Riding celebration marks the boundaries of the common moss on the moor. This incredible display of community solidarity has taken place every year for over 200 years. There are historic disputes regarding the ownership of the common moss which are still deeply felt today by the people of Langholm. Through a community ownership, the people of Langholm will have secured the land for generations to come.

Land reform in Scotland is a hot topic and a community buyout of this scale has so far never happened in the South of Scotland; but what will the people of Langholm do with the land? The Langholm Initiative has a plan and at its heart this project is about building on the incredible natural and cultural heritage.

It is not only important to the people of Langholm but on a global scale it is important in the fight against one of the biggest threats humanity has ever faced, climate change.

The Langholm Initiative is likely to seek to have the land designated as a National Nature Reserve. This is a landscape scale climate action project and on this vast area of land we will aim to reverse decades of drainage to our vital peatlands, promote the natural regeneration of native woodland and provide a mosaic of habitats and species that make the area more resilient to climate change.

Our vision will encompass sustainable and responsible outdoor tourism. We hope to deliver environmental education and try to reconnect people with the land around them. In this pioneering project our hope is to demonstrate that nature based tourism can be an economic driver of conservation. The community are also investigating the feasibility of small scale renewable energy on the least sensitive parts of the sale area which will bring a direct benefit to the community. Sensitive and sustainable development ownership of the land could be the first step in the regeneration of a once vibrant town and a giant leap for communities taking responsibility for the natural environment on their doorstep. The Langholm Moor Community Buyout is a project of vision and of hope at a time when humanity needs it most and perhaps above all it is a project for our future.

# LOOKING TO THE FUTURE: ECOLOGICAL RESTORATION, CLIMATE CHANGE AND THE BIODIVERSITY CRISIS

*John Thomas*

"It's a green island in the midst of a denuded landscsape, an oasis for plants and wildlife in a sea of bare hills" thus spoke a visitor from the National Trust for Scotland as we emerged onto the plateau from the Carrifran valley below and viewed the hills far and wide around us.

Carrifran Wildwood is not sufficient in itself. We need to do more, much more, if we are to recover the wildlife – plants, insects, birds and animals that once flourished in these hills and with them the diversity of livelihoods that they will support even in the modern world.

Reviving the plants, woodland and wildlife of the Wild Heart of Southern Scotland is part of a wider picture of how the uplands can deliver the public benefits of ecological restoration, namely storing carbon, combating biodiversity loss, reducing air and water pollution, improving health and well-being, improving flood management and outdoor education and learning.

The rapidity of rising carbon dioxide ($CO_2$) levels in the atmosphere resulting in global warming and more frequent extreme weather events is of grave concern. Restoring rich and diverse plant-life is one of the simplest, cheapest and most beneficial ways of combating these rising $CO_2$ levels. Mature trees, because of their size and extensive canopies, store carbon in their wood and as leaves and woody debris builds up on the forest floor so a proportion of the carbon from their leaf fall is stored as organic soils accumulating beneath the canopy, a change we have observed in the first 20 years of the Wildwood in the Carrifran valley. The roughly 600 hectares (1,500 acres) of planted and planned woodland across the three sites of Carrifran, Corehead and Talla & Gameshope, plus the recovery of extensive areas of sphagnum combined with peat restoration at three peat bogs and the planting of montane scrub on the site, once well established will sequester around 500 tons of carbon each year averaged over 100 years.

What we are showing at Carrifran, Corehead and now Talla & Gameshope is that unimproved grassland high up in the hills is capable of growing rich and diverse woodland and forests if a little less rapidly than lowland plantations and therefore a little slower to store carbon.

An interesting variation on this theme is that on the lower ground at Corehead we intend to develop a small productive forest of mixed species managed on a continuous cover basis along with some coppiced woodland. This may result in increased carbon storage as there will be a higher proportion of young growth than in a forest allowed to grow old without any intervention but this will be offset by more disturbance of the forest floor and consequent release of carbon when it comes to the extraction of selected trees. The extraction will be small scale and may be minimised by using 'low tech.' approaches such as horse logging but that will be a matter for the next generation to decide. The trees have yet to be planted!

## CONCLUSION

The land and how we use it will play a vital part in meeting the huge challenges set by climate change and biodiversity loss. Whilst this is a global issue we cannot confidently and honestly call for others to take action if we leave our own backyard in the uplands denuded and impoverished.

The Wild Heart based on the Talla-Hart Fell Wild Land Area can contribute to tackling these great global issues, especially if they are part of a Land Use Strategy which takes in the surrounding landscapes and valleys. It would become the wild core of more actively managed and farmed areas in each of the main valleys surrounding it, similar to the model of the Biosphere in Dumfries and Galloway.

Reviving the Wild Heart is not a task that can be completed in a single generation. The project is already on a sufficient scale to attract a new generation of volunteers inspired by the opportunity to help plant and care for the woodland and plants in such a wild and impressive landscape. Through volunteering they are being equipped to help sustain and maintain the Wild Heart in perpetuity in order to deliver those intergenerational goals set out in the bullet points at the start of this Part of the book.

The Wild Heart of Southern Scotland will provide a wonderful naturally wild place to visit, rich in wildlife and plants comparable to anywhere else in Scotland. As the land recovers its heart and wildlife begins to flourish so it becomes more and more rewarding to visit. There is so much to observe and so much to enjoy that even those who are feeling stressed or at odds with the world come back refreshed and revived. The Wild Heart will attract visitors from far and wide and be easily accessible to everyone in central Scotland and the north of England, providing footfall and customers for many local businesses generating jobs and income.

Photo: John Thomas

# EPILOGUE
# REFLECTIONS ON A JOURNEY

*Myrtle and Philip Ashmole*

As you have read through – or browsed in – the diverse sections of this book you will have become aware of the magnitude of the voluntary as well as professional efforts to revive the countryside in the Southern Uplands of Scotland, welcoming nature back to a restored landscape. On a worldwide scale what we at Borders Forest Trust and other organisations are doing is tiny, but it is a contribution. This is something that so many people can play a part in.

Our personal journey started half a century ago. We had lived in the United States for a decade and had travelled to many wild areas. We were appalled by Rachel Carson's 1962 book *Silent Spring* and Paul Ehrlich's 1968 *The Population Bomb*. We had three children, but Myrtle became intensely aware of the problem of human population growth and was an early organiser for *Zero Population Growth* (ZPG) in eastern USA. We were also influenced by the work of our mentor David Lack, who emphasised the role of competition for resources in limiting animal populations. So, if humans became too numerous for our resources, our numbers would eventually be controlled by famine, pestilence and war. We hoped that as intelligent beings, we would be able to do better than that.

In the same period we also became uneasy at the anthropocentric tone of nearly all discussions of the environment. Humans naturally strive to ensure the welfare and survival of our descendants, but not many people seemed to be thinking about the other living organisms with which we share the world, and many of which provide us with benefits. Their demise is a by-product of our failure to accept responsibility for the damage caused by our surging populations and careless lifestyles.

Near where we lived in Connecticut was a tiny patch of 'wild' land between housing developments, and passing it on the way to school our eight year old daughter commented that it should have a high fence built round it to keep people out, leaving it entirely for nature. This idea, that some space should be found for wild nature even in the crowded modern world, stayed with us, but we only slowly began to respond to the challenge of doing something about it.

Soon after moving to Scotland in 1972 we had become aware of the large extent of the denuded – almost skeletal – hillsides in our local landscape, and of the ubiquity of grazing farm animals. We checked the few studies of fossil pollen for the area, and confirmed our

*Carrifran valley in January 1999, with sheep*

*Carrifran Wildwood in September 2018, with trees*

hunch that this was an environment transformed from its natural largely forested state. Humans and their animals had degraded their environment. People now are appalled if this degree of destruction occurs rapidly in far-off places, but here in southern Scotland it had taken place gradually, over many centuries, and had rarely been noticed. Little room was now left for nature.

During the 1980s Myrtle and some friends formed *Peeblesshire Environment Concern* (PEC) and organised two series of evening classes to foster awareness of worldwide and local environmental issues. We also became aware of the work of *Trees for Life* and *Reforesting Scotland*, and when Philip retired in 1992 we began to focus – with a remarkable and diverse group of local people – on the possibility of enhancing part of our own environment in the Scottish Borders.

The 1993 *Restoring Borders Woodland* conference organised by PEC focused on the denuded state of much of the Scottish borderlands and on opportunities to restore more natural habitats. A few years later, when we were looking for sites of 1000-2000 acres, a supportive but sceptical landowner commented on the 'enormity' of the enterprise. But if one is to make an impact – both ecologically and in the public mind – scale matters. A quarter of a century later, Carrifran Wildwood shows 'What rewilding looks like' and the ambitious work in progress on the other two large sites owned by Borders Forest Trust ensures that the Trust's vision of ecological restoration on a truly landscape scale no longer elicits such a cautious response.

During the past few years we have welcomed to our sites scores of groups of students who will become the land managers of the future, and many hundreds of dedicated individuals and members of activist organisations, who demonstrate by planting trees that they can make a personal contribution to the worldwide effort to limit climate change and curb the loss and decline of so many species. These young and older people contribute so much in their personal lives – eat less meat, use less plastic, use less fuel – as well as planting lots of trees. Many also put time and emotional resources into demonstrations, pleading with our politicians and prominent people to accept their responsibility to do something on an international scale to prevent collapse of the ecosystems of the world.

The year 2019 saw a revolution in public awareness of the need to halt the warming of our world before it is too late, and in 2020 we have been rudely awakened by Coronavirus (COVID-19) to one of the hazards of globalisation. All is not yet lost, however, and as we celebrate the 20th Anniversary of the planting of the first trees in Carrifran valley on Millennium Day, and see the progress in the restoration of Corehead & Devil's Beef Tub and of Talla & Gameshope, we take pleasure in the knowledge that the past and future achievements of Borders Forest Trust can shine a ray of sunshine into a gloomy world, illuminating a pathway by which all of us can help to restore the beauty and vibrancy of life to some small parts of our wounded planet.

# AT CARRIFRAN, WHERE THE WILDWOOD GROWS

When I was there at Carrifran,
In the valley in Moffat hills,
I saw a vision realised, where
New wood, new leaf, new life sprang forth
And everything was good, there where I stood,
Upon the slopes that once were bare.

When I was there
I gazed in wonder at the scene.
Broad hillsides rising high
Above the stell,
Clothed in a fine mosaic of trees
In many, many shades of green,
From valley floor to skyline wide.
Below them there I saw in shade
Where Bluebells grow in Spring again
Upon the broad hillsides
That once were bare.

When I was there
I saw the Oak and saw the Ash
And saw the trembling Aspen fair,
Rowan and Bird Cherry too.
The Alder, Hazel and Hawthorn
I saw them growing there anew,
In this place that once was bare.

When I was there, one day in June
I saw, with flowers virgin white,
The Guelder Rose in fine full bloom
Before it formed red berries, shining bright,
Come Autumn in the sunlit glade,
Amidst the thriving wildwood trees
On the banks that once were bare.

When I was there
I saw the butterflies, bugs and bees,
Spiders, slugs and Bufftail moth.
And nearby, some Rowan trees
Above the valley bottom burn
That flows downslope
In foaming swirls and rushing rills.
Through the rocks and over falls
It spills, and hastens onward

Down cutting through the great moraine.
Endlessly it runs on by the place
Where white Sea Campion now grows
Beside the burn at Carrifran
That once was bare.

When I was there
I saw the natural springs
That ooze and spurt
And slowly trickle down the hill
Between the rounded stones,
Past pale-leaved clumps of Butterwort.
Then, steeply down through vegetation thick,
Past Honeysuckle and Holly bush,
Not quick, it slows still further now,
Inexorably passing by,
Drip, drip, drip,
In a steady measuring of time
Since Carrifran became so bare.

When I was there
I saw a dream that had become reality,
Where panting folk climbed hillsides steep,
When planting Oaks and Juniper
And other trees they hoped would make a bid
To cling to life upon the heights,
And so survive, despite the doubts.
And did! on land no longer grazed by goats
Or nibbling sheep
That kept the hills always so bare.

When I'm not there
I close my eyes, remembering
The Willows waving in the breeze,
The lichens, moss and Lemon-scented Fern,
Where everything I saw did please
At every turn
Along the paths.
There in the valley, in the hills
That are now no longer bare.
At Carrifran where all life now thrives
On gentle slope and hilltop high.
At Carrifran, where the wildwood grows.

T. Astley, *June 2019*

# INDEX

**For general topics, please refer to the list of Contents on pages V-VI.  In the Index, bold type is used in a few cases to indicate the main treatment.**